MULTI/RACE/
LESS/NESS

ALSO AVAILABLE FROM BLOOMSBURY

Alienation and Freedom, Frantz Fanon
Black Art and Aesthetics, ed. Michael Kelly and Monique Roelofs

MULTIRACELESSNESS

A Process Philosophy

Jon Ivan Gill

BLOOMSBURY ACADEMIC
LONDON • NEW YORK • OXFORD • NEW DELHI • SYDNEY

BLOOMSBURY ACADEMIC

Bloomsbury Publishing Plc, 50 Bedford Square, London, WC1B 3DP, UK
Bloomsbury Publishing Inc, 1385 Broadway, New York, NY 10018, USA
Bloomsbury Publishing Ireland, 29 Earlsfort Terrace, Dublin 2, D02 AY28, Ireland

BLOOMSBURY, BLOOMSBURY ACADEMIC and the Diana logo are trademarks of Bloomsbury Publishing Plc

First published in Great Britain 2026

Copyright © Jon Ivan Gill, 2026

Jon Ivan Gill has asserted his right under the Copyright, Designs and Patents Act, 1988, to be identified as Author of this work.

For legal purposes the Acknowledgements on p. viii constitute an extension of this copyright page.

Cover design: Ben Anslow
Cover image © Concept of a human walking near the sea
Contributor: Vincenzo Dragani / Alamy Stock Photo

All rights reserved. No part of this publication may be: i) reproduced or transmitted in any form, electronic or mechanical, including photocopying, recording or by means of any information storage or retrieval system without prior permission in writing from the publishers; or ii) used or reproduced in any way for the training, development or operation of artificial intelligence (AI) technologies, including generative AI technologies. The rights holders expressly reserve this publication from the text and data mining exception as per Article 4(3) of the Digital Single Market Directive (EU) 2019/790.

Bloomsbury Publishing Plc does not have any control over, or responsibility for, any third-party websites referred to or in this book. All internet addresses given in this book were correct at the time of going to press. The author and publisher regret any inconvenience caused if addresses have changed or sites have ceased to exist, but can accept no responsibility for any such changes.

A catalogue record for this book is available from the Library of Congress.

ISBN: HB: 978-1-3504-3547-6
PB: 978-1-3504-3548-3
ePDF: 978-1-3504-3549-0
eBook: 978-1-3504-3550-6

Typeset by Deanta Global Publishing Services, Chennai, India
Printed and bound in the United States of America

For product safety related questions contact productsafety@bloomsbury.com.

To find out more about our authors and books visit www.bloomsbury.com and sign up for our newsletters.

Dedicated to my paternal grandmother, Antoinette Cain Gill. Your heart, soul, and body permeate this text, and I feel all of you in this work. *Gracias por todo y mucho más.*

Dedicated to my maternal grandfather, Robert Lee Turner. Your creativity creates through me always. Infinite gratitude for your authorship in every morsel of art.

CONTENTS

Acknowledgments viii

Prolegomenon to any Future Philosophy of Race x

Introduction 1

1 "Black" Is Dead: A Moorish Un-sure-ing of a "Sure Thing" 11

2 Who Keeps the Gate?: Identity Politics and the Composition and Maintenance of the Racial "Us" and "Them" 31

3 Alternate Race Theories in Motion: A Discussion with Dominic Pettis-El/I.B. Fokuz 53

4 Period, Full Stop: The Oversights of Cancel Culture(s) 75

5 The Lure of the Shroud: The Question of the "Mattering" of the Conceptual Human Illusion 99

6 Multi/race/less/ness: A New Name for Timeless Ways of Human Becoming 121

7 BioDigital Jazz: Reflections on Emergent Multi/race/less/ness in Hip-Hop and Belize 143

8 Self-Study: Scattered Thoughts on Genealogy as a Facet of Multi/Race/Less/Ness 167

Breve Epílogo 183
Notes 187
Bibliography 213
Index 223

ACKNOWLEDGMENTS

I literally write this at the very end of the text. Whew. It was a ride. Thanks to all those who inspired this work in any way, shape, form, and non-form of continuous energy. Special shout out to my parents, Lavern and Eustace Gill, who urged me to continue and challenged me when they thought I was moving in the wrong direction. This is valued. Steve and Sharon Andrews, my brother and sister-in-law, and Clarice, Leslie, and Shaun, my niece and nephews, thank you for everything. Y'all mean a lot to me, and I want you to always know that. Much obliged to ALL my family from near and far. You are ALL felt in all these words. Thank you for confirming my insanity on several occasions. Gratitude to Monica A. Coleman for teaching me process thought in ways that no one else would and could. José Francisco Morales Torres, you've been a more than adequate friend, and your "wondrous" scholarship is a "starting point" for much of my own." Here's to EGL. Thank you for reading the manuscript and offering insightful thoughts. Huge shoutouts to Josh Brown, Lisa Heldke, Peg O'Conner, Mike Shaffer, and Tommy Valentini for having me as a member of the dopest Philosophy department in the world at Gustavus Adolphus College. You all are doing some really cool thought experiments here, and I'm honored to test ideas in the lab of Old Main alongside you. Tomorrow Kings, this one is for you. If a rap I penned in the super tough writing sessions with y'all were a text, it would look something like this. Echoes of Oratory Muzik, let's get it. It's been an honor to rock with y'all for the better part of 15 years. It's appreciated that you took me in. Bless up. Itzpapolotl, you're magnificent and such a great friend to have. We gon' keep panche be In Xochitl In Cuicatl til' di shitstem fall. InnerSections! Much love to Jonathan Calvillo. Your work is super awesome and inspiring. I'm honored you took your valuable time to read through parts of the drafts of this and offer some excellent ways to fine-tune my "sky rhyming." Shoutout to Roy Whitaker, a sometimes unsung pioneer in the field of Hip-Hop studies in general and Hip-Hop and religion studies in particular. Thanks for all your encouragement and setting an example I was compelled to follow in many ways. All respect due to Catherine Keller. I'm grateful that you saw fit to introduce my first text, *Underground Rap as Religion*, to your students on various occasions. Your thoughts have significantly helped me develop my own, and for that I am grateful. Gotta give a huge "Peace!" to the Doc Daniel White Hodge. You've set an impeccable example for prolific and challenging scholarship while navigating the academy's dark side. Major shoutout to my good friend Elonda Clay and all your groundbreaking scholarship that still fuels many of my classes and writings. In no particular order, thanks to Christopher M. Driscoll (I always think about how dope your work is as I'm critiquing and brainstorming my own), Monica R. Miller, Jim Perkinson, Jennifer Lisa Vest, Erin Manning (many thanks for your openness to share your brilliant ideas with me), Petra Carlsson Redell, Elisabeth Belgrano, Matthias Knörrer and Andrea, The Opus, Epik1, STILLRIFT, NIZM, Lyric Versatile, Belize, Señor Jesus y Señora María y su familia (muchisimas gracias!), Christopher Britton, Joe Woods, Saint Peter Good Neighbor Council (Trish, Bill, and Dana, I appreciate you), José Pimienta-Bey, Phantom Thrett (Let's get this Crystal Radio shit out there and quit the fucking around! Love you, my Brother!), Maria Jackson (thank you for being such a good and longtime friend, and for reading and offering thoughts on portions of the manuscript) Gusties Thia Cooper, Joaquín Villanueva, Blake Couey and Angelique Dwyer (the professional support in a critical time is super valuable and won't EVER be forgotten) and EVERYONE else I may not have mentioned. You're not forgotten. Special thanks to Dr. Sheila Otieno and all the wonderful faculty of the Religious Studies and Philosophy departments at Elon University. You were so kind to have me give the Powell Lecture in Religious Studies in October of 2024 where I was able to try out some of the ideas of this text on a critically appreciative and gracious group of scholars from students to professors. I'll never forget that, and I look forward to seeing you soon.

Finally, but nowhere near trivially, thank you to Prophet Noble Drew Ali. What you left us has truly transformed my thinking. While I do it my way, I do it through a serious grappling with what you divinely *prepared*. ISLAM.

PROLEGOMENON TO ANY FUTURE PHILOSOPHY OF RACE

> I walk on streets that are paved with spinned clips
> Only vacations I go on is head trips
> And I see visions and dreams
> But they're never what they seem, yeah
> I reach out to touch them and they go
> When I come down, reality meets me there
> And I sing the song of how life's not fair
> Look and my reflection
> Reflect on my direction
> Holding on to a past that isn't there
> We need to "Let it go…"[1]
>
> **TUNNEL RATS, "CHANGE"**

This time of night, I always get agitated. You have no idea. I'm usually awake this time. I don't know [if] I've had a sleep-filled night since that boy was born. Most nights my eyes fly wide open out of a sound sleep. Heart beating so hard I feel it throbbing in my ears. Always right about this time. Too late to go back to sleep, too early to get on with the day. You [the husband socially constructed in the context as "White"]…just snoring away. Usually, I go stand in the door to his room…and listen to him breathe. Sometimes, I go in and…touch the muscle on his neck. Or shoulder. Stand there and bullshit myself, 'Don't worry, Kendra, he is big and powerful. This world can't hurt him.' Until that nagging feeling comes back and I dwell on how fragile he is. And whatever nightmare that has just woke me up, someone texting in an SUV or an errant punch in a bar fight, a ruptured appendix in some third world country. Most…most mothers can sit there in the dark and get rational, go back to sleep. But sometimes, in my nightmares, I see nooses and crosses and white men with Brylcreem crew cuts.[2]

AMERICAN Son

I inaugurate this voyage into a shift in thinking with a musing on dreams. In the text of the Tunnel Rats, we see Dax Reynosa "waxing philosophical" (if you know, you know) on being trapped in the past. The past is deceptive. It can ensnare us within its passageways of repetition. But, as a process thinker, the past is also a very valuable and active part of the becoming of all. In "Change," Dax showcases a certain type of past wrapped within an active *rehashing* of that which has come before. Think of one of the original printing presses. In the manufacture of a book using the letter "k," in each instance of words using "k," this particular character will show up as it has in every other instance. There will be virtually no deviations, and if slight alterations happen to appear, they could be attributed to some flaw in the empirical form of the character itself, the machine, and so on. But under normal circumstances, "k" will always disclose itself on the paper as "k." Switching this into the "key" from which Dax writes/sings, he alludes to this sort of rehashing of the past, seemingly without the possibility of novelty. The "mirror" referenced in this captivating second verse, instead of engaging adventures in front of him, "rehashes" "a past that isn't there." This is a past of "streets with spinned clips" and vacations of head trips. I wonder what one would find if one could pull open some of these lines and lay bare the types of personal and perhaps collective trials Dax's somewhat general words beautifully cover here. The mirror repeatedly rehashes a form of the human, potentially persuading one of the misplaced concreteness of their permanence and not the inevitability of their flux. This has a bit more "sticking power" when thought of in a "purely" figurative tone. What does it mean to live as the rehashing of a reflection you deceivingly think is synonymous with yourself, a past not really "there?" One might not only become the prisoner of their wonders but also of their tragedies and feel doomed to forever remain returned to them. Dax, mostly concerned with the *trauma* of his past in this verse, creates a sledgehammer to shatter the mirror by coming to the realization that this particular *intersection* between himself and the past is something he needs to "let go."

But what happens when this rehashing shows up in the case of Kendra Ellis-Conor, played by Kerry Washington in *American Son*? In the movie, the totality of which takes place in the waiting room of a Miami police station, Ellis-Conor has just received news that her teenage son had a run-in with the police and is anticipating further information from an officer, who is eventually exposed as being nowhere near as helpful as he could have been. Ellis-Conor identifies with and is identified as the category "Black" by her context, and the so-called "White" officer assisting with the case interacts with her, mediated by the rehashing of the negative stereotypes difficult to separate from thinking about said category. The officer expects Ellis-Conor's son to be a "mirror" of the category "Black," and is dumbfounded when he turns out not to be. The quote at the beginning of this chapter reveals Ellis-Conor's unintentional obliteration of the category "Black," a category she instinctively dons again right after violently taking it off. Both Dax and Ellis-Conor employ the idea of "dreaming," a psychological recurrence not particularly pleasant for either of them. For Ellis-Conor, the dream is literally a nightmare, full of the rehashing of that which constitutes the category of "Blackness," such as discrimination, death, a need to prove oneself worthy to exist within a "White" hegemony by showing how well one can abide by its tenets, and so forth. This movie focuses on a mortal fear of the police encoded into the intersectional categories of "Black" and "male." Because Ellis-Conor's son identifies and is identified as "Black" and "male," she understandably fears for his safety. The quote showcases a deep *trauma* Ellis-Conor feels, an "eternal return" overtaking not only her dreams but also her waking life.

For quite a long time, numerous writings in the philosophy of race have engaged racial trauma in its various manifestations. Perhaps most, if not, all have dealt with the traumatic nature of racial biases by default. But what has not been seriously considered is race *as trauma* itself. In the admission of many theorists that race is indeed a social construction tailored differently in and by different contexts and not a universal "fact," there is a tendency to return to race in a sort of essentialist way: while it indeed becomes construed as a construction arising from various types of trauma, it is still seen as a valuable identity in a way similar to how Ellis-Connor rips it to shreds before or even while attempting to recover her bare *becoming* in it due to a seeming obligation to it. In this clip, it seems as if there is no recourse but to ingress the racial category of "Black" with all the negative connotations associated with it and, in some way, try to struggle through it and be "proud."

This is *trauma*.

Kant, in his deviation from Hume's empiricism and its lack of ability to provide a solid and, to him, necessary ground for metaphysics, gives an alternative starting point of epistemology from the physical world impressing its ideas onto the mind (Hume) to the mind imposing its own reality upon objects (Kant). This move changed the trajectory of the philosophies of the "West" forever, giving rise to varying positions on his system, which reverberated throughout the annals of everyone from Hegel to Heidegger and still shakes the pillars of the present discourse. New questions were raised, forward movements ensued, and positions in opposition produced more insightful and interesting streams of thought. This prolegomenon suggests a similar novel move of its own in shifting from race as that which trauma befalls to race *as* trauma itself.

Why do I call for such a move? What justifies a reconceptualization of race *as* trauma?

"Trauma" can be defined as "a tragic experience that drastically shapes the contours of the future of an experiencing entity." After a traumatic event, one potentially perceives the world through it consciously. In other instances, said transformed perception may be subtle. A woman may not notice that she becomes unusually defensive and dismissive when she encounters a man flirting with her due to the PTSD of a horrible experience in the past, such as harassment or rape. Trauma "rehashes" itself in these instances, replaying the tragic event in memory and tormenting the experiencer. In the case of race, trauma is a mirror perpetually reflecting a past of the category of race, which arbitrarily came into existence and is not really and/or not necessarily "there."

The racialized body is a traumatized body.

The text aims to show the totality of this as it unfolds, but it suffices to say at the outset of the project that the key of race *is* trauma, and that not addressing race as such dooms us to infinitely mirror the tragic initial events of its creation, which are revisited in detail in the first chapter and referenced throughout the text.

Of trauma studies, a relatively new field drawing from the insights of poststructuralism, psychoanalysis, and postcolonial theory, among other methodologies, practices, and disciplines, Michelle Balaev says,

> The idea that a traumatic experience challenges the limits of language, fragments the psyche, and even ruptures meaning altogether set the initial parameters of the field and continues to impact the critical conversation even while alternative approaches displace this notion.[3]

In Ellis-Connor, we witness the challenge of language to describe the events that have befallen those whom the system of racial and race-related classifications calls "Black." What she tries to convey to the officer, who has been socialized into the experience of "Whiteness," is something he just can't fathom. Not only can she not communicate what it is like to be subsumed under this racial category to the officer, but in my read of the movie, she also can't articulate a clear separation *between* race and trauma. Her son, Jamal, who she fears for in her dreams and while awake, is never distinguished from the trauma of "nooses and crosses and white men with Brylcreem crew cuts" precisely because he is "Black." To *think about* and *think* (referring to the possession of the possibility of the idea of Jamal, which provides the content of analytic and emotional thoughts) Jamal, the mark of the social construction of "Blackness," filled with all its hierarchical and oppressive contents, must be thought of as the same side of the same coin. It is the contention of the text that race must be considered precisely as this kind of psychological trauma with its physical consequences.

Philosophy of race has yet to make an explicit experiment in which race is tried on for size *as* trauma. For Freud, a precursor to modern-day trauma theory, Baalev says, "Traumatic events create conflicts in the ego which "split off" from the unity of the ego and are repressed but return later often in dreams."[4] Through the colonial projects starting in the late fifteenth century and changing the landscape of the globe, the trauma of race is not a preexistent unity of consciousness upon which trauma is inflicted. Rather, race *happened to* previously raceless[5] individuals in its stripping some humans of personhood and elevating others above personhood.

It was a sword of international law that perpetually split the pre-racial "self" just enough to erect the category of race in between the spaces so cunningly that eventually the fact that human becomings weren't always thought of and thought in the key of race gradually sank into the collective subconscious of even those who are keenly aware of its origins. This causes many so called aware individuals to reify the trauma of race in their attempts to reform it, as the text will attest to as I engage various interlocutors throughout its development.

Succinctly, I assert this prolegomenon as a foundation for the project at hand: *race, the colonial event of reducing the human to categories separate from pre-colonial methods of identification, is a traumatic psychological experience perpetually rehashed by dominant systems and those of us willingly and unwillingly governed by them.* When someone is referred to and/or accepts that they are any racial and/or race-related[6] category such as, but not limited to, "Black," "White," "Latinx," "Indigenous," "Native American," "African American," and "Asian," I assert that they partake in the "mirror," repeating the traumatic experiences from which the categories emerge and confusing it *as* "themselves." The text aims to establish, on this novel proposition, that the category of race itself, as opposed to being an authentic identity in some significant sense standing outside of the oppressive confluences of social forces chaotically converging into the category (this seems to be the position assumed by many critical race theorists and philosophers of race covered in the text), is like a notion of panentheism, where God is the world but also beyond the world. Is race the creation of identities inseparable from said confluences of oppressive social forces? <u>Here, I want to attempt to think of racial and race-related categories *as* slavery, theft of land, forceful renaming of people, arbitrary demarcations separating those who may have previously perceived no separation at all, various types of discrimination from redlining to lack of access to necessities, and much more.</u> Such a shift allows for not only a more critical analysis and deconstruction of racial and race-related categories. If the assertion of race *as* trauma, or what I will hereinafter refer to as "race/trauma," is plausible, it provides a solid reason for the abolishing of race not seen in more utopian or differently grounded philosophies.

Further, if race *is* traumatic, then perhaps it can be reconceived as a *problem* that needs to be excavated and overcome by the psychoanalytic therapist, the "self," the community, and so on. It is not common to seriously consider race as the same or similar to any other traumatic experience, and this text aims to take our imaginations there. I'm inspired by the work of poststructuralist thinkers such as Alfred North Whitehead, Judith Butler, Monica A. Coleman, Brian Massumi, Erin Manning, Gilles Deleuze, and Roland Faber, as thinking through their bodies of work enabled me to come to this explicit experimental articulation of race *as* trauma (especially the work of Butler, who arrives at a similar place with her theories of gender negotiation through performance and the societal acceptance and/or rejection of multiple instances of performance). If race is indeed traumatic, then a psychological approach to rid the human of it seems warranted. The aim of this text is not intended to be philosophical work in psychology or psychoanalysis, but the conclusions presented could be developed further in this very direction. Trauma studies, as it stands has yet to venture into the realm of playing with the hypothesis that race is trauma. For example, psychologist Alex Klein can be construed as taking for granted race's separate identity from trauma in his definition of racial trauma. He says,

> Racial trauma is the ongoing result of racism, racist bias, and exposure to racist abuse in the media. Racial trauma can affect many aspects of a person's life, including their ability to have relationships, concentrate on school or work, and feel safe. Racial trauma is widespread among marginalized groups. This is particularly true among Black people in the United States, the majority of whom say they have experienced racism. Media depictions of racism, such as police violence against unarmed Black people, may also trigger feelings of racial trauma.[7]

This quote, much akin to the work of other thinkers on racial trauma such as Sheila Wise Rowe's *Healing Racial Trauma: The Road to Resilience*, Connesia Hadford and Ariel D. Marrero's edited volume entitled *Racial Trauma in the School System: Naming the Pin*, and Guiliane Kinouani's *Living While Black: Using Joy, Beauty and Connection to Heal Racial Trauma*, all start with the background assumption that race stands independent of trauma and undergoes traumatic experiences. This starting point obscures the dependence of race on trauma for its very existence. In leading with the proposition that trauma is "widespread among marginalized groups. . .this is particularly true among Black people," one misses various justifications to make what Henri Lefebvre would refer to as a metaphilosophical move, a supersession of philosophy, which in his words, "opens a way neither positivism nor philosophism, neither a philosophically systematized materialism nor idealism, suffices to determine."[8] Studies in racial trauma as they stand have yet to seriously conceive of an end to the system of racial trauma itself, which I assert is activated by an in-depth look at the traumatic aspects characteristic of the very category of race and the reasons I give in the body of the work for adding this important element to the discourse.

In a word (really), the text as it develops aims to show that the category of race is inevitably traumatic and argue for its dissolution from this proposition.

To return to the examples that began our brief setting of a foundation for the remainder of the work, both Dax Reynosa and Kenda Ellis-Connors deal with the past in ways that cause it to seem as if they are bound to it. The mirror reflects us and there's nothing we can do about it. We must accept what we see, whether in Dax's figurative mirror or Ellis-Connors' seemingly accurate reflection of the "universal" category "Black." However, what they both discover opaquely is that the door between the mundane and the novel is actually wide open. The following pages are faint steps toward a *process* by which race, the very definition of trauma hereinafter referred to as "race/trauma," can be abolished. This is, along with Dax, the undying lure that sings, "Let it go, let it go, let it go. . .seasons change."[9]

INTRODUCTION

For as long as I can remember, I have been trying to figure out what race is and what it means. Is it a color? Is it an ideology? Is it my and other humans' true identity? Does it originate in the Middle Passage or transcend it? Is it solely a legal construction or solely the making of religion (of course it can't be "solely" either of these things since nothing this complex is ever that simple)? Can I put it on or take it off like I can clothes? Should I want to preserve it? What is the relation of race to the current "cancel culture"? Can I ever abandon it? Does walking away from it make me a "sellout"? How does race exist? *Does* race exist?

For my entire young life, I have walked largely in the shadow of "Blackness" in particular and racial language in general without having ever really understood the meaning(s) of the shadow under which I was subsumed without my express consent; the shadow that was said to define my "origin" from the continent now known as "Africa" to an assumed enslavement of my ancestors and forced travel to the areas I currently write to you in (well, if Van Sertima, Ben Jochannan, and Noble Drew Ali were right, then people who looked like me were already here; we'll get to that). As a child, I told my Chicagoan mother with Chahta (now transformed through colonial alchemy into the term "Choctaw") roots in Arkansas and Mississippi and ancestry in various countries of the continent now known as "Africa" that I was "multicultural." Not long after these words came out of my mouth, she quickly illuminated the error in my ways, telling me in no uncertain terms that I was "Black." At this early age, I was attempting to express my confusion with the angst of this category. This is an angst that I would become all too familiar with as I grew up in the South Side of Chicago and caught strange looks from my friends because I'd rather listen to the Doors than Ice Cube (I grew out of this, but never totally), overheard comments in undergrad from the "White" students marveling that the "Black" kid knew more about Sixpence None the Richer and the book of Isaiah than they did, and people showing intense shock when they saw the "Black" dude frying tortillas and making empanadas at my and Phantom Thrett's record store, Serious Cartoons Records and Tapes (my father and his family are from Belize, and my great-grandparents raised my grandmother and her siblings in Puerto Cortés, Honduras, where three of my father's siblings were born and reared for some time). There was something about racial categories that has never sat right with me, and one of those "somethings" was that racial categories reduce rather than expand identity.

What do I mean by "reduction" and "expansion?" Well, this is something that we all are familiar with and is certainly not novel to any academic discussion on race. Many who participate in critical race theory, from the armchair enthusiast to the university professor, would accept that what we call race, this method of grouping people based on similar biological and phenotypical characteristics in ways that denote conceptual and essentialist homogeneity (e.g., the background assumption that people who happen to have ancestry in a certain part of the world and appear similar to onlookers must also have corresponding metaphysical similarities such as character traits and intelligence, among other things), is a social construction. Race has always bothered me because this social construction is one that we can historically locate in the approximately mid- to late fifteenth-century colonization projects of Spain and Portugal and was utilized to subjugate people who were already in the lands, as well as subdue and dehumanize those forcefully taken from their original homes to create currently existing capitalist systems. Race, in a resistance of "expansion," has the magical power to "reduce" the "other," an entity who is "strange" at first contact to the subject and possesses a being/becoming that exceeds the limited ability of the colonizing agent to perceive them as they are and are not simultaneously (the mystery of culture that can mystify even those who are part and parcel of it), to a well-known entity that corresponds to and complies with the dominant power's systematization of them as subordinate pieces of the "New World," which he has come to inscribe on top of ancient ways of becoming. I say "he" because those who identified as "male" were the ringleaders of this, and said category corresponded to the "Whiteness" that said malehood manufactured and assumed. I don't expect to get much argument here.

As I began to reconceptualize my own identity through writing and listening to edge-piercing rap music, reading more about my own personal and more than tri-national histories, reflecting on the boxes in which society says a person who looks like me is supposed to reside in and what happens when these "lines of scrimmage" are transgressed (over a period of twenty plus years), and studying the philosophies of Noble Drew Ali's Moorish Science Temple of America (one of the major philosophical foundations of this work), racial categories began to break on my frame similar to how the braces on Forrest Gump's legs cracked into pieces as his stride transformed from a severely impaired limp into a sprint. After a series of ruminations on race and what it meant over the past fifteen years, one of which was an encounter with a then fellow graduate student who, during a conversation around ethnicity, told me that I was "Black Black Black Black!" in disregard of my multinational identities in the United States, Belize, Honduras, and so on (keep in mind that I never said that I wasn't "Black" to this person, but only communicated to them that "African American," the equivalent of "Black" to this person, did not in my estimation encompass the totality of how I understand myself), I rejected the use of racial categories from my own vocabulary. I pledged to live a life that would not impose this ever-evolving conclusion on others. I write this in part to serve as a faulty rubric for those who may want to do the same in their own lives.

A major source of fuel for this labor is the interesting fact that while many brilliant thinkers within and outside the academy affirm that race is a social construct and acknowledge not only the arbitrariness of its existence but also the rootedness of this arbitrary category in "White" supremacy, there have been few serious moves of thought made to renounce the nomenclature of race. In the fourteen-page pamphlet "A History: The Construction and the Deconstruction of Race," the authors expose the history of racial language while simultaneously appealing to the same racial categories it has so eloquently deconstructed (e.g., after gutting the colonial history of the term "Asian," this word is still used to refer to a certain group, assuming that such a group even exists after the language that the group is contingent upon is deconstructed). The pamphlet ends with an appeal to the term "people of color" and its usefulness, but dangerously reifies racial language on the grounds that even if race does not have to exist, it does exist, and its existence affects the social, economic, political, historical, and cultural aspects of life.[1] This is plausible, and elements of this are implemented in what I refer to in the second half of the text as "responsible post-race." However, is an approach that does not take the implications of the conclusion to the next level, the renouncing of racial categories altogether, radical enough?

What would a world where racial categories are nonexistent look like? Is this possible? Should it be possible? Is this what the later James Baldwin and Octavia Butler were dreaming about? And the flies want to hang out on my computer as I type on the verandah in an undisclosed location in Belize. They're welcome to. As I was saying, these and other thinkers do lure us into a framework where the ideas of race we are so wedded to, both by the lot of being born into them and finding it difficult and maybe even impractical or even realistic to live outside of them, either do not exist or are not a primary means of identity. Baldwin, in a 1984 interview with Julius Lester, stated that the task facing "Black" writers of any era is the task of making the question of color obsolete. Baldwin went on to talk of the terror that faced "White" people in light of a literary era in which "White" people were objects as opposed to subjects, and in that objectivity were incapable of any objection, much like the subjectivity colonization forced upon bodies colonially and post-colonially renamed and subsumed under the category "Black," "Latina/o/x/é," "Red," "Coolie," and other distinctions, arguing that this would lead to the obsolescence of the shadow of race.[2] While somewhat shortsighted in that Baldwin failed to realize that reacting to "White" subjectivity with "Black" subjectivity would only reify the reality of the color schematic he wants to deconstruct in a passive admission of its actuality, his objective to abandon color as a primary means of identity and collective individuation (or what we recognize as color and appearance but is really something more) is as illuminating now as it was then, and still guides the subjective aim of this text.

Also, in an interview, Octavia Butler stated that when she created characters in her science fiction, work that has been inducted into the loose canon of what is now known as "Afrofuturism," she indicated that she wanted her characters to speak nonverbally in ways that are irreverent to the boxes we are asked to check on job applications in this world.[3] Novels such as *Parable of the Sower* showcase Butler's literary genius as she tricks readers into ingression into the lives of characters who are anything but what they might be typecast as by the film of race, removable glasses we have been bewitched into believing are our eyes. As with Baldwin, Butler's forward-thinking still falls short in that she still appeals to the nomenclature of race, even though these categories may take longer to appear in her storylines. Ytasha Womack, in her text *Afrofuturism: The World of Black Sci-Fi and Fantasy Culture*, takes the notion of race to the brink of extinction, reasserting that it is the "creation" of the transatlantic slave trade and the justification for the domination of the unfortunate subjects of these "business negotiations" and their descendants (and contemporaries of the slaves who looked like them but never actually underwent the crises of the slave trade), a notion that she develops in her text *Post Black: How a New Generation Is Redefining African American Identity*.[4] Womack makes great strides toward the possibility of negating racial identities, work that this text tends to both build on and challenge in the philosophico/street language articulation of my goals in this lyrical excursion.

What is the value in a deconstruction and abolishment of racial language? I'm glad you didn't ask. When Sri Aurobindo talks about Maya as the illusory emanation/creation of the divine essence in the tangible world, he says that the divine essence is the play, the player, and the playground of Maya. In other words, Maya as the self-representation of the divine essence (what we might call the empirical world) is inseparably intertwined with the divine essence despite descriptions that would assert some substantial and actual distinction between the two, such as the substances perceived through the senses. As a reflection of essence, Maya *is* essence.[5] Are race and Maya similar? Is the category of race the illusory emanation of not just humanity but a "divinized" humanity of a specific sociohistorical context? And if race is a reflection of this specific socially located human, what could that tell us about the emanation, the shadow that virtually all parts of the globe are overcast under? If we conclude that race is indeed the stratified reflection of this "divinized" humanity of Spain, Portugal, England, Germany, France, Belgium, and other nations from the mid- to late fifteenth century onward (as much of the historical information and scholarship in philosophy of race, sociology, critical theory, and cultural studies has indeed concluded), we must seriously question what it means for us, people who have experienced complex spectrums of subjugation and domination through these categories both in actuality and ancestrally, to perpetuate that which many of us have perhaps rightly called an "illusion." We must ask if we see ourselves or the spellcaster when we accept racial language as descriptors of ourselves, even when we are critical in our acceptance of this nomenclature. What or who is this "spellcaster?" The Kantian-inspired first offering of the text, entitled "Prolegomena to Any Future Philosophy of Race," suggests a shift in perspectives on race. Instead of equating the categories of the spellcaster as inseparable from, if not synonymous with, the experiencing self enduring or benefiting from the traumatic occurrences of colonial oppression, I suggest that subsequent philosophies of race experiment with viewing race and race-related categories as synonymous with trauma itself. I argue that race *is* literally trauma and has its initial clash with humanity in the colonization projects of the mid- to late fifteenth century. Further, this trauma is perpetuated whenever racial and race-related categories are applied by the metaphysics of language and related to how the self is viewed by the self and others, which is every second of our lives. Racial and race-related categories are readily referred to in the text as "race/trauma" after this potential new starting point is posited in the Prolegomenon.

A different way to query the value of the abolishment of racial language would be to ask somewhat of a converse question: What are the disadvantages of living in societies that maintain racial language, something that many of us agree is the arbitrary residue of colonization, much like ideas of transcendent Goddesses and Gods of "Western" Christianity? In a time of "Black Lives Matter," I've asked the question (perhaps to the dismay of some) if it is possible for a "Black" life to "matter" insofar as the language of "Blackness" was created and inserted into social systems for the purpose of domination and the removal of the human significance of people defined by and defining as the category. These images of identity have been reflected back to the power system that bestowed them upon us by us in a defiant acceptance as opposed to the more subversive deconstruction and discarding of these very images. José Pimienta-Bey encourages those socially constructed as "Black" to reject the language of "Blackness" for this reason. The first chapter, entitled "Black Is Dead: A Moorish Un-Suring of a Sure Thing," appeals to the work of Pimienta-Bey and Noble Drew Ali, the founder of the Moorish Science Temple of America. In this chapter, I rehash and attempt to recontextualize a well-known history of the category of race through an appeal to aesthetics and elaborate on several benefits of the abolishment of not just "Blackness" but all racial language taught by the MSTA.

Another thing that arrests my attention in the discussions of the philosophical, religious, and anthropological notions of race is the sense of community that it seems to engender between people who find themselves grouped in a certain way by colonial outsiders and take for granted that this grouping is a sui generis monogenesis sort of thing. Many people under the shadow of several strands of geographical oppression and grouping from the late fifteenth century until the present commonly refer to themselves as "one people." But would they have seen themselves as "one people" if dominant powers did not (1) both create and emanate racial categories that combined self-identifying nations in the same or neighboring geographical regions with heterogeneous practices, histories, and origin stories, and (2) force them to reduce their diversity to the narrow view of how they were perceived by the dominant power systems for the purposes of survival and a fragmented attempt at maintaining "historical" "identities?"[6] Chapter 2, entitled "Who Keeps the Gate?: Identity Politics and the Composition and Maintenance of the Racial 'Us' and 'Them,'" deals with this insufficiently explored problem in detail, excavating what it means to say things such as "us," "we," and "my people" as living results of the underside of the colonial project. This chapter engages the work of Ann Cudd, Kwame Anthony Appiah, Jorge Gracia, Naomi Zack, and Jennifer Lisa Vest, all of whom offer various valuable perspectives on the manufacture, malleability, and utility of race (Appiah, Zack); the creation/definitional oppression of dominant and subordinate social groups (Cudd); the constraints of what the language of the social group is capable of meaning (Gracia); and the negotiation of racial multiplicity disseminated through the un/category of "Mixed Race (Vest)." These thinkers are the interlocutors I chose to assist me in questioning the complicity that racial language has in reifying the "we," "us," and "my people" colonization has created and may continue to create at the expense of uncovering more equitable means of understanding the self who is inseparable from colonial history yet existing before and perpetually becoming after.

The third chapter's musings (maybe this entire work is more a text of musings than anything else), entitled "Alternate Race Theories in Motion: A Discussion with Dominic Pettis-El/I.B. Fokuz," revolve around the concept of nationality. As a transcribed conversation between myself and Dominic Pettis-El, founder and member of the rap collective Tomorrow Kings (a group of which I am a proud particle) and Sheikh of Temple No. 1 of the Moorish Science Temple of America, we have a conversation about something we always discuss "off the cuff:" the ways in which the categories of race rob an individual of (1) nationality, and (2) a substantial connection to land, two pieces that for many are significant within several constructions of personhood, among a plethora of other things. MSTA founder Noble Drew Ali, in the creation of the Moorish Science Temple of America, admonished his followers to not refer to themselves as "Negro," "Black," or "Colored" because of the inability/intentionality of these terms to deny those subjugated/described by them in a national capacity, which he argued is necessary for one to be acknowledged by the nations of the world as a human. In an age where discussions of reparations to Afro-diasporic US citizens are at an all-time high, we are reminded that up to this point in the history of the United States, only nationalities and ethnicities have been given reparations (e.g., "Native Americans" and the Japanese). We must ask the question if "Black" people or any non-national-identifying historical recipient of colonial oppression by descent are legally eligible for reparations since it could be quite persuasively argued that race and race-related terms are neither ethnicity nor nationality, thus not eligible for reparations. This conversation between Dominic and myself investigates the importance of the MSTA in dialogues on nationality and how that might be attained for those who have found themselves on the underside of the racial system of classification in the passage of history "from then 'til now."[7] Also, there is a resurgence of interest in the MSTA by the academy, such as Judith Weisenfeld's lauded text *New World A-Coming: Black Racial Identity During the Great Migration* (NYU, 2017) and Larry L. W. Miles' monograph entitled *Afro and Indigenous Intersectionality in America as Nomen* (Lexington, 2023).

The fourth chapter of the text, "Period, Full Stop: The Oversights of Cancel Culture(s)," encounters the idea of "cancel culture" vis-à-vis what I would argue are its foreparents, racial categories. In cancel culture, certain bodies and conceptual identities frequently described by the undersides of racial categories as "Black," "Latina/o," "Hispanic," "Native American," "African American," "Asian," "Indigenous," and so on tend to oppose others categorized by these same mechanisms who choose to transgress the colonial and postcolonial identities said others have accepted as sui generis identities. When Kanye West asserted that slavery is a choice and that a United States with Donald Trump as president is more of an opportunity than a hindrance to "Black" people, he committed sacrilege to the "sacred cow" championed by many who have been identified by and now identify with the repurposed undersides of racial taxonomies, and without a deconstruction of the categories themselves, they "canceled" West, dismissing anything else he had to offer subsequently or anything of value embedded in that particular conversation. Nick Cannon's 2020 remarks in conversation with a former member of the legendary political rap collective Public Enemy on the oppressive behavior of those who identify as European Jews in the entertainment industry caused him to be canceled without (1) a serious attempt at verification of the charges and (2) the historical complexity of the social group "Jewish" in terms of who is/can/should be included in that particular social group. Rachel Dolezal's adaptation of "Black" identity also secured her sentence to be canceled, overlooking the complexities around the category of race a surface-level look at her situation glosses over. The chapter explores critical questions around cancel culture in relation to West, Dolezal, and Cannon, respectively.

Following from this discussion, the fifth investigation, "The Lure of the Shroud: The Question of the 'Mattering' of the Conceptual Human Illusion," which begins to move toward the solution I propose, will interrogate the ideas of race and racism in more detail, exploring the connections between both. To put it bluntly, is it at all possible to eliminate racism without eliminating the category of race? In *Method as Identity: Manufacturing Distance in the Academic Study of Religion*, Monica R. Miller and Christopher M. Driscoll, in relation to the work of scholar of religion Charles Long, point out that "Blackness" (and race as a category for that matter) is rooted in imagination. And we know that imagination is arbitrary and materializes in reality the way it does due to certain interests, needs, and "natural" emanations of the historico-cultural situations in question.[8] Again, I will ask the question: Can a "Black," "Hispanic," "Latina/o/x," "African-American," "Asian," "Pacific Islander,"

"Native American," or any other non-"White" life matter due to the possibility of an assertion of value in the face of concepts that by definition and rootedness in systems of domination and subordination, can only have limited value as symbols of full human value determined by systems of governance as old (or young) as and created by the colonization projects of Spain, France, England, and so on? If we conclude that we indeed cannot eliminate racism without eliminating race, where does this leave our impressions of our actual historical identities, identities that for many of us are perpetually consumed (and I mean "consumed" as in fire, for the category of race forever scorches, especially when the implications for and of its underside are forced upon you by societies powered by hegemonic systems of oppression) and bound up within ways of being? These questions have been asked before, but I hold that a more concrete philosophical suggestion as to how we move forward is missing in the discourse. Can we move forward without the category of race, seeing that we've preserved it and used it to create and recreate ourselves for so long? It is my hunch that we can indeed leave it behind and may need to for the survival of the human psyche as a whole. While the first chapter is similar in that it deals with the *advantages* of dismissing racial language, and the third chapter involves how *nationality* is not afforded to an individual through racial categories (with "Whiteness" perhaps being the only category i.e., not in need of nationality, for it has the power and the universal social capital to transcend it even when it seems to subscribe to it), this chapter deals with the possible *impossibility* of ever ending racism without a collective abolishing of the category of race like an outdated currency that just can't be spent anymore anywhere on the globe. This chapter places the implied and clearly stated answers by scholars to the question of whether race itself is raced on a spectrum, considering the theories of Ibram X Kendi (antiracism), Mahzarin R. Banaji ("mind bugs"), Cornel West (race as utilitarian), Judith Butler (categories as power dynamics), and Ania Loomba (the comparison of race to caste).

Chapter 6, "Multi/race/less/ness: A New Name for Timeless Ways of Human Becoming," outlines my solution to the category of race, which I have called "multi/race/less/ness" in my first book, *Underground Rap as Religion: A Theopoetic Examination of a Process Aesthetic Religion* (hardcover 2019, paperback 2021). As the book really hinges on this idea, the chapter gives an outline of it that is disconnected from underground Hip-Hop culture in general and the manifestation of underground rap in particular, which is, of course, different from its appearance in the aforementioned text. In multi/race/less/ness, I argue that the realities of a world conducted by the arbitrary categories of race can be authentically encountered while simultaneously rejecting said arbitrary categories, hence possibly avoiding the pitfalls of ascribing to "Blackness," "Whiteness," "Hispanicness," "Latina/oness," "Native Americanness," and more. As ancillary to multi/race/less/ness, I present in detail a Whiteheadian process approach to primordial[9] and futuristic means of identity and explore the implications of a transformation of personhood for both self and world if multi/race/less/ness is adopted as a means of abolishing race. Multi/race/less/ness in my formulation is both theological and philosophical, and since it is my contention that the facets of race most responsible for the seemingly irreversible spread of these arbitrary ideas across the globe are its theological and philosophical components, my theory draws from both of these wellsprings as it offers an alternative. To this end, the chapter reforms the theological underpinnings through an appeal to the philosophy of religion as explicated in Whitehead's *Process and Reality* and *Science and the Modern World*, as well as Philip Clayton's theories of emergence, the Derridean-influenced work of John Caputo, and Hunbatz Men's teachings on the deeper meanings of Mayan cosmologies. The philosophical revisions of multi/race/less/ness draw from the racial deconstruction found in the thought of Monica A. Coleman, the postcolonial pioneering writings of Frantz Fanon and the concepts of the *occurrent arts* and *activist philosophy* found in the work of Brian Massumi.

Chapter 7, entitled "BioDigital Jazz: Reflections on Emergent Multi/race/less/ness in Hip-Hop and Belize," develops through an appeal to experience two of the three manifestations of multi/race/less/ness I posit as more equitable concepts of identity than race/trauma, namely the manifestations of culture and nationality. I will engage two cultures very familiar to me that I would argue function with varying degrees of multi/race/less/ness: the religion of Hip-Hop Culture/Kulture and Belizean nationality, scanning them for insight into the possible effectiveness of such a move enacted within (and possibly to the destruction of) spheres where the social groups of race reign supreme. Hip-Hop is connected to the "culture" manifestation and further develops multi/race/less perspectives on ways of becoming in relation to heated current debates around whether "Blacks" and "Latina/ox," or solely "Blacks," are responsible for founding the Culture, demonstrating how Hip-Hop as multi/race/less in theory and practice arguably bypasses this discourse. The complex histories of identity formations in Belize are raised as an example of the "nationality" manifestation of multi/race/less/ness, exploring how either being born or inaugurated into Belizean citizenship provides more equitable (though in some cases problematic) legal and experiential transcendence and bypassing of race/trauma.

Chapter 8 is referred to as "Self-Study: Scattered Thoughts on Genealogy as a Facet of Multi/Race/Less/Ness," and as the title indicates, it offers an aesthetically motivated rendering of the "genealogy" aspect of multi/race/less/ness. The chapter explores what might happen if, instead of accepting singular or multiple racial categories *deductively* as reliable descriptors of one's identity, one studied themselves and the history they are aware of and based their understanding of their perpetual human becoming on an authentically *inductive* coming to terms with what is discovered both through the learning of family histories and the transformations that said knowledge is a catalyst for in lived experience. The assertion of the chapter is that a "real" encounter with genealogy makes evident that our complex ancestries not only defy racial categories and render them logically inconsistent but also detract from fuller understandings of the self in community.

Whether flight or crash will occur is yet to be seen, and either is welcome. This script is not written from end to beginning but is more like a freestyle tournament or hostile street cypher like those I used to participate in in a past life that now seems as far away as Panama from Tuvalu (well, I still show up in these from time to time to be completely honest). Sometimes I'd win, and sometimes I'd lose. But whatever the outcome was, I learned many things. Let's observe the game. The DJ just dropped the beat. The next page is my first battle rhyme. Maybe by the time the record needle plays the last instrumental (or the bibliography), the category of race will be in a casket. I hope you're as eager to start this treacherous journey into racial blasphemy as I am. Shall we start?

1 "BLACK" IS DEAD: A MOORISH UN-SURE-ING OF A "SURE THING"

Do we still hear nothing of the noise of the gravediggers who are burying God? Do we still smell nothing of the divine decomposition?

Gods, too, decompose! . . . The holiest and the mightiest thing the world has ever possessed has bled to death under our knives: who will wipe this blood from us? With what water could we clean ourselves? . . . Do we ourselves not have to become Gods merely to appear worthy of it? . . . Finally, he threw his lantern on the ground so that it broke into pieces and went out. "I come too early", he then said; "my time is not yet. This tremendous event is still on its way, wandering . . ."[1]

FRIEDRICH Nietzsche

Introduction

Perhaps the time of this work, similar to the time of the madman in Nietzsche, is not yet. Maybe the time of this work will never come, unlike the madman in Nietzsche. I mean, what am I even embarking on? There's no possible way to foresee the end of racial language. Unhinging that might mean unhinging "us" and everything "we" have fought for "us" to be. There is no turning back. We just have to deal with this unfortunate sleight of hand and, more accurately, slip of tongue. Or be accused of betrayal of our "races." What else can we do?

Fuck That. We Can Do a Lot.

In this chapter, I aim to take a serious and maybe for some uncomfortable look at the language of race, language that many would assert is part and parcel with their "authentic selves." What philosophical, ethical, legal, and religious harm is inflicted by self and community when one chooses to become the "Black," "Latina/o," "Native American," "Asian," or other person that one is expected to be? If one chooses to transgress the category of race that they are said to fit into by those within and without the group, what happens to one's status not only within broader societal frameworks constructed by the category of "Whiteness," but also within the cultural fabrics of those who subscribe to the social group that has been formed for them *before* them but not *by* them (e.g., a person's relation to "Black" people who may see them as strange for rejecting "Blackness")?

Gradual answers to these questions will begin in this chapter. In keeping with a keen focus on the Moorish Science Temple of America's understanding of the detriments of racial categories, this chapter will begin with a brief history on the idea of race as we know it, continue with a philosophical analysis of how Western philosophy has reified the "biological" notion of race, and conclude with the insights of Noble Drew Ali and José Pimienta-Bey, who both argue that not only the idea of race as existent by necessity but also the philosophical and religious categories supporting the idea of race are the main reasons why racial categories are detrimental to the human situation.

A "Brief" Rehashing of the Modern Origins of the Category of Race

In philosophy of race, critical race theory, cultural studies, sociology, religious studies, theology, and other disciplines in the academy, the street corner cypher, and other places, the notion of race as "social construct," or a sort of confluence of several materialist occurrences and not an essential systematization of humanity, is accepted by many. However, many of these same thinkers reconstruct the category of race after they've done so much to deconstruct it. Why is that? Is it because it's easier to resort to what's been known? Is it because they believe that it is a helpful one that can serve the process of progressive liberation, or what Anthony B. Pinn might refer to as "complex subjectivity?"[2] Is this not an issue for them because they understand racial terminology to be synonymous with self-naming post-deconstruction? Whatever the reasons are, the fact that not much work has been done on the possible inherent problems of holding onto and "caretaking" of racial language, to draw from Miller and Driscoll's use of religion scholar Russell McCutcheon,[3] indicates that this large beam in the eye of critical race theory, philosophy of race, sociology of religion, and studies in religion and race must still be addressed. And with several very marginal movements presently gaining steam in this area, it's a fine time to encounter it thoughtfully and critically.

An Aesthetic Shaping of Time, Space, and Matter

In *Mothership Connections: A Black Atlantic Synthesis of Neoclassic Metaphysics and Black Theology*, Hartshornian process philosopher and theologian Theodore Walker, in conversation with esteemed religion scholar Charles Long, states, before transatlantic slavery, there were no people calling themselves "African." Prior to transatlantic slavery, people on the continent we now call Africa identified themselves by reference to particular tribes and nations (Ashanti, Hausa, Mendi, Yoruba, Zulu, etc.) without adding reference to color (black) or continent (Africa). "Black" and "African" identities were born during the Middle Passage and matured in subsequent years and generations.[4]

Race is an aesthetic movement in Walker's quote. Portraits do not have to exist by necessity. The portraits created betray the innermost thoughts of the artist. Some portraits have started revolutions, ended free nations, enslaved and liberated humans, committed murders, and started religions (word to Jim Morrison).[5] Any conceptual category is the creation of historical, theological, sociological, anthropological, and random amalgamations of energy bursts that are conducted by several human (and non-human) wielders. Here, we will engage the nature of the artists who created the modern idea of race at a much deeper level.

A Portrait of the Category as a Sketch

As we know, several critical race theorists and philosophers of race would assert that elements of what we now know as "race" were not "painted" until a little over 500 years ago. Even though substantial evidence as charted in the work of historian Benjamin Isaac calls for a broadening of what "racism" is and points to systemic categorization and types of oppression existing in early Greco-Roman societies,[6] many theorists working on race as a conceptual category that has given birth to modernity and its many components still cite the last years of the fifteenth century as its beginning. While my work uses a more recent nativity as a point of departure as well, I'd like to consider some of the insights of Isaac on more "antiquated" time periods before we fast forward. In *The Invention of Racism in Classical Antiquity*, Isaac states that

> It may be useful again to note what we should not be looking for in Greece and Rome. Greek and Roman antiquity did not know the sort of racism that western civilization developed in the nineteenth and twentieth centuries, since they had no concept of biological determinism. There was no nationalism in the modern sense of the Greco-Roman world, nor was there any concept that a specific ethnic group should live within defined borders. What the ancient world did have was a range of prejudices, phobias, and hostilities toward different groups of foreigners . . . Clearly racism is not a way of looking at people based on genuine scientific observation of their physical and mental qualities. It is a construct of underground theories of discriminatory commonplaces elaborated with the specific aim of establishing the superiority of one group over another, based on presumed physiological characteristics.[7]

Race is the practice of making a group out of people who have similar physiological characteristics, share intangible characteristics and abilities (or disadvantages), and possibly establishing a hierarchy based on said characteristics. Racism is not necessarily traceable to the ancient Greek and Roman societies that Isaac is interested in. However, there were "underground theories of discriminatory commonplaces," which were no more based on an essentialist understanding than the modern understanding of race. The existence of political enforcement of bias in ancient societies such as ancient Greece and Rome is important to note in that it draws attention to the underlying consciousness which created illusory boundaries not equivalent to but in many ways very reminiscent of modern categories of race.[8]

In many ways, the modern portrait of race has as its paint the very "range of prejudices, phobias, and hostilities" that Isaac tells us were present in ancient Greece and Rome. When the Moors were ousted from their occupation of Al-Andalus by Christian forces, the area experienced conversions of Muslims and practitioners of Judaism to Christianity to ensure their safety and tenure there. In an attempt to establish a unified religious state different from that of the Moors, Ferdinand and Isabella expelled first Jews and then Muslims from the realm in 1492 and 1502, respectively. Regulating the massive conversions happening at this period, the new monarchy only allowed converts who could trace their ancestries to Christian families resisting the Moorish invasion to remain. Under the grand inquisitor Torquemada, confessing Christian faith was not enough. This ushered in the idea of *limpieza de sangre*, or "purity of blood," a concept that George Fredrickson cites as possibly the first instance of occidental proto-biological racism.[9]

As the portrait moves from sketch to flesh, this obscurity of the hegemonic negotiation of identity politics through theological ideas is sublated as more "empirically based" systems of science become the face of this process of becoming. This changing of the form of identity politics progressed to "biological" and "anthropological" conceptions of what eventually becomes the secular category of race. In the Iberian Peninsula under the auspices of Portugal, the theological idea of not enslaving Christians but readily enslaving those who did not practice the dominant Christianity[10] gradually progressed to establishing connections between not only certain phenotypical features and types of work (e.g., lighter-skinned slaves having tasks deemed to be less arduous than their darker-skinned counterparts) but also associating Christianity or the lack thereof with physical appearance.

These ideas of Christian-influenced pure blood that are outlined in the conceptual imagination of the world conquerors of the sixteenth century take shape in what is articulated in the natural philosophy and biological science writings starting in the late seventeenth century. In "A New Division of the Earth," published in 1684, Francois Bernier systematized his encounters with humanity in Persia, Egypt, and India in such a way that the differences he described between these people became the means by which "Europe" defined humanity. Based on his experience, he understood the world to be divided into four "races," the first race being those from the places commonly referred to as "Europe" and "North Africa" (who for Bernier had similarities in types of hair and bone structures), the second being the people south of the Sahara (physically characterized by their wooly hair and dark skin, thick noses and lips, etc.), the third referring to the inhabitants of east and central "Asia," Siberia, and Russia (classified by their "white" skin, among other characteristics such as flattened noses and eyes that were thinner than the other "races" Bernier creates), and the fourth representing the inhabitants of northern Scandinavia (categorized by Bernier for their comparatively short and stocky stature). In Bernier's taxonomy, there is a fifth race, and that is the race of the inhabitants of the "Americas" at the time of Spanish, British, French, and other strands of colonization. However, Bernier said that this fifth race can also be subsumed into the first.[11]

Bernier is credited with being the first to apply the existing idea of race to physical distinctions.[12] Bernier's work was followed by the writing of Johann Friedrich Blumenbach in his dissertation "On the Natural Variety of Mankind," which was published in 1775, with a revised edition coming on the scene in 1781. Blumenbach maintained a structure of races similar to that of Bernier, which was systematized into the people of "Africa," "Asia," "Europe," and "America," with "South Pacific" being a fifth category added in the 1781 edition of the text. In another revised edition in 1795, Blumenbach amended the work to introduce the term "Caucasian" to refer to the inhabitants of "Northern Asia," "Europe," and Northern India. The 1795 edition also put forth the term "Mongolian" to refer to those people of "Asia" who did not fit Blumenbach's portrait of "Caucasian," "Ethiopian" to refer to the non-"Caucasian" peoples of Africa, "American" as those who inhabited the places referred to by many as the "Americas," and "Malay" as those native to the "South Pacific."[13] While Bernier's discoveries were said by some at the time to lack scientific rigor due to him founding his racial distinctions on the base of skin color, Blumenbach based his own varieties on cranium size, which supposedly gave him more scientific credibility.[14]

Early work of the natural sciences on race was also established by the research of Francis Galton, who introduced the term "eugenics" in 1883. Applying the conceptual framework of Darwin's idea of "natural selection" to the process of reproduction, Galton, one of the first proponents of Social Darwinism, advocated that the intentional breeding of certain "upper echelons" would produce the human with all of the desirable dispositions,[15] characteristics that certainly were not associated with those labeled "Ethiopian," "American," or "South Pacific." Galton argued that eugenics should even be thought of as a "religion" the US government should enforce.[16]

Unlike Galton, Houston Stewart Chamberlain put a more conceptual and "essential" component on eugenics. For Chamberlain, the things we call distinct races emerge from geographical situations in which people who are in certain parts of the world began to intermingle.[17] This belief led Chamberlain to conclude something similar about the cultural productions of certain people, culminating in his assertion that the most celebrated cultural productions of the world were the result of the genius of discrete natural selection of the Aryan race. For Chamberlain, the Reformation is a very important point in the history of the Aryan race because it unites various groups (German, Slavic, Teutonic, and Celtic) in a dialectical move.[18] The tenuous polarity between the Aryans and Jews exists, according to Chamberlain, because Judaism contains in a continual reflection on history and its repetition in the present, while the Germanic impulse looks toward the future as it asks the reflective question "Who am I."[19]

As artists contributed to the dominant portrait and continued to create subordinate portraits, the portrait that served as the pinnacle mystically gave birth to parts of the other less desirable pictures ingressed by those the dominant society understood as "other." Some of the undesirable features associated with the non-"White" image did not have to always be explicitly drawn, even though they were in many instances. In other instances, these "shades" appeared on the subordinate conceptual portraits when human entities antithetical to the pinnacle conceptual portrait appeared in empirical eyesight. The "hues" that these humans radiated were in unintentional opposition to "Whiteness," which Jim Perkinson refers to as "a power of opposition . . . it is the racial inverse of blackness, a negative conviction that 'whatever else I might be, at least I am not that, not black.'"[20]

This systemic ridding of the other also appears in the work of Madison Grant, a proponent of US anti-miscegenation. In Grant's book *The Passing of the Great Race*, published in 1916, he argues that racial boundaries that are the foundation of US identity by this time and are widely accepted by many of its citizens should not be crossed, so as not to pollute the "White" race.[21] Grant's influence caused miscegenation to impact immigration laws and interracial marriages in thirty states, only overturned in 1967 in Loving vs. Virginia.[22]

While biological arguments about the reality of race have a considerably long history in their formation starting in the seventeenth century and "mature" in the twentieth century, Franz Boas was one of many biologists to dispute determinism. Since much of the study of biological race held that cranium size was an indication of the "stock" from which one came, Boas argued that cranium size was determined not by genes but by environmental variables. From this move, Boas ushered in an acceptance of ethnic groups as not biological but cultural. If ethnic groups are predominantly cultural and not biological, then they are mutable, thus problematizing a fixed notion of deterministic race.[23]

Another important denial of the notion of biological race in the twentieth century came from anthropologist Ashley Montagu. Montagu argued that the real determining factors of appearance were genetic. This challenges biological notions of race, since various physical features can be either the result of the perpetual passing of genes within a discrete group from parent to child or the result of genetic mutations.[24] After the work of Montagu, the United Nations Educational, Scientific, and Cultural Organization (UNESCO) released an official statement that denied the biological foundations of race in 1950, with the American Association of Physical Anthropologists (AAPA) issuing a similar denial as late as 1995.[25]

The Results of the Conceptual Made Physical

We've been given portraits, which have painted for us what our "essential" selves are. Race is the paintbrush, wielded by witting and unwitting agents of history upon the canvas. Aesthetic criticism, disguised as critical race theory and philosophy of race of various types, has pointed out several possible origins of the paintings, with the most profound revelation being that we were humans before we misplaced ourselves in the portraits created for us. And even though we know we could ban the paintings from the gallery like the swastika or the "N-word" (well, they tried with that one, but to no avail, really), they remain. Next, we turn to the works of Western philosophy, which served as bulwarks for the biological and anthropological portraits of race.

The Ghost of/in the Racial Machine

In Walter Benjamin's classic essay, "The Work of Art in the Age of Mechanical Reproduction," he introduces what he calls "aura," the actual thingness of the work of art, as the physical manifestation is merely an accident of this more "transcendent" category.[26] For Benjamin, physical works of art lose their original relatedness to their history when they are detached from the spatial and conceptual location that gave birth to them.[27] However, in a turn of Benjamin's argument in my own direction, I would suggest that there is still a residue of the original mountain range that, while detached, intentionally and by social natural selection in something tangible, like a postcard, retains its "cultic value." Is the portrait of race a portrait that will always possess its original aura?

Of the novelty of mechanical reproduction in 1935, Benjamin says,

> An analysis of art in the age of mechanical reproduction must . . . lead us to an all-important insight: for the first time in world history, mechanical reproduction emancipates the work of art from its parasitical dependence on ritual. To an even greater degree the work of art reproduced becomes the work of art designed for reproducibility . . . Instead of being based on ritual, it begins to be based on another practice – politics.[28]

In their mechanical reproduction and possibly even mechanical mutations[29] over hundreds of years in places far removed from their origin, have works of art lost their cultic value in their present stages, or has their transmission from context to context simply transformed what their original cultic value looks like? Is the idea of race simply a brain that constitutes and facilitates the mundane functions of "essential" human natures, or is it a mind that "consciously" conducts interhuman relations, the aura of the past that is presently nowhere, hence everywhere?

In the moment of the critical scholar's recanting of categories that are deemed as "unintellectual" and "primitive," they take on the method of dissecting the data of people who inhabit parts of the world with strategies that appear unbiased. The communal ritual of the conceptual aesthetics of the modern category of race transcends the Iberian Peninsula of the late fifteenth century and is applied anywhere in the world without reference to the conflict between Islam and Christianity in Spain that gave birth to it. The ritual that originated out of somewhere becomes essentially out of nowhere. Benjamin uses the metaphor of the surgeon and the magician and says the magician works healing through the conduit of her own body, referencing contextual traditions and beliefs. The surgeon, disconnected from "primitive" ideas of medical practice, is also disconnected from their patients through the impasse of the surgical instruments, unlike the immediate reach of the magician's hands.[30] While Benjamin in my reading adequately outlines the break between cultic ritual and mechanical reproduction, his own words imply something that he does not intend to focus on but at the same time does not deny: the idea that the surgeon is still the magician. There is a ritual dimension to the fascist mechanical reproduction. Of fascism, Benjamin says,

> Fascism sees its salvation in giving these masses not their right, but instead a chance to express themselves. The masses have a right to change property relations; Fascism seeks to give them expression while preserving property. The logical result of Fascism is the introduction of aesthetics into political life. The violation of the masses, whom Fascism, with its *Führer* cult, forces to their knees, has its counterpart in the violation of an apparatus which is pressed into the production of ritual values.[31]

At the end of the essay, Benjamin states that fascism mechanically reproduces ritual values. It is my contention that the philosophical development of the category of race is a clear example of fascist conceptual mechanical reproduction that is indeed ritualistic and has an aura hidden due to the obfuscation of its genealogy.

Race as Philosophy

The philosophical shaping of the portraits by various thinkers helped spread these arbitrary ideas into the global imagination as necessary. In Bernier's coining of "race" to refer to various types of physical appearances, he did not answer a burning question of whether all humans share the same root.[32] This becomes important in some philosophical discussions in the seventeenth century due to the consequences of the side one took in this argument. If a philosopher wanted to reflect on the biological superiority of "pure blood" as exemplified in what was becoming the "White" race, one might refer to polygenesis. This does not connect the other races to the "White" race. However, if one argued for monogenesis, one could still argue for the supremacy of the "White" race, but with obvious logical difficulties since the "White" race would have to also include the manufactured demarcations of people groups that "Whiteness" was and is established to subordinate and emerge from.

In this important debate between monogenesis and polygenesis, David Hume was a prominent voice, contributing statements that could be construed to support either side. In the infamous essay "Of National Characters," Hume famously states in a footnote,

> I am apt to suspect the negroes, and in general all nations other species of men (for there are four or five different kinds) to be naturally inferior to the whites. There scarcely ever was a civilized nation of any other complexion other than white, nor even any individual eminent either in action or speculation. No ingenious manufactures amongst them, no arts, no sciences. On the other hand, the most rude and barbarous of the whites such as the ancient GERMANS, the present TARTANS, still have something eminent about them, in their valour, form of government, or some other particular. Such a uniform and constant difference could not happen, in so many countries and ages, if nature had not made an original distinction between these breeds of men. Not to mention our colonies, there are NEGROE slaves dispersed all over EUROPE, of whom none have ever discovered any parts of ingenuity; though low people, without any education, will start up amongst us, and distinguish themselves in every profession. In JAMAICA, indeed, they talk of one negroe as a man of parts and learning, but it is likely he is admitted for slender accomplishments, like a parrot, who speaks a few words plainly.[33]

Firstly, while the essay itself does support that differences between various cultural groups classified by the eighteenth century taxonomy under the label "White" are the results of nurture and not nature, the footnote could be taken to argue for a polygenesis which would subordinate all races under the "White" race. It is important to note that Hume singles out the "Negro" in his footnote, using the distinction as a prime example on which he builds his case for natural differences between the races, which could arguably be read as polygenesis.[34] Secondly, in stating that "Negroes" were ignorant and could at best parrot the intellectuals of Europe, he adds to a collective assumption of the day that "Negroes" are unintelligent. Thirdly, Hume asserts that mostly all non-"White" people are inferior to the "Whites" in cultural contributions to civilization, and in the footnote, Hume tends to tie this supposed inferiority to natural and perhaps polygenetic differences. For the Hume of this infamous footnote, it seems as if the cultural improvements available to the "White" race are not possible for other "primitive" and "inferior" races.

Immanuel Kant, on the other hand, gives a strong philosophical defense of monogenesis in his essay "Of the Different Races of Man." For Kant, all humans did in fact descend from common human ancestors, and those ancestors originated in the areas commonly known as "Europe," and what came to be known as the various races are the results of migration to areas with various climates and continuous inbreeding. Kant held that after discrete inbreeding over long periods of time developed distinct physical characteristics, they would be more or less finalized unless some person or people of foreign stocks were introduced into the gene pool.[35] In Kant's taxonomy, the distinct races that come from this process of migration and inbreeding are the "noble blond" of Northern Europe, the "black" of Western Africa, the "red" found in the Americas and East Asia, and the "olive yellow" of Asian-India.[36]

Like Hume, Kant's racial categories enforced the existent and perpetually forming racial hierarchies of the era. Kant held that the "Native Americans" are of the lowest status because they lack the capability to be trained as slaves, and "Negroes" are a bit higher because they can be taught to serve the "Whites" as unpaid laborers. Those of India can be educated but are still not able to understand abstract concepts. In the drafts of Kant's anthropology lectures, he points that "Native Americans" and "Negros" are incapable of self-government, thus conveniently offering a philosophical argument as to why it was necessary for then to be subjugated and enslaved by the "Whites."[37] However, in the 1790s, Kant's racial theories take a turn, as he shifts several of his views on non-"Whites." In *Toward Perpetual Peace*, written in 1795, Kant denounces the practices of slavery and colonization, and even goes as far as introducing a concept called "cosmopolitan right," which holds that all people have equal legal rights as humans. From this, it would follow that no land should be utilized in any way without express legal permission from the occupants of the land.

It is important to note that in this "conversion experience," Kant does not relinquish the concept of biological race, but only the connection between phenotype and intellectual capabilities.[38] Kant's later acceptance of cosmopolitan right fits into his support of monogenesis, as it affirms the implication of equal humanity that could be said to follow all humans being of the same species. The demarcations of race are still held onto by Kant, who argues that the blending possible and evident in the co-creation of two people from different racial stocks supports monogenesis. In racial blending, physical characteristics of both races are evident, something not always readily evident in discrete procreation. Thus, interracial breeding creates individuals who in many instances did not visibly fit into the prescribed characteristics of the racial categories of Kant's era.[39]

In spite of counterarguments to polygenesis from the likes of Kant and Blumenbach, the idea was still very much a live option in the mid-nineteenth century, espoused by anthropologists such as Louis Agassis. After studying medicine, zoology, and paleontology (among other things) at several universities in Germany, his belief in monogenesis was shaken when he went to the United States and encountered a "Black" person for the first time. This led him to believe that there was no biological relation. Agassis announced his turn to polygenesis at the 1850 meeting of the American Association for the Advancement of Science.[40] Race theorist Arthur de Gobineau held that while the other races were governed by the impulse of repulsion, humans of the "White" race followed their impulsive attraction to those of different racial stocks. This allowed the "White" race to perpetually progress toward higher levels of civilization.[41] Through the success of the theory of evolution as argued in the work of Charles Darwin, polygenesis began to die out, as Darwin's work indicates a common human family that produces differences partly through natural selection and partly through continuous mating among people with similar physical characteristics.[42] After Darwin, polygenesis was replaced with natural and sexual selection as a much stronger explanation of the differences among people.[43]

This trajectory of monogenesis is further developed in the annals of the transcendental philosophy of G.W.F. Hegel. When Absolute Spirit realizes itself fully in the world story, the dialectical tension that Hegel argued marked historical eras would be sublated. Hegel, a lifelong Lutheran, asserted that the fullness of Absolute Spirit happened in the isolated occurrence of the life, death, and resurrection of Jesus. For Hegel, the actuality and the figura of Jesus could be said to represent the "thesis" of divinity merging with the "antithesis" of humanity; that moment when Absolute Spirit becomes a tangible reality. In the resurrection, when the physical Jesus disappears and disperses the Holy Spirit to remain and distribute the enlightenment of Absolute Spirit to the world, the "synthesis" of Spirit and human is the consciousness that enjoins the human family into a collective oneness where they clearly understand the impulse of universal logic, in a sense understanding that they are that logic.[44]

Hegel's notion of philosophical Christianity isn't a clean slate but is encoded with theological, philosophical, anthropological, and cultural presuppositions and concerns. Spirit's "second coming" is localized in the "White" race as its conduits to the world.[45] In the *Lectures on the Philosophy of History*, Hegel outlines various stages of human development from the "Orient" of ancient times to the German era of his day. Evident in Hegel's work is a similarity between his division of people groups and the racial categories that had been created and accepted by the 1820s and 1830s. Hegel, in resonance with the anthropological work of Gobineau, articulated in *The Lectures on the Philosophy of History* an idealistic understanding of the progression of Absolute Spirit from the "Oriental World" to the "German World."[46] While Gobineau holds that the progression of humanity culminates in the "White" race as it subordinates yet depends upon all the racial mixtures that precede and constitute it, Hegel argues that the progressive manifestation of *Geist* appears through conceptual evolution most clearly in the "White" race, with the German people being the preeminent exemplars of it.

In *The Lectures on the Philosophy of History*, Hegel defines "Freedom" over against "Nature," with the latter indicating actions that bend to desires unbridled (thought of as irrational), and the former indicating a recognition of a universal logic that the enlightened human consciousness becomes one with. The antithesis of the desires of Freedom and Nature is overcome when the human consciousness embodies the universal logic so that one's Nature acts according to the knowledge of Freedom.[47] Hegel goes on to say that

> When man is spoken of as "free by Nature," this mode of his existence as well as his destiny is implied. His merely natural and primary condition is intended. In this sense a "state of Nature" is assumed which mankind at large are in the possession of their natural rights with the unconstrained exercise and enjoyment of their freedom . . . Examples of a savage state of life can be pointed out, but they are marked by brutal passions and deeds of violence; while however rude and simple their conditions, they involve social arrangements which (to use the common phrase) *restrain* freedom.[48]

If we are to interpret this quote within the tapestry of the newly created and more or less agreed upon racial categories of the nineteenth century, we can see how Hegel's statements on Freedom and Nature interface with the contemporary hierarchical view of humanity: the non-"Whites" in his sketch of the history of ideas become the "savages" that Hegel says not only are devoid of the ability to act beyond the whims of their passions, but also are devoid of history, as the acts of Nature alone lack the "dignity" of history. This subordination to Nature is by no means foreign to the "White" race, but in Hegel's idealism, the "Whites" can and do escape it through the progression of history into higher stages, something that the non-"Whites" seem to never be able to do collectively.

Friedrich Schleiermacher's *On Religion: Speeches to its Cultured Despisers*, published in 1799, also served as an indirect reification of the concepts of race that the collective imagination of Germany, England, France, the United States, Spain, and others had come to accept as empirically factual. Schleiermacher offers a then non-traditional understanding of religion as feeling and not necessarily dependent on a traditional notion of "belief" in a conscious and purposeful God.[49] In the Fifth Speech of the text, Schleiermacher alludes to several traditions that would now be known in academic studies as the "world religions." In this allusion to and explicit naming of these traditions, Schleiermacher intends to problematize the idea of a one true religion, thus opening his vantage point of Christianity to a pluralism that many of his clerical contemporaries dismissed. Schleiermacher decenters the singularity of a "right" religious belief manifested in Western Christianity, a singularity that fueled the beginnings of race in the late fifteenth century in the Christian reconquest of Al-Andalus from the Moors. He says,

> If you do not want to have only a general concept of religion . . . then you must abandon your vain and futile wish that there might be only one religion, lay aside your loathing of its plurality, and as impartially as possible, approach all those that have already developed out of the eternally rich womb of the universe in the changing forms during the course of humanity, which is also progressing in this respect.[50]

This sounds amazing at first read! At this final point of *On Religion*, Schleiermacher seems to dislodge "true" religion from this localized space of Christianity common to several European articulations. If Schleiermacher's postulate that there is value in more than one religion is true, then the hierarchical philosophico-religious underpinnings encoded into the modern idea of race are in jeopardy. But Schleiermacher, perhaps unknowingly, carves a way out: a return to the all too familiar idea of "progress."

Toward the end of the Fifth Speech, Schleiermacher states that

> However fortunate you may be at deciphering the *crude and undeveloped religions* of distant peoples or at sorting out the many types of individual religions that lie enclosed in the beautiful mythology of the Greeks and Romans is all the same to me; may their gods guide you. But when you approach the *most holy*, where the universe is intuited in its highest unity, when you want to contemplate the different forms of systematic religions – not the *exotic and strange* but those that are still more or less present among us – then it cannot be a matter of indifference to me whether you find the right person from which you must view them. (italics mine)[51]

Here, we see that Schleiermacher, similar to Hegel, sets up a conceptual schematic that inseparably links "positive" types of Christianity as practiced by colonizing nations to the idea of an actualization of a pure universal intuition.[52] Because of this, the revelation of the universe's totality that Schleiermacher says can be accessed from several religions can really only be accessed in its most perfect state from the "true" religion of Christianity as practiced in his context, as it is *most holy* and neither *crude and undeveloped* nor *exotic and strange*. These distinctions between the "holy" and the "crude" that Schleiermacher and other influential thinkers of the era shape the conceptual landscape of subsequent theology, philosophy of religion, and various other intellectual movements in the "West," reifying watershed moments in the biological and philosophical development and maintenance of the category of race.

The Reclaiming of a "Lost Estate"

This chapter starts with a poetic and possibly theopoetic remembering of the infamous "Death of God" narrative. In my reading, Nietzsche's insight about the death of God can be used as a fluid hermeneutic through which we can approach the category of race, especially since this text, like J. Cameron Carter's *Race: A Theological Account*, elucidates the interdependence of the modern category of race and religion (specifically Judeo-Christianity in the "West"). If we accept Nietzsche's claim that this Judeo-Christian God is indeed "dead," or never really existed in the first place, what happens to the category of race, which draws much of its impetus from and was in many ways "drawn" in the perceived likeness of this God and derived from Judeo-Christian theism? Are we unaware of race's "death" in the same way that Nietzsche says we are unaware of God's? Enter Noble Drew Ali, who gave detailed answers to both of these pressing questions through the lens of "Blackness" being a category in a casket but moving throughout the globe as a powerful apparition.

Noble Drew Ali and the Moorish Science Temple of America

A discussion of the history of Islam in the United States is incomplete without a discussion of the Moorish Science Temple of America.[53] Founded by Timothy Drew, who was born in North Carolina in 1886,[54] the MSTA evolved as a unique mix of Islam, nationality, and a reorientation of the descendants of enslaved humans in the United States to citizens among the nations of the world. Drew's ancestral origins as rendered by various sources are both convergent and contradictory, connecting him to both Morocco and the Cherokee (originally known as the Aniyunwiyah) Nation. Some reports assert that he was the child of ex-slaves adopted into the Cherokee nation after his parents died. Other sources hold that Drew's mother was Cherokee and his father was Moroccan. The oral tradition surrounding Drew also puts forth that he went to Egypt as a teenager and studied esoteric arts under a priest of these disciplines.[55] After this period, Drew, who took on the name "Noble Drew Ali," established The Canaanite Temple in 1913 in Newark. The movement in its infant stages suffered factions that caused it to be split into two groups: The Holy Moabite Temple of the World, which remained in Newark, and Drew Ali's sect the Moorish Holy Temple of Science, which moved to Chicago in 1925 and was changed to the Moorish Science Temple of America in 1928. Subsequently, temples began to appear in the Midwest, the East Coast, and the South, with Ali's Moorish Divine and National Movement of North America as an organization under which all MSTAs were autonomously united.[56] Members who joined the rapidly growing movement added the surnames "El" or "Bey" to their existing names, with "El" referring to chiefs in the Onondaga ("Iroquois") language and "Bey" being both a distinction of "governor" or "provincial ruler" and the name of a clan in pre-colonial Sudan.[57]

Drew Ali taught a version of Islam that asserted that Afro-diasporic US descendants of slaves or so-called "Black" humans who came from non-slave lineages should not refer to themselves as "Black," "Negro," or "Colored," but as "Moors," a name said to refer to the original people of modern day Morocco, Mauritania,[58] Mali, Niger, Senegal, Mozambique, Chad, Zanzibar, and other sub-Saharan "African" regions to which the Moors were connected, such as Ghana.[59] José Pimienta-Bey makes the point that the term "Moor" was used to identify people with "Africoid" features "who were of mixed African and near-East origins."[60] In other usages of the word "Moor" appearing when the categories of race that we now know began to take shape in the late sixteenth century, we see that it reverently referred to anyone with "Africoid" features as cited in several English dictionaries[61] and sometimes those considered by many accounts to be "European."[62] This ties into MSTA teachings that the Moorish domain and people were by no means restricted to the countries of the "African" continent but extended to the pre-Columbian "Americas" and even to the mythical city of Atlantis.[63] The MSTA holds that colonizers encountered Moors with "Africoid" features in the "Americas" and "Caribbean" who arrived long before the enslavement period. The term "Moor" is also said by some to have ties to the land known in the Hebrew Bible as Moab. Of the Moabites, Drew Ali starts the MSTA holy book, The Circle 7 Koran, with these words,

> The illustrious acts of the Moslems of northwest and southwest Africa. These are the Moabites, Hamites, and Canaanites, who were driven out of the land of Canaan, by Joshua, and received permission from the Pharaohs of Egypt to settle in that portion of Egypt. In later years they formed themselves kingdoms. These kingdoms are called this day Morocco, Algiers, Tunis, Tripoli, etc.[64]

In this beginning, Dew Ali connects the Moabites with the Hamites and the Canaanites, who are linked genealogically and said to have been the ruling powers of Moorish North Africa. The Canaanites (Cushites), who inhabited the area now known as Western Sudan, are said to have descended from Ham, the son of Noah, who is understood to have been dark-skinned.[65] Simply put, Drew Ali argued from burgeoning yet unpopular historical information of the time that the enslaved in the United States referred to as "Negro," "Black," "Colored" "Native American," etc. had linguistic, ancestral, and diplomatic ties to the Moorish empire and were Moors, a legally respected title, by nationality.[66] Drew Ali presented this information to followers in such a way that suggested that the labels "Black," "Negro," or "Colored" denied the descendants of the US chattel slavery period (whether or not their ancestors were enslaved) true personhood among the nations of the world and the national government, and that this personhood could be gained only by a reclaiming of their nationality, which was connected to the ancient Moors (a distinction that José Pimienta-Bey argues applies to all non-Eurpoeans),[67] or Moabites, as members of the MSTA were called by Drew Ali.[68]

The idea of "nationality," or a rejection of the category of race, is paramount to the teachings of the MSTA. In rejection of these terms, which Drew Ali deemed as destructive to Moors, the MSTA espoused a legally sanctioned nationality called "Moorish American" to replace the labels of "Black," "Negro," or "Colored." The title "American" is not rejected as in some of the radical movements of the time such as Marcus Garvey, who Drew Ali cites as his forerunner, but embraced as the government under which US Moors were born.[69] Because of a loyalty to both nationalities, chapters of the Moorish Science Temple of America publicly display both the Moroccan Flag and the US flag. In Chapter XLVII of the Circle 7 Koran, Drew Ali lays out the basics of Moorish American nationality as championed by the MSTA's status as a legally classified religious corporation, which solidified by the US law that claiming and living a Moorish American identity is practicing religion, thus taking nationality out of the realm of anything that could be legally challenged.[70]

Historically, Morocco is the first country to recognize the United States as a nation in 1778, and Many Moorish Americans cite the 1787 treaty between the United States and Morocco as the bilateral agreement that grants them protection in the United States as the descendants of people who were under the jurisdiction of Morocco before the creation of the United States. US citizens in Moorish domains were also granted protection. This led to slave traders capturing some Moors under the jurisdiction of the Moorish empire and bringing them to the United States, but eventually having to free them due to their nationality as Moors.[71] The fact that some Moors directly connected to Moorish domains were taken as slaves indicates that their appearance was that of most "Negros." For Drew Ali, race truly takes the form of an idea that leads to a "Blackness" that can and must be abandoned if Asiatics[72] are to experience full humanity.

The Moorish Science Temple was created on the backdrop of the "Black" nationalist traditions of the early twentieth century, with Marcus Garvey's Universal Negro Improvement Organization (UNIA) serving as a major springboard. The Circle 7 Koran of the Moorish Science Temple of America states,

> In these modern days there came a forerunner, who was divinely prepared by the great God-Allah, and his name is Marcus Garvey, who did teach and warn the nations of the earth to prepare to meet the coming Prophet; who was to bring the true and divine Creed of Islam, and his name is Noble Drew Ali: who was prepared and sent to this earth by Allah, to teach the old time religion and the everlasting gospel to the sons of men.[73]

The position of some of the members of the MSTA is that the larger and more well-known Nation of Islam utilized much of the foundational doctrinal structure (a return to Islam, dietary restrictions, pushes toward self-sufficiency, etc.) but 1. denies that this structure is in fact Moorish American in origin and 2. became subject to the "White" supremacist scheme by returning to the term "Black" and "Negro." The Nation of Islam's Minister Louis Farrakhan, in an address uploaded to YouTube on May 27, 2020, states that Noble Drew Ali was the "prime predecessor" of Master Wallace D. Fard in *introducing* Islam[74] to the descendants of those classified as "Black," "Negro," and "Colored" in the United States. He also says that when members of the MSTA moved to the NOI with Islamic surnames, The Honorable Elijah Muhammad saw no need to change these names again (as is the custom when entering the NOI), since the titles "El" and "Bey" were already Islamic in origin.[75]

Several mysteries surround the death of Noble Drew Ali in 1929. He passed following his release on bail after in prison beatings due to police suspecting him and several other members of the MSTA as culprits of the murder of Claude D. Greene-Bey, Drew Ali's business manager.[76] The death certificate lists the cause as "tuberculosis broncho-pneumonia."[77] Drew Ali's suggestion that "Blackness" is, was, and will always be a "dead" category, similar to God's "death" in Nietzsche, seems absurd to many. However, he leaves us a picture of identity as nationality that provides a progressive reimagination for pictures formerly subjugated under the dominant portrait with no escape.

The Benefits of Noble Drew Ali's Death of "Blackness"

For Drew Ali, the difference between race and nationality is the difference between being a person (who by definition receives the benefit of the law) and being property (warranting said entity no protection under any law). Drew Ali first approaches the death of "Blackness" from a legal perspective, arguing the impracticality of desiring to be treated as a human while treating oneself as non-human.[78] In nationality, one is connected to a history, lands, traditions, and communities within which one can practice all of these. This is why, in concert with the sociological function of religion, Moorish Science Islam is ostensibly only required to orient the displaced Moor with her national name and heritage, which *is* the practice of religion for the tradition.

Drew Ali and the MSTA's emphasis on nationality as a renouncing of race brings us to the question of reparations. While some would argue that reparations have been given to "African-Americans" in various forms such as recently repealed DEI scholarships and providing state and national holidays for "African-American" leaders,[79] others would argue that this is not nearly enough. Some argue that writing a check to all of those Afro-diasporic US citizens disenfranchised by US participation in the transatlantic slave trade is not only financially unfeasible (and this of course can be debated) but also leaves structural injustices as they are.[80] Possibly, the proponents of the various mainstream forms of reparations understand "African-American" or "Black" to function as a nationality, or at the least, an ethnicity or culture. But if these labels are interrogated as legal categories, one must think through Drew Ali's admonition from the pamphlet entitled "A Warning From the Prophet," which states,

> The citizens of all free National Governments, according to their National Constitution, are all one family, bearing one free National name. Those who fail to recognize the free National name of their Constitutional Governments are classified as – Undesirables, and are subject to all inferior names and abuses, and mistreatments the citizens care to bestow upon them. And it is a sin for any group of people to violate the National Constitutional Laws of a free National Government; and cling to the names and principles that delude to slavery.[81]

It could be said that nationality makes one eligible for reparations of various types, while subordinate categories of race would technically classify one as an "undesirable." Drew Ali calls us into the ancient methods of identity that Jennifer Lisa Vest tells us are before race and "White" men don't know.[82] As a side note, it is interesting that the United States has only provided solely economic reparations to legally recognized nationalities, such as the "Cherokee" and the Japanese. According to Drew Ali, the citizens of both of these nations are due reparations if wronged because of their status as citizens of a nation and persons. "Blackness" and its descendant "African-American" remain locked in a slave verbiage that, in the words of Pimienta-Bey, indicates "persons legally transformed into property."[83] Miles reminds us of the shakiness of the Fourteenth Amendment to ensure citizenship to "African-Americans" since it was forced upon them as property and not agreed upon as persons having previous histories legally protected by nationalities.[84]

Related to the legal benefits of nationality that Drew Ali raises, Pimienta-Bey also discusses the psychological benefits of a disassociation from "Blackness." It is not a far leap logically from "Blackness" as the absence of personhood to "Blackness" as a mental state of inferiority perpetuated by disenfranchisement. After a period of time, one begins to believe that they are "Negro," "Black," and "Colored," the legal constructions of what they have been named by a colonizing system for the benefit of the system's survival. In the life of Malcolm X, this issue comes up when Malcolm Little is confronted with the literal definition of the word "black" in English dictionaries that hold definitions of its usage that predate and are directly responsible for the creation of "Black" people. In concert with Drew Ali, Malcolm finds that the word means "nothing," "absence of light," "vile," "ill-repute," "savage," etc.[85] Pimienta-Bey says that the historico-psychological concept of "Blackness" has a connotation that is very difficult to overcome. The perception of "Blackness" is inherently derogatory, and the problem of its redefinition is a problem that nationality provides an answer to by not confronting it at all but rather reverting to ancient Moorish identities in modern "American" ways.[86]

The psychological and nationality benefits that come from a rejection of "Blackness" that Noble Drew Ali advocated also bring with them a historical component. Drew Ali would argue that "Blackness" causes a people to wander in a wilderness wearing a name that does not suit them.[87] This opening to nationality is a gateway to learning about the several cultures that converge in the post-colonized so-called "person of color." If one is aware of one's nationality(ies), one may be more prone to seek out the history of said nationality(ies) as opposed to seeking out the history of "Blackness," which arguably is a null (empty) set. This is perhaps easier to do in the present with DNA testing (of course, the difficulties the accuracy of such tests must be acknowledged as well). When we consider Anderson's assertion that this adherence to an ontological Blackness "calls into question 'African-Americans' interest in fulfilled individuality,"[88] we see a possibly strong connection between the created portrait of "Blackness" and a knowledge of self that is left unfulfilled by the category.

At what point does the descendant of chattel slavery with roots from Yorubaland to Spain become "Black?" If a person is "Black," that's often all they are allowed to be in many conversations about race and identity that take place within and without the so-called "Black" community. Historian Francisco Bethencourt asks, "How is it that the same person can be considered black in the United States, colored in the Caribbean or South Africa, and white in Brazil?"[89] Pimienta-Bey, while focusing his work in *Othello's Children of the New World* on Moors who looked more or less like Wesley Snipes and Whoopi Goldberg, also stressed that Moors came in all shades and were what many would currently describe as "multiracial."[90] As I have mentioned before, Noble Drew Ali took account of his own specific ancestral composition, according to some accounts stating that his father was Moroccan and his mother was Cherokee. In my understanding, Moorish American identity is more equipped than the rigid boundaries of many instances of "Blackness" to handle what many anthropologists and sociologists might refer to as genealogical multiplicity.

Thirdly, an abolishment of "Blackness" as advocated for by the MSTA causes us to reconsider the effectiveness of activist movements that continue to hold on to it as a useful category. If the terminology of "Blackness" is 1. not a term which our ancestors used, 2. a term which meant "inferior," "absence of light," "of ill-repute," and "of low moral character," and 3. a term which could be argued to function presently in the same way in a legal sense, is it far-fetched to suggest that the title of "Blackness" is unfit for use for liberation due to it being a logical and legal inconsistency in that "Black" is synonymous with dehumanization? We must consider the sobering possibility that a statement such as "Black Lives Matter" is and can only be a poetic assertion. This torturing of the pictures of race, demoting it from its status as a series of pre-given portraits to shining a light on its biological, anthropological, theological, and philosophical constructions and introducing the thought of Noble Drew Ali as a possible route toward a more liberating approach to the fluid person, is an essential ground floor of the house of multi/race/less/ness.

Conclusion

Through a reiteration and recasting of the well-known anthropological, biological, religious, and philosophical history of the modern idea of race, I have attempted to take seriously at a different level the arbitrary existence of racial categories without the usual return to a use of the categories themselves as a method of critique. I have chosen to attempt to leave the master's house without using his car. In offering the thought of Noble Drew Ali and the Moorish Science Temple of America, I present an example of a transgression of race that occurs by a death of "Blackness" that many efforts of resistance to racial oppression inevitably return to in varying capacities, such as the "Black" Panther Party, "Black" Lives Matter, the term "African-American," and other related symbols. It is left to the reader to decide whether such a religio-cultural renunciation of "Blackness" as articulated by Drew Ali and taught by the MSTA is plausible and realistic. This work operates from the experimental position that Drew Ali's philosophical theology is a move toward a liberation in the destination of multi/race/less/mess that does not only deal a natural death to "Blackness" but also all race/trauma.

2 WHO KEEPS THE GATE?: IDENTITY POLITICS AND THE COMPOSITION AND MAINTENANCE OF THE RACIAL "US" AND "THEM"

Introduction

The insights of the history of the development of racial categories explored in Chapter 1 lead us to an important question engaged by several philosophers of race: to what and whom is one referring when one uses power system-derived terms such as "White," "Latino/a," "Hispanic," "Native American," "Black," "African-American," "Indigenous," etc.? When they emerge from the speakers, (1) which speakers mean to indicate that all people socially constructed to fit into any of these have a common history, identity and social norms, render chastisements for supposed members transgressing these norms, and are more or less the "same people?" (2) Which speakers mean to identify a group of people who are only a group because much of the outside world sees them as such, which may result in them being treated in certain ways by those in other groups, having larger or smaller access to resources than other groups, and assumptions by non-group members that all group members have certain characteristics? Which speakers mean to identify both (1) and (2)? Which speakers mean to identify something other than either (1) and (2)? While philosophy of race has thoroughly explored the question of the "us" and the "them," the discourse has yet to lead to a widespread nuancing of what racial categories can mean.

This chapter will initially take a turn toward analytic philosophy, utilizing the skill set of Ann Cudd's description of what makes and maintains a social group. From the implications that Cudd's work provides, we will, through an appeal to the language that constitutes dominant and subordinate social groups, consider if racial social groups can (1) ever provide authentic identity for a human self and (2) if they can ever be non-oppressive. The second section will examine the work of philosophers of race such as Kwame Appiah, Jorge Gracia, and Naomi Zack as we try to get a clearer grasp of what is actually meant when "us" and "them" racial language is used, especially when the essential "us" and "them" of racial groups are of the type that Cudd argues. Finally, we will turn to the work of Jennifer Lisa Vest on the philosophical underpinnings and conceptual breakthroughs of mixed race identity as a possible strategy for "passing the impasse" of racial social groups.

Ann Cudd and Social Groups

The contention of analytic philosopher Ann Cudd's work in *Analyzing Oppression* is that "social groups play an essential role in oppression, in the sense that members are oppressed only as members of social groups."[1] She also holds that many social theorists, philosophers, and scientists reject the reality of either one of the two types of social groups that she points out: voluntary social groups (those that the members agree to be a part of) and involuntary social groups (those groups which are created to include individuals without their consent). The definition of social groups that she articulates means to include both the willful and determined aspects that go into these categories.[2] For Cudd, in order to account for oppression, one has to affirm that social groups do exist, regardless of their type of existence (constructed or natural).

Cudd outlines three ways in which the content of groups is amalgamated: 1. naturally, 2. socially, and 3. accidentally. In the natural force of collective naming, Cudd refers to certain seemingly objective structural epistemological factors that are shared by entities, thus causing them to be placed into a category. We can conceive of a natural labeling of rocks based on a particular region of the world from which they come as a type of cataloging that is largely unrelated to a social categorization of those same rocks into their countries of origin, which at this stage would indicate a strictly imposed cartography including lines of demarcation and decided by governmental decisions and human history on the natural region, among other factors. The accidental facet could be represented by imagining that half of these rocks were at some point lost in transit, and a set of the lost rocks emerging from the mere knowledge that there are lost rocks can be utilized as a strategy for locating them.[3]

Going further, Cudd also states that of those who do actually hold that social groups are real, there is one disputed question: how are social groups formed and maintained? Intentionalists, such as Weber, Sartre, Nietzsche, and Gilbert (among others), would assert that groups are formed and maintained by those who consider themselves part of said group. This is a voluntary type of social grouping. The structuralists, such as Marx, Durkheim, and Folbre, hold that social groups emanate from the structures which situate life in the context in question, thus causing them to persist as long as the structural conditions that give rise to them remain. Examples of the types of social groups that concern structuralists are race, class, gender, and culture. While both structuralists and intentionalists conflict with each other, Cudd argues for a compatibilist approach which agrees that some social groups may be of either the intentionalist or structuralist ilk. She also asserts that some social groups can be both intentionalist and structuralist.[4] She says,

> On my view, individuals whose actions are intentionally guided, though perhaps not toward the ends they achieve, exercise social control of the social constraints. But at the same time individuals act within socially determined constraints that guide and shape their intentions. And so on. The intentionalist is correct to see that the action begins with the beliefs, desires, and capacities (both psychological and material) of the individual acting agent, but wrong to suppose that that rules out social forces beyond the control of that agent, forces that affect her beliefs, desires, and capacities. The structuralist is correct to see that from the point of view of the acting individual, there are groups to which she can choose to belong and those unchosen groups to which she either belongs or does not, but which she cannot choose to enter or leave. But the structuralist mistakenly attributes these to immutable forces of history located beyond the influence and responsibility of individual human beings.[5]

While Cudd argues for a compatibilist approach to social groups, she cautions against internalist compatibilist positions such as that of Richard DeGeorge and Larry May, who hold that the intentional and structural aspects of social groups become the identity of group members to the point that personhood and the social group are inseparable. For example, the internalist compatibilist perspective is revealed when person X is categorized as a so-called "Latina." This category becomes not just how they are externally classified but how they understand their internal identity. Cudd's compatibilism must allow for people who may be classified as a certain social group but reject membership (e.g., an individual socially constructed as "Black" who identifies with their Nigerian ancestry but not with "Blackness"). These are prime examples of what Cudd calls "involuntary social groups."[6]

Cudd offers an externalist compatibilist view of social groups. While assenting to the construction of social groups, many times by those outside of the group but eventually accepted by those within the group (intentionalism) and the maintenance of said groups through historical forces beyond the control of the members (structuralism), Cudd states that "What makes a person a member of a social group is not determined by any internal states of that person, *but rather by objective facts about the world, including how others perceive and behave toward that person* (Italics mine)."[7] The "Native American" is really only "Native American" in a structural sense because the society sees and treats him as such. Whether or not the person sees themself as a part of the group or believes the group exists is irrelevant to how others react to the group, favorably, disparagingly, or both.

What happens when personhood is conducted as part and parcel of an oppressed racial group by either group outsiders or group insiders? If Cudd's line of reasoning is indeed valid, it may lead us to some extremely potent strategies for providing answers. This question raises several subsequent issues, such as what to do and how to interact with non-consenting members of a racial group, and the problem of voluntary members of the racial group who don't completely fit into the group for various reasons (possessing a phenotype not typically associated with the racial group, etc.). The most captivating question (at least for me) is this: does any participation within and acceptance of an oppressed social group as personhood not only perpetually predispose the group to racism but also perpetually self-inflict racism on members of the group? To be clear, the first chapter addressed some of these same concerns from the vantage point of the history of colonization from the fifteenth century onward, philosophy, theology, and Moorish Science. However, the work in this segment adds on to the previous chapter in its analytic focus on oppressed races as social groups. To make this distinction more "clear" in a related analogy, what are the effects of the Moorish American leaving the race/trauma social group of "Blackness" but being forced by group insiders and outsiders back into it?

Cudd remarks that we do not need to know we're in a social group to be a part of one, which is the definition of a nonvoluntary social group. But tensions can emerge when an assumed member of the group rejects membership. This occurs frequently in discussions of the limits of the racial group. The Moorish American may be told that regardless of how they see themselves, they are "Black," "Latino/a," "Hispanic," "Native American," or any other distinction given to those whom Noble Drew Ali referred to as "Asiatics." Obviously, when this happens, we are experiencing a "failure to communicate," or at least a failure to communicate with comprehension and/or acceptance. Cudd, in a conjuring of the work of Margaret Gilbert, asserts that when one refers to "we" and "our" as in "our people" and "we who are Asians," certain criteria should be met by group members, and the criteria that Gilbert is referring to is not prima facia, like visible physical features. For Gilbert, group membership requires that all group members have a goal in common and are collectively aware of this.[8] Would the person who rejects any racial category qualify for racial group membership under Gilbert's definition? Rejection of the category could be argued to imply that the goal of solidifying the group's identity (possibly the goal of maintaining said racial identity) is not shared by the individual in question. However, much of the outer world and many of those within the group would consider this dissenting individual to be a group member, and their lived experience would reflect those who are placed into said group with and without their consent.

Gilbert holds that a social group can only refer to individuals in close proximity to each other, where there is a more realistic chance of members meaning the same thing by group identity.[9] In the case of racial social groups, a person from the United States categorizing a person from Mexico they encounter in Chicago as "Black" and being offended if/when said person rejects the group membership is engaging in a surface-level inclusion of a person with different goals and motivations in their own "we" and "our." What must precede this inclusion in the "we" and "us" is the plural consent of both partners. Gilbert lets us know that most of the important social groups governing our daily lives do not meet the criteria of consent.[10] The "we," "us," and "our," of social groups, then, should perhaps not be so frivolously distributed as they many times are in racial social groups. What are in many cases referred to as "social groups" are, to Gilbert, simply

> large and anonymous collections of persons, for whom neither the willed-unity condition or the common knowledge condition could be satisfied except for under rare circumstances (perhaps during revolution for example). So if these collections are social groups, then there is a second social group to recognize.[11]

The reason that I am considering race as a social group in the sense that Cudd and Gilbert are dealing with is due to the widespread opinion that race is the type of social group that either provides or denies foundational human rights. Cudd points out that the constraints of some social groups are naturally determined, such as the social group including those who are over 6ft. tall. Such a group is nonvoluntary, but membership is not generally thought of as something that its members would dispute. Also, this situation may or may not come with the types of existential assumptions that accompany social groups associated with human identities. There are other types of social groups that are determined by social constructions. These social constraints refer to the access or denial of some social groups to resources that make human flourishing possible.[12] Many would agree with the axiom that racial groups have the power of liberating or constraining their members. Cudd also discusses social group constraints that seem to be freedoms. Several theorists, such as Jim Perkinson, understand "Whiteness" to be a category that transcends all other categories. But this freedom is also a "death" of sorts, in that in transcending all other racial identities and being the measure against which other said identities are measured, it in turn relinquishes a right to having its own identity.[13]

If race is the type of social group that functions by necessity on group constraint even when constraint seems to be a type of freedom, then we could plausibly argue that the voluntary (or involuntary) claiming of involuntary racial social groups participates in a type of social constraint and is in turn oppressive. However, it may be possible to conceive of a racial social group that does not necessarily function by constraint. In the "Black" and "Brown" power movements, "Asian American" student organizations, and "Native American" resistance efforts at Standing Rock, the perception by many is that these racial social groups are not intrinsically oppressive but have been made so by a manipulation of external forces. But if what

Cudd has said so far is true, do the metaphysics of racial social groups allow for them to operate without the social constraints associated with racism?

One could assert that nonvoluntary social groups such as racial social groups are oppressive by nature in Cudd's general definition of social groups, which is that "*A social group is a collection of persons who share (or would share under similar circumstances) a set of social constraints on action.*" If "oppression" at its base level for *Homo sapiens* is anything that constrains the human's pursuit of the benefits of humanity as ends-in-themselves as opposed to means-to-ends, then many racial social groups would qualify at the least as being agents of oppression if not the "primordial" foundation of it. Cudd, drawing again from Gilbert's understanding of social groups, points out that members of a social group share something that is socially significant, whether voluntarily or involuntarily. In many instances, that something shared does indeed shape how those within and outside the definition of the social group perceive others within the definition and how they are perceived by those outside of the definition.[14]

Those who by definition fall within in the confines of a social group perhaps inadvertently created for the purpose of domination could be said to exist within oppression as long as (1) the social group exists or (2) group members choose not to renounce the group and make explicit to those who by default claim them as part of the group that they are not members. While Chapter 1 dealt with how race as a social construction regrouped and reshaped perhaps preexisting social groups, this section strictly focuses on the experiential effects of the linguistic metaphysical nature of social groups. If a racial social group due to the history of the category of race by nature must be hierarchical (the proposed consideration of Chapter 1), then racial social groups by definition are either subordinate or dominant. Therefore, there can be no racial social group without a root of racism encoded into its definition. According to this logic of social groups, races are not only social groups that demarcate a collection of people with things in common (such as the social group of drivers who text while driving, a social group that is also in serious need of abolishing), but also are the borders erected between humans that metaphysically imply the superiority of some groups and the inferiority of others.

Philosophers of Race on the Problem of the "Us" and the "Them"

While I am certainly concerned with what is actually being said and implied metaphysically when one uses racial language to describe themselves, I am more intrigued by the consequences waged on those who reject the racial categories that they are "supposed" to fit into by those socially constructed to be both within and without the social group. What needs to be examined more thoroughly is not the act of chastising of those who don't identify with the group they are commonly associated with by insiders and outsiders but the seemingly pre-reflective background assumptions identified with a racial category to the point that rejecting said category when possessing certain "defining" characteristics of the group seems irrational at best and delusional at worse.

The work of Kwame Anthony Appiah, Jorge Gracia, and Naomi Zack provide insights into the structural dimensions of racial categories that not only provide valuable insight into the implications of racial categories when used from general conversation to intentionally philosophical discourses, but also assists in elucidating the possibilities of dissenting group members transcending the group in substantial and meaningful ways.

Kwame Anthony Appiah: Not "Race" but "Racial Identity"

Kwame Anthony Appiah's perspective of reductionism concludes that there is nothing at all real about race. Appiah states that since this is true, the most we can relate to an unreal category that metaphysically structures how several societal structures conceptualize humanity is to *identify* with it, perhaps out of necessity and perhaps out of volition, as in Cudd's definition of a "social group." Appiah is making the claim that when we think we're using race as an objective essentializing category, we're actually using it as an identity that is separate from the human histories in question.[15]

In "Race, Culture, and Identity: Misunderstood Connections," Appiah says,

> Even ordinary users of the term "race," who operated with what I have called vague criteria in applying it, thought of themselves as using a term whose value as a tool for speaking the truth was underwritten by the experts. Ordinary users, when queried about whether their term "race" really referred to anything, would have urged you to go to the experts: the medical doctors and anatomists, and later the anthropologists ad philologists and physiologists, all of whom together developed the scientific idea of race.
>
> This makes the term "race" unlike many other terms in our language: "solid," for example. "Solid" is a term that we apply using everyday criteria: if I tell you that material scientists say that a hunk of glass is not a solid but a liquid, you may feel well that they are using the term in a special sense, resisting semantic deference. Some people might want to defend the word "race" against scientific attacks on its legitimacy, by denying, in effect, that semantic deference is appropriated here. Of this strategy, I shall make just this observation: if you're going to go that route, you should probably offer some criteria – vague or strict – for applying the term. This is because, as we shall see, the arguments

against the use of "race" as a scientific term suggests that most ordinary ways of thinking about races are incoherent.[16]

Appiah's conclusion in this quote is something I've taken to the form of conversational thought experiment, and most of the times that I've done it, it's been met with confusion, frustration, dismissal, and even emotions that border on the type of anger that Whitehead describes as a feeling that quickly looses its "object" as fast as it "attains" it in the transmission from idea to physicality.[17] When someone would begin to state a racial universal such as "Blacks naturally want to be around their own kind," I posed two poignant questions: What do you mean by "Black," and what do you mean by "own kind?" Many of the initial responses were befuddlement, like I know or should know exactly what these things mean. With some of my more inquisitive interlocutors who actually "played along," their response to the "Black" query, while answered rhetorically, got us to a similar point: "Black" refers to a person of African descent. When I would respond with the contention of many anthropologists that *Homo sapiens* came into existence in the region we now refer to as "Africa," thus making every human "Black," the retort would be something like, "No, that's not what I'm saying." But yes, they did. This begs the question, what do they mean when they say "Black?"

To this question, I would suggest that maybe what they were really referring to by "Blackness" is someone who has kinky hair, possibly light to dark brown skin, thick lips, wide nose, and/or possibly a descendant of the enslaved in a particular country, etc. If "Blackness" is guised as signifying people with a human ancestral connection to the region we now refer to as "Africa" but can really be abstracted into an independent concept based on appearance that contains virtually no cumpulsory connection to "Africa," the conversation on what race is has drastically been complicated. As Appiah suggests, the scientific definitions of race correspond to and largely center on phenotype, but the "folk" usage reads a self and selves onto this bare skeleton of analytic discovery. "Black" has become a people and a consciousness in popular discourse when a strict analytic usage of the terminology initiated by the scientists who developed the idea requires it to be neither.[18]

In light of the "What do you mean by 'our people?'" question, I mostly received the same initial response that I garnered from the "What do you mean by 'Black'" question. This came up during a discussion with a person who stated that if they were in a country where there weren't many of their "own kind," they would want to find out more about that person and why they were in this particular region of the world where many of their "own kind" were not present. I then asked this person what they meant by their "own kind." They paused at this question for a moment, and then responded that "our people" are those who look like us. Further, they offered that when you encounter a person who looks like you, there's a good chance that you will have a lot in common with them. I began to push further, asking if the person knew beyond a shadow of doubt that when they saw a stranger who by their definition could be placed into the "own kind" category that they shared any other similarities besides appearance. They paused again, as if the obvious answer was "Yes" and this was something that I should know, but after their brief hesitation, they conceded that it may be likely that there are similarities but that this may not be the case. They continued with a question about a particular circle of friends that I have—my rap collective, the Tomorrow Kings. All of the members in the group at this time would be socially constructed as "Black" by the "common" uses of the term in public US discourse. My unintentional "thought experiment participant" suggested that the things we have in common are in some way metaphysically tied to the fact that they are my "own kind," which for this astute conversation partner was initially known by appearance. My response to this excellent observation was a question (and of course, they tell us to never answer a question with a question, but philosophical investigation has always been hampered by a strict adherence to any rule): is the fact that most members of the Tomorrow Kings share physical similarities primary to our being of the "same kind" or are these phenotypical characteristics arbitrary in comparison to other shared properties (e.g., being fans and artists within the realm of underground Hip-Hop, having friendships that predate the rap group, etc.)? I introduced a different definition of "own kind" that corresponded more with my authentic experience than the one presupposed and weilded by my interlocutor. Appiah's illuminating of the transformation that racial language has underwent and its disputed interpretations (both legal and everyday) does much to substantiate the point that the language of racial groups does not refer to anything "real" at all.

Appiah's use of "racial identity" is his way of coming to terms with the fact that racial language structures many societies in the world while also eliminating any undercurrent or overt belief that the verbiage is anything more than an arbitrary by-product of the British, Spanish, Portuguese, and other expansion projects of the fifteenth century onward. He says in defining racial identity that it is

> a label R associated with *ascriptions* by most people (where ascription involves descriptive criteria for applying the label); and *identifications* by those that fall under it (where identification implies shaping role for the label in the intentional acts of the possessors, so that they sometimes act as an *R*); where there is a history of associating possessors of the label with an inherited racial essence (even if some who use the label no longer believe in racial essences).[19]

From Thomas Jefferson to Matthew Arnold (and other pitstops along the way), Appiah goes through a great deal of biological, philosophical, and sociohistorical scholarship to show why race isn't "real." In reflection on DuBois' wrestling with the race concept, he argues that race and racial language lack any sort of essence that could unify all who should fit into one of the several categories based on sensory perception as one "kind." However, because race is (1) a measuring stick by which we are many times regarded whether we like it or not and (2) many hold that race is the basis for how people are treated, there is a utility to racial identity in that it "keeps it real" with how much of the world functions while not claiming that race is anything more than an arbitrary grouping at its root.[20] But in this understanding of race, Appiah does assert that ways of being in the world that some may refer to as "culture" and "ethnicity" do develop as a result of the metaphysical racial constraints under which bodies are subjected due to appearance.[21]

Appiah does go on to state that even though racial language at the present time serves a certain utility of identifying and potentially addressing the metaphysical structures of injustice that certain phenotypes are forced to function within, we do need to "ask whether the identities constructed in this way are ones we can all be happy with in the longer run."[22] Appiah's merit is that he lays the groundwork for a restructuring of logical symbolisms that govern how bodies are perceived. It is not enough for a negatively racialized body to eventually gain respect and meaning. Appiah states, "If I had to choose between Uncle Tom and Black Power, I would of course choose the latter. But I would like not to have to choose."[23] In "Race, Culture, Identity," we're asked to imagine a time in which racial social groups aren't useful, one of the primordial prehensions of multi/race/less/ness.

Jorge Gracia: Not "Racial Identity" but Definitional "Race"

Jorge Gracia's ideas of race share some similarities to Appiah's "racial identity," but also diverge from his project in some significant and critical ways. However, Gracia outlines a separate understanding of race and ethnicity, as he, unlike Appiah, is uncomfortable with blurring the lines between the prima facie characteristics which make one a part of a social group and the shared ways of becoming that social groups tend to explore over time. Gracia refers to his idea of race as the "Genetic Common-Bundle View" and to his idea of ethnicity as the "Historical-Familial View."[24]

In *Surviving Race, Ethnicity, and Nationality: A Challenge for the Twenty-First Century,"* Gracia says,

> Consider a person who has all the external marks of being "Black" and yet denies he is one, thinking himself rather Latino. Is there a conflict between being "Black" and being Latino? Are these categories of the same sort? And for that matter, is there a conflict in being Latino and Puerto Rican, or Hispanic and Jewish when Jewish is not taken as religious designation? Some think

so, whereas others disagree, although most of the time these agreements and disagreements are based on gut feelings or folk psychology rather than well-developed views of race and ethnicity.[25]

Here, Gracia has perfectly set up the dilemma that fuels this chapter: (1) the metaphysical impossibilities of seriously escaping the racial constructions placed upon us and (2) the difficulties of conceptualizing how one person can embody two or more of said distinct racial and race-related constructed categories due to the exclusionary definitions that create racial social groups. The postcolonial human psyche has difficulty envisioning humanity as anything that does not fit within the parameters of colonial-constructed race and adjacent categories. Therefore, when a human becoming asserts a transcendence beyond the categories, some voluntary and involuntary members of the social group remind them of 1 and 2, thus chastising the human in question back into the construction which society says people with their phenotype (and maybe their ancestry) are "supposed" to wear.

Theoretically, from the vantage point of Gracia, a racial social group dissenter may be justified insofar as said dissenter holds not that they aren't a part of the racial social group that they are "supposed" to fit in (which would imply that the set of race X does exist but person Y does not fit in it). Rather, it might be justified if the social group does not exist as an essential category, but exists due to labeling.[26] It is a different move for the Belizean and Honduran to assert that they are not "Black" while maintaining that someone is. A chess move of social group chastising may be more justified in this instance because the individual in becoming may possess all needed defining characteristics. In Gracia's definition of race, that is the only thing required.[27]

Gracia's conditions for membership in a racial group are as follows:

> (1) each member of the group is linked by descent to another member of the group who is in turn also linked by descent to at least some third member of the group and (2) each member of the group has one or more physical features that are (i) genetically transmittable, (ii) generally associated with the group, and (iii) perceptually perspicuous.[28]

For Gracia, inclusion in racial group membership cannot be derived from either (1) and (2) independently. Both must be true for the subject to be a part of the particular racial set. According to Gracia's definition, the US "one drop rule" would not be sufficient for "Black" racial group membership to include President Warren Harding if the historian J.A. Rogers' work on the lives of Presidents Harding, Lincoln, and Eisenhower (among others) were proven to be accurate. This demonstrates once again how cut and dry Gracia's definition is, and reinforces race as nothing but a superficial identifier that holds no substantial cultural and ethnic information. In this framework, to deduce anything more than the sum of the parts from a racial whole would be impossible; there is nothing else that radiates beyond the whole due to the metaphysical capability of incapability showcased by racial language.

For Gracia, modified ideas of ethnicity and nationality are possible alternatives to the conflation of identity with physical descriptions and maybe some other nonphysical properties that can be associated with race. In what Gracia calls the "Familal-Historical View," ethnicity is philosophically separate from race and other observable characteristics that undergird certain racial-esque concepts of ethnicity by postulating the most important characteristics that determine ethnicity emerge from a shared history. Gracia states as an example of the Historical-Familial View that "a family does not get its unity from common features among its members, but rather from the particular historical relations that tie its individual members, which in turn produce features common to some of those members."[29] For Gracia, the Familial-Historical View of ethnicity does what race cannot: transcend the metaphysical schematics of grouping by appearance to observe the collective identities that sensory-based renderings of race are not equipped to recognize. For example, in the Familial-Historical View,[30] a person from Haiti who lives in Tijuana and becomes an integral part of Baja California culture(s) while maintaining their own in a syncretism and possibly having children with a parent from Tijuana could be said to be developing a Tijuanese ethnicity. There are instances in which the Common-Bundle View happens to correctly guess the ethnicity a person identifies with, but would exclude some people who many if not most members of the ethnic group would identify as a part of the group due to them not having observable features an outsider might look for (such as phenotype or speaking a particular dialect) that place them in said group.

Gracia's partiality to the Familial-Historical View should in no way be taken to indicate that ethnicity is a realm in which identity is mediated anywhere near adequately. He says of race, ethnicity, and nationality,

> On the one hand, this language and these concepts appear inadequate, and their use is objectionable on various grounds; on the other, we need them to make sense of the past and to chart a better future devoid of the abuses resulting from their use. So what do we do? The only procedure that makes sense is to turn to race, ethnicity, and nationality, and explore whether there is any way of understanding them that can help us decide whether to keep them in, or permanently banish them from, our thought and discourse. The answer will depend on whether we articulate coherent notions that capture the fundamental elements of these concepts, while avoiding the obvious mistake of such views as the biological conception of race prevalent in the nineteenth century.

For Gracia, race, ethnicity, and nationality must be reckoned with in some way; something must be done with them, and it would be irresponsible to mechanize subconscious thinking to not recognize the way the metaphysics of these categories operate. The question is what do we do with them. We've already seen that Gracia's take on ethnicity in the Historical-Familial View separates him from the use of race and identity that Appiah performs and even regretfully asserts is necessary. So, how does Gracia treat nationality?

Gracia's understanding of nationality follows from a critique of David Miller's definition in *On Nationality*, which basically states that a nationality is a group of human individuals who (1) have ostensible identities that rely on the geographical region, or the "nation," within which they were born,[31] and (2) the shared beliefs, histories, ideas, customs, and ways of behavior that may emerge due to the certain demarcated geographical region, or the "nation," within which they were born. This definition, while helpful, is too vague for Gracia, as its ambiguity could refer to ethnicities, who could also be said to have certain geographical territory associated with them, history, shared beliefs, and distinct from other communities due to their own methods of life.[32]

Gracia, in concert with Drew Ali, goes on to say that a characteristic which distinguishes race from nationality is that it is legally constructed. The ways of becoming a member of a nation can vary from birth to naturalization, but the advantages of nationhood are the same irrespective of how one joins the nation.[33] Further, in some cases, from the notion of nation radiates some of the characteristics of ethnicity, such as the loose association of a certain nationality with a cultural practice (such as Brazil with soccer) or religious tradition (such as Libya with Islam), but these characteristics are just that: radiations.[34] They are not intrinsic to the definition of "nation." The "radiations," or the more or less synthetic a-priori and a-posteriori by-products of the idea of nationality, are covered by Gracia's emphasis on his discussion of the "will to identify" with the nation both (1) commonly and (2) politically, where (1) indicates that a person subscribe to the national ideals as opposed to their own, and (2) that the political system is a means of transmuting the national ideals into semi-"innate" and "inalienable" ideologies and enforcing them. To this point, Gracia states:

> In this conception, nations are groups of people that have a common will to be organized politically under a system of laws within territory. Accordingly, the members of nations are subject to a body of laws they are expected to accept and abide by, and that regulates the relations among them. This does not mean that they actually agree with or obey these laws. Members of nations frequently disagree with some or even many of the laws governing them, and it is obvious that they frequently violate some of them, even when they agree with them.[35]

In the term "will to identify," Gracia subverts the use of "will" as conscious choice by employing it to mean a sort of uncontested "instinctive" affirmation of the metaphysical structures that govern the conceptual unity of the nation. In my estimation, this sort of involuntary national identity is analogous to race and race-related categories in that the choice of what constructed and arbitrary category one is in becomes the choice of the rules of the categories themselves and not the person. Even though the contours of race may not be legislated by governments in the way nationality is, the presuppositions and assumptions of race can act as laws that critically trouble societal understandings when transgressed due to the ingrained expectation that they be upheld.

Naomi Zack and Racial Eliminativis

While Appiah and Gracia are critical of the idea of race yet maintain it to differing degrees, Naomi Zack argued that race as a biological construct should be eliminated. Since societies hold that race is a biological reality in spite of the admission of many physical sciences that it is not, the category gives off an image of being something that is as inconvertible (at least easily inconvertible) as becoming a human lacking a nose without removing the nose in question, assuming one was born with a nose. While being reverent of the works of thinkers working in philosophy of race such as Lucius Outlaw and Jorge Gracia, Zack put forth the idea that the acceptance of race as a biological phenomenon fuels racism. This "minimal physical realism," or the belief that science holds that race is biological, a belief that science has not been able to and has been candid about its inability to demonstrate, grounds Zack's assertion that biological race should be eliminated.[36] Zack says,

> The best option is . . . remove biological race from secular ontology . . . because the modern idea of biological race originated in modern biology and spread through application to medicine, social science, common sense, public policy, the arts and liberatory theory, the emanation of the idea of biological race requires thorough criticism of many disciplinary as well as informal subjects and practices. This criticism and elimination would constitute a major paradigm shift in an important area of human life in society.[37]

The impetus of Zack in her push to eliminate *biological* ideas of race could be said to be in harmony with Appiah and Gracia (Gracia is critical of the eliminativism he employs in *Philosophy of Science and Race*) in that both of these thinkers have a relationship with race that is symbolic and hence not fixed to an unstable physical foundation.[38] Insofar as the *biological* understanding of race is taken to be synonymous with race as whole, both Appiah and Gracia would reject the push to eliminate it, as the pushback by several philosophers of race has been that such a stance erases both the privileges and detriments that all of us as inevitably racialized people experience.

I would offer that in her work entitled *White Privilege and Black Rights: The Injustice of U.S. Police Racial Profiling and Homicide*, Zack does acknowledge the effects of racial categories without resorting to what some would call a reductive argument, suggesting that the deaths of Trayvon Martin, Tamir Rice, and other instances of police brutality could be remedied by an eliminating of the idea of race. While staying close to racial elimativism in this text by focusing on the metaphysics of "White" privilege and "Black" rights as power systems that are not intrinsic but associated with certain humans through the historical passage of events and contexts, she addresses head on the ways in which racial categories effect the everyday life of "Black" people detrimentally.

Zack's philosophical premise could be said to deny the racial "us" and "them." If there is no race, then "us" and "them" could not mean the racial distinctions that have carved the world into its present state are like the arbitrary lines we call national borders. If employed plausibly, they would have to refer to a type of difference that actually and usefully exists. Zack is not an opponent of difference, but she does argues fiercely against a certain type of difference that is intrinsically hierarchical and based on a common belief practiced as scientific and hence certain and unchanging: the difference of race.

Jennifer Lisa Vest and Categorical Disturbance

Jennifer Lisa Vest's philosophical work highlights the instability of the racial and race-related categories which structure understandings of the "us" and "them." Racial and race-related language erects and keeps gates restricting humans to presupposed "cells with open doors" in which they are expected to live within due to their obligatory reverence for the laws of race. The disruptions (Carolina Hinojosa-Cisneros) of Vest find a theoretical fleshing out in the poem "Names," her notion of the "New Dialogic," and the categorical disturbance of her theory of "Mixed Race." These ideas are deconstructions of racial and race-related gates, obscuring the boundaries once imagined to be as natural as the Chicago Cubs losing after an exceptional season of baseball. I can say that because I'm a Chicagoan, but I might diss you if you were to say the same.

"Names"

In the poem "Names," originally published in 1997, Vest explores the Florida Seminole side of her history in ways that illuminate the complexities, making it what it perpetually becomes. Vest recalls the formation of the Seminole from an amalgam of formerly enslaved humans with substantial roots in the continent commonly referred to as "Africa" and various nations who were in the area before, as well as discusses the Seminole in Mexico and the Bahamas, among other places.

She stated that she wrote the piece after growing tired of the misinformation that had been spread about the nation by scholars.[39] In "Names," Vest displaces and deconstructs the types of distinctions placed upon the Seminole by outsiders, opening up not only the multiplicitous nature of the nation but also some insights into how the "us" and "them" of this section function. Vest states in the poem,

> Before Jackson
> Before rabid flesh-hunting Carolinians came
> We were fluid and raceless
> Ibo, Dahomey, Gan Fon, Hausa, Yoruba
> We were Ewe and Dogon
> farmers teaching hunters
> clans expanding
>
> We were Mikasukee, Tallahassee, Muskogee
> allies and kinfolk
> Before they called us
> Mulatto, Mestizo
> Stolen propery
> Creek[40]

Vest makes it a point to connect names such as "Negro," "Mestizo," and "Mulatto" not only to a sacrificing of authentic fluidity and racelessness, but also to the power of the colonizer to rename the humans and lands they encounter. In a contrast of the names the nations gave themselves with the names provided by the colonizer, Vest reveals the maligning effects of the reidentification projects of race and race-related language, and can be taken as a silent argument that the acceptance of externally applied "us" and "them" categories as one's authentic identity may be dangerous at best and disastrous at worse. "Names" is an exercise in fluidity.

An additional function of "Names" is the poem's decentering and challenging of the modern idea of national borders, which conceptually partition one part of land from another. If we weren't systematized into thinking that the militarized maintenance of human traffic flow from one side of the arbitrary line to the other was the result of deduction and not induction, the fluidity that Vest refers to as the worldview of first nations before colonization may be recognized. Perhaps it would not be recognized because in some ways such fluidity may have been so entangled within the life intersections of people that it was an undercurrent not critically reflected upon. Hunbatz Men reminds us that the "Maya" worldview had a difficult time conceiving the personal subjectivity which fueled the expansion projects of Britain, Spain, Portugal, and others because the self was fluidly synonymous with one's other (in lak'ech).[41] In "Names," Vest draws the reader's attention to a time in which difference emerged without the antagonistic trappings of the power dynamics of outside empires. We must remember the significance of the fact that many of the names for the first nations and lands of the "American" and "African" continents are not the names they were known by previously. Vest lures us into a deconstruction of the act of naming, and one of the implications that can be drawn from this is that the modern idea of nation naming and demarcation not only formats but creates identities that did not previously exist. What does it mean to claim as your objective to own the name the colonizer called the land in which you were born?

The "New Dialogic"

In "The Promise of Caribbean Philosophy: How it Can Contribute to a 'New Dialogic' in Philosophy," Vest holds that the "Caribbean" is a region that complicates and even possibly deems untenable a singular "us" and "them" rendering of identities. In the "Caribbean", identity and belonging is/can be fluid and resist the ossification of racial and race-related categories. Vest says,

> The Caribbean, both in its fantastic diversity and its political and historical unity, promises to give birth to a philosophy unique and specific in its own right and it must do more than build upon prior work in African, African American, and Native American philosophies. Because the Caribbean is characterized by a complex coming together of various racial, ethnic, linguistic, and cultural traditions and identities because it is generated from a fusion of Asian, African, Indigenous and European cultures and peoples it makes sense for Caribbean philosophy to dialogue with these other traditions. This is especially true given the fact that the articulation of new academic fields in philosophy entails the identification of texts and traditions from which to depart.[42]

Vest suggests that due to constitution of the "Caribbean," it would benefit philosophers from the region commonly known as "the Caribbean" to dialogue with the ancestral philosophical roots that compose the thought and life-worlds of its inhabitants such as China, Nigeria, and India (just to name a few) as opposed to forcing it to be conversant with the dominant idea of "Western" philosophy. In other words, Vest subverts the possible crystallization of a "naturally" fluid discourse and way of thinking/living, which may occur in dialogue with the dominant philosophical "canon." The alternative is to establish communications in a South-South direction as opposed to the common East-West direction that "minority" perspectives in philosophy seem to be bound to.[43] This conversation and critical examination that occurs when "Caribbean" philosophers engage interlocutors other than those in the "West" is what Vest refers to as the "New Dialogic." Vest states,

The *New Dialogic* calls for the creation of new philosophy through the critical insistence on South-South dialogues that shift the discursive center. As such, it both initiates and requires a breaking down of current disciplinary and sub-disciplinary boundaries. Motivated as it is by a richer and more extensive pursuit of wisdom, this new approach will be open to question and all limiting devices will be retained only insofar as they aid the larger goal of enriching the study of philosophy, where philosophy is defined as the asking of endless questions in pursuit of wisdom. Thus, dialogues will not be constrained by divisions between Analytic versus Continental, or Western versus non-Western schools of philosophy, nor will they be limited by a need to find transcultural universals.[44]

In this decentering of Britain, Spain, France, and Germany that is the philosophical project of the "New Dialogic," Vest also argues that her intent is not to foster the sort of discourse that would engender a centering of any other philosophical frameworks. Because of this, the "New Dialogic" has an interesting role within what has come to be known as "African philosophy" and "Africana philosophy," or African and Afro-diasporic bodies of work and schools of thought produced by thinkers trained in and teaching philosophy in institutions of "higher learning." Vest argues that in the disregard of the "Western" "center," there is the tendency to reimagine the various strands of African and Afro-diasporic thought as several streams of one river. For Vest, if we follow the "New Dialogic" to its dialogical end, we may find that the similarities we assumed were shared between thinkers and regions aren't actually there, thus challenging the idea of creating an "us" possibly fashioned from "center" of the "West." The "New Dialogic" is destabilizing and potentially unable (and unintended) to support even progressive notions of personhood emanating from ideas of race (such as the idea of a collective "African" identity that philosophers such as Luicus Outlaw and John Mbiti articulated),[45] as the decentering of the "West" upon which racial and racial related categories emerge is perpetually deconstructive.

"Being and Not Being, Knowing and Not Knowing"

In the essay "Being and Not Being, Knowing and Not Knowing," a chapter in Tina Fernandes Bottes' edited volume *Philosophy and the Mixed Race Experience*, Vest further troubles easy and folk allocations of group members to the "us" and "them" categories by presenting the prism of "Mixed Race" multiplicity to parse out the logical impossibilities of racial categories. Vest, harmonizing with the lead of Zack, argues that since "Mixed Race" doesn't register on the scale of race due to its transgression of either the "us" or the "them," and race is a scale which determines and measures humanity (to many), it is a site where humanity is of limited availability or flat out denied to the "Mixed Race" person. Vest says,

Mixed people cannot exist qua mixed. The hope for existence for the Mixed person is in partial existence in the form of monoracialization. The only human kinds to which Mixed people can legitimately belong are monoraces; the only identity a Mixed race person can assert is a monoracial identity (i.e. a partial identity). In a society such as ours the urge to monoracialize is strong. Everyone must assert a monoracial identity. To do otherwise is to live in a fantasy world of one's own making. Any person claiming to be mixed is always asked "But who are you really?" Anyone with an ambiguous phenotype creates confusion for onlookers in a racially stratified society. The urge to monoracialize requires that a race be assigned, even if it is not obvious which race should be assigned. A race must be found. A fix must be found to the confusion. Without the assignment of a race, social existence is not possible.[46]

For Vest, the "Mixed" individual is perpetually between various *puentes tumultuosos*, tenuous intersections in which each section pulls them toward itself. The result is a psychologically, socially, religiously, and racially stretched human who inevitably gambles with their status as a person daily. Until the "Mixed" person picks or is forced into a racial side, they cannot be "known."[47]

Drawing from the work of legal theorist Cheryl Harris, Vest points out that if "Mixed Race" individuals exist, then property rights and privileges granted because of "Whiteness" also don't exist since said property rights are granted due an eventual connection of European ancestry and certain phenotypical characteristics to an idea of "Whiteness." If this was the case, the children produced by the rape of the enslaved by the overlords would be the beneficiaries of this privilege, but history and the present era shows us that in many instances they were and are not.[48] Flowing from this discussion on "White" privilege as counter logical in light of the existence of "Mixed" individuals, Vest also discusses how the "Mixed" person is the reminder of the oppression of colonization, and refers to the work of Theo Goldberg, who argues in order for the "Mixed Race" person to exist, that which they are mixed with must also exist. According to this logic, Goldberg states that "Mixed" identities actually reify the oppressive mechanisms of racial categories.[49]

Vest lifts "Mixed" identity as a way to see through and possibly beyond racial categories in that they blatantly illustrate their inconsistencies overall. After all that has gone into a historical, cultural, scientific, theological, philosophical, etc., cementing of the folk and legal definitions of race from legislation to imagination, the "Mixed" individual fucks it all up—in a good way. While Vest values but is not pushing for the racial eliminativism of Zack and Appiah, she is indeed instigating a utilization of the messiness of "Mixed" identities to further the conversation and forward thinking on race.[50] In service of Vest's argument of the logical incongruency of racial categories, she raises how the category of "Blackness" when presumed to be a visible component of the "Mixed" person's racial make-up overrides all other categories under which they might be perceived or identify with.[51] She also highlights how a "Mixed" person in the United States may be categorized within a fixed race in another region of the world, such as Trinidad.[52] But the potential multiplicitous, multi/race/less, and hard to bridle energy of the category of "Mixed" for Vest presents what Homi Bhabha would refer to as "Third Space" in which the relevance and power of racial and race-related languages is caricaturized and satirized by person who embraced living as "Mixed." A conscious enactment of the volcanic potential of "Mixed Raced" identities allows for the subversion of colonial and postcolonial ways of becoming by those who were disenfranchised by them. Vest makes the point that the first thing many people recognize about a person is what society would label them racially or sexually. "Mixed" categories of identity destabilize racial rules and norms, thus chaotically rescrambling race, one of the most predominant organizing schematics of humanity.[53]

Vest employs the mechanism of "Mixed" identities to trouble not only where/if lines of distinction can meaningfully be drawn between the "Us" and the "Them" and the logical inconsistencies of monoracial essentialism but also the involuntary and sometimes intentional act of the creation of racial groups by the observer (arguably the genesis of racial groups). Vest says poetically and biographically,

> Some people are confused by me and ask what I am but many people are not confused. They are sure they know who I am. By the same token, I am not confused about what I am. I am sure I know who I am. It just so happens that my knowing and the knowing of most people I encounter do not converge. There is no consensus. Our knowledges do not line up, do not converge; they fail to coincide. They are irreconcilable. What I know is not what they know. And this inability to know has nothing to do with identity. I am neither confused or tragic but have always lived in a tragically confused world of non-knowers.[54]

"Mixed Race" identities provide an intense difficulty for the categorizer, a benefit in that the hierarchies, logical difficulties, and biological and psychological embellishments of racial categories are confounded, but a detriment in that those who take on "Mixed Race" identities become sites of unwelcome scrutiny as the question "What (not Who) are you?" is a constant refrain. However, Vest seems to find value in the unrest of the categorizer not "knowing" where to insert the "Mixed Race" person in their metaphysical *cajas* of human becoming. The interruptions of the categories of race by "Mixed Race" identities and the fixed behaviors they are expected to adhere to serve not only to reveal their contradictions but also to seriously question their usefulness.[55]

Conclusion

This discussion of the "Us" and the "Them," significantly linked to analytic philosophical and metaphysical approaches to language, causes us to seriously consider what we are indicating with racial language and what is possible to indicate with racial categorization. Cudd adequately shows how social groups are both voluntary and involuntary, paying close attention to how an intentionalist and a structuralist approach can ground critique in real lived experience, as humans are categorized in ways that involve the interpretative assumptions of properties that are more or less brute "facts" (e.g., skin color, place of birth, sexual organs, etc.) in arbitrary ways. The construction of the social group obviously does not create said observable features (structuralist), but depends on said data for its constructions. While Cudd gives an extremely useful and coherent account of the mechanisms of social groups, her constructive project in *Analyzing Oppression* favors a sort of bracketing of this information in that her conclusion, which aims toward a feminist theory that reassembles social groups and uses them for liberating ends in some ways ignores her stance that a large part of categories we hold to be metaphysical necessities are (1) manufactured and (2) manufactured for the purpose of oppression. Cudd pushes toward not an abolishment of the categories, but a feminist philosophical restructuring of them for the purpose of a perpetual teasing out of their oppressive tendencies/compositions. For me, it is difficult to see how her thesis can rest on any category such as race and gender due to her exceptional deconstruction of them in the first parts of the text.

Philosophers of race such as Gracia, Zack, and Appiah, like Cudd, offer starships that take us to the edge of the universe where a relinquishing of the categories of the "us" and "them" as we've known them is plain sight, but stops short. Gracia's Historical-Familial View shows us volatile stars our stares can't make clear images of in its appeal to shared histories as a means of determining group members and non-members, but still maintains a type of appeal to racial categories as that which could possibly be restructured for justice. I wonder if the Historical-Familial View would prove even more valuable if it were to be consistently applied outside of the paradigm of racial categories, as the Historical-Familial View seems to lend itself more to ethnicity and nationality (with of course a recognition of the difficulties with these categories as well) than to race. In Appiah's notion of racial identity, his mention of preferring "Black" power over Uncle Tom but not wanting to have to choose either points us toward a thought experiment that his notion of racial identity is incapable of testing. Appiah's racial identity attributes a utility to racial language that while plausible is something a holistic human (and perhaps transhuman) future may require us to acknowledge and deconstruct while transcending. While Appiah's racial eliminativism is conditioned with the caveat that the category of race is useful to identify the ways in which humans are structured in societies, Zack's racial eliminativism is boldly unconditional. Her philosophy calls for the erasing of biological race in no uncertain terms, since for her, the category of race is intrinsically problematic. A meticulously systematic extension of Zack's eliminativism and "concrete" examples of this already at work in the world (which is lacking in her own) is what I intend to actualize with the possibilities of multi/race/less/ness.

The energy of the "Mixed Race" category as Vest presents it stretches us to reconsider not only those who the society may readily systematize into the category of "Mixed Race" but also all humanity, as the concept of "Mixed Race" identities are microscopes through which we are able to observe the incoherencies of pure racial categories. The existence of the "Mixed" individual makes a mockery of the hegemonic iterations of societal norms that equate existence with a neat fitting in one of the several racial and race-related categories. However, like Appiah, Cudd, Zack, Gracia, and others, Vest has thought through the category of race via "Mixed Race" to the point that even "Mixed" identities are not only deconstructed but surpassed. Could we take her argument that "Mixed" identities reveal the inadequacies (and perhaps the non-essential existence) of race to indicate that the insights of "Mixed Race" are means to an end and not the end in itself? This is not to assert that she indeed sees "Mixed Race" as a final destination, but I propose to take her insights a step further as arguments to dissipate race itself and forge a tentative experimental future.

They've led us to the bridge. But what if we actually crossed it?

3 ALTERNATE RACE THEORIES IN MOTION: A DISCUSSION WITH DOMINIC PETTIS-EL/I.B. FOKUZ

Customized as the fallen for fallen knowledge
A mother's good intent when its clergy was formin' vices
When the backs was broken for private islands
You could read his story and plummet, we numbin' to the sky
Violence employed
We rose from the ashes of a broke crack slave with his vision recoiled, shattered
A little to do
The only thing is filling his shoes
Riddle me this, what you envision is you
What's up nigga, what's up black
I guess we good enough, we hood enough for that, or,
Until they tell your ass you good enough for half
In order for reparations need a nation and a flag
But who cares
We still money hungry
A license to kill if another brother takes it from me
Internal Revenue Service still lurkin'
And baby girl around the block is outside still twerkin'
Crippled by the pillars, we killers to advertise
I'm a Moorish American Moslem
Descended from Moroccans
Sitting on Northwest Amexem, pissin' out toxins
Cus' being free never was an option
So many bodies underneath nobody's conscience
Downing a bottle, we follow, we hobble for ignorance
The pot sizzlin', we livin' in spells
Before a slave, it's a reason we fell…

I.B. Fokuz on "Black Power in Hell"[1]

I had the esteemed honor of talking with longtime friend Dominic Pettis-El and founder of Tomorrow Kings (a Chicago-based rap collective of which I am a member) on the possibilities of living outside of the shadow of racial and race-related identities. Pettis-El, a member and Sheik of the Moorish Science Temple of America's Temple No. 1, not only provides a history of the MSTA but speaks from personal experience on what he takes to be the human benefits of shedding the racial identity of "Black." This discussion is very central to the "architechnology" (shout out to Chicago's own Hip-Hop production duo of solar conductors Rubberroom, who I directly draw the use of this term from) of multi/race/less/ness as many of bursts of energy surrounding this rhizomic InnerSection leapt out of intensely spirited conversations between Pettis-El and I over the years. This discussion is also paramount due to the fact that an increased interest in the MSTA by religion, Africana studies, and cultural studies scholars has yet to do ethnographic work on the ways in which Moorish American identities impact the lived reality of members of the MSTA or those outside of the Temple who adhere to various aspects of the teachings (such as myself in some ways). I am in no way claiming that this interview is ethnography. However, I am asserting that, along with providing a window into what it might be like to sidestep race as a primary structuring category of human existence, it indicates that a deeper look into how Moorish identities work in praxis is needed for more complete pictures of the simplicities and complexities of this categorical abolishing that happens in the philosophical theology of Noble Drew Ali.

> JIG: You and I have had these discussions about nationality and about how the concept of race is not really equipped to provide nationality. We both have been described by the term "Black." I've been described by the terms "Black" and "Latino" and "Hispanic." You know, we don't [physically] see any of those terms. So, I just wanna kick off with quickly asking you how did your notion of identity shift and how was it in some ways maybe ruptured and reconstructed?
>
> DPEL: Um, sort of like how people would say you know what, they're going through a different environment, and it's almost like a culture shock. It was sort of like that type of element. A lot of changes. Moorish Science was sort of like that for me because . . . growing up in a Christian household, there were a lot of things that I was taught at home with my mom, where it gave me morals and values, but there still was . . . a void, that was missing, that I still wasn't able to connect the dots entirely. And because of that lack of being able to connect the dots, I sort of rode the fence of "am I religious or am I spiritual?" . . . And so when I proclaimed my nationality . . . on the nationality part, It says, you know, "I herenow declare that you are Moslem." And I remember when they said that it was a weird feeling because all I knew all my life was Christianity. You know

what I'm saying? All I knew was what my mom taught me. And here now I have someone telling me "I declare that you are a Moslem." And I didn't know how to accept that at first. It was something in the back of my mind. I started to question, like, "Am I a Moslem? How do I feel about being a Moslem?" You know what I'm saying? Like, what does that come with? You know, is this really the decision I wanna make? . . . And see when I came across Moorish science, truthfully, I came across it from a civic point of view. Of how I can, you know, know more of law and how to manipulate it in my favor . . . That's how a lot of brothers and sisters come across Moorish Science . . . If you know how to manipulate it for yourself, why not? And so, being a truth seeker that kind of connected me to "Oh, I could fill my toolshed with how to navigate." . . . But then when I actually stepped into the Temple, it was introduced to me in a totally different light. And I think that's where I was a little conflicted but still interested . . . So, I knew there was something there that was pulling me in, but I still didn't get it yet. You know, I was still on the fence about it. That was the same time I knew that it was revealing something to me that I never had revealed to me anywhere else. It was something promising about it, but I couldn't put my finger on it. So, I proclaimed my nationality, you know, believing that this will make a difference in my life and my family's life. You know . . . I'm at a that point where [I thought], "Well, if this is not what I thought it is, then what is it?" Because I'm here now . . . My family's here now. And so, another conflict came when I started seeing the debates of who's who, and it made me start to question if I was even in the right place to begin with. Or was it legitimate? . . . So that in itself made me want to challenge anything that I came across or what was presented to me. Which ultimately was beneficial in the long haul. And so, I remember one of the first verses out of the Holy Koran of the Moorish Science Temple of America that really like stood out to me was where the Prophet said, "If you ask me what to study, I would say yourselves. And when you will have studied that well and will ask what to study next, and then I will say again, yourselves." And that stood out to me because in so many ways it's saying "Don't take my word as fact." Challenge what I'm saying so you could stand on what you're learning. And I never had anybody present it to me in that way because usually when it comes to religion it's "believe and don't question." If you do question, you can only ask certain questions, but certain questions are forbidden. But here I was challenged to ask any question that made me feel uncomfortable because I'm studying myself.

JIG: That's powerful, man. That's a very powerful intro . . . So . . . what was your perception of this language of race that we've been subjected to being deconstructed and dismissed by the Temple? What was your first impression of that . . . when you were first hit with the information that you're not "Black," you're not "Colored," you're not "Negro," what kind of revelation was that for you?

DPEL: Well, the information definitely was kind of embedded in the information I got before I stepped into the temple, but just obviously unfolded more when I stepped into the temple to get a better perspective of it . . . the one thing that was intriguing to me, that sort of brought it to change the way I just thought about everything, was, you know, it's certain things we take for granted . . . We all know that . . . there is a North, Central, and South America. But we're conditioned to believe that you cannot be an American unless you're in the United States of America. But when you think about it, a Mexican is still an American because they [were born in and possibly reside] in North America . . . You would never call a Mexican an American . . . and so when you look at it from that light, that's sort of the awakening of like, "How stupid am I to be looking at things in that way when I know the game, I know the truth? But because I'm conditioned in such a way, I've convinced myself that that's not what it is because of how I've been taught." And so, I use that analogy for the "Black" demo, because the simplest thing is if you're "Black," then prove it. And one of things you can ask that's been asked that made me think about was, "Okay, what is 'Black?' 'Black' is a color. And it describes something. And if you are talking about a something that describes something, then it's an adjective. Right? And an adjective describes a noun. Well, what am I? I'm a noun. So, I can't be an adjective." And when you're not conditioned to break things down like that, you can be caught up with the hype; you can be sold on an illusion.

JIG: I went through similar things . . . in different ways. But, you know, I remember being a kid and asking my mother because . . . I was young, and I heard this discussion about "Black" and "White ["people"]" and I didn't know what they were talking about. At this time, I'm seeing people as my friends. I don't really see them that. Then I [had to ask], "Mom what's a 'White' person? What's a 'Black' person?" And then from that point on, I was taught I had to see the world through those lenses. And I always had problems with that. It never made sense to me, you know. And when I would tell my mother about it, like, "You know what? This doesn't [make sense], she's like, "No, your 'Black' and that's it," you know. There was no kind . . . of extended dialogue . . . you're this . . .

DPEL: It was a point of no return at that point . . . When you destroy somebody's reality, you really can leave them naked and abandoned. And that might not always be a good thing at the moment in time . . . You strip somebody of everything they know . . . So if you strip their reality, it's like, "Man, well what else do I know how to do? What can I lean on?" So, it's like the moment you accept that, it's a point of no return . . . That was what was so intriguing. But at the same time, it was a burden you have to carry. Because if you don't figure it out, it's a lost estate.

JIG: It's basically like leaving a job and not having a new one lined up and you have to provide for your family . . . You know, that's difficult, because what we've done for so long, [is identify] race with ethnicity. So, the idea becomes if I neglect my race, I neglect my ethnicity [and culture] . . . But race was never ethnicity [or culture] . . . have you ever had to deal with people who said that you're a traitor to your race because you don't use the term?

DPEL: Yes, I have.

JIG: And how did you deal with that?

DPEL: The only interaction I could probably think of where I wasn't as seasoned, but my soul was set on fire if you may, was when I came home and told my mom that I proclaimed my nationality and that, I'm a Moorish American Moslem and Noble Drew Ali was my prophet. And her first thought was, "So you with Farrakhan now?" Since that's the only thing she equates to an Asiatic brother in a Muslim demonstration . . . And to fast forward . . . maybe two years ago, I ran across a brother who was at my job. And at this point in time, especially being more seasoned, I don't allow people to call me "Black." I correct them immediately. I mean, this particular brother was like, "Aight [alright], Black Man" at my job. He's one of the tenants. And I said, "Peace, brother. I'm not 'Black.'" He said, "What?" I said, "I'm not 'Black,'" And he said, "Well, what are you, then?" It's like at that point, people almost get offended that the extension of what they consider "brotherly love" has been denied because I didn't accept "Black" as an identification for myself. So, when I explained to him what I was, and what I stand for and why I don't accept that, his only response was "Well I don't care what the hell you think you are, the 'White' man gon' always consider you a n**** and you will always be a n**** in his eyes. You will always be a *** in the world." And I said, "I don't accept that." And I could see hatred and anger even within him being mad that I don't accept that reality. And like, there was a measure because, you know, if I wasn't seasoned, I probably would have felt some type of way going back and forth with him. But because I identified "truth" versus "falsehood," truth is the only thing that changes not, and falsehood is the illusion of what seems to be. But it will pass away. So, I have to realize that he had more attraction to falsehood than to the truth . . . You can't make anybody believe in a construct if it doesn't have a duality in it. If it doesn't have a balance to it. So, it's easier for us to accept being "Black" as long as there's somebody who's "White." But if there was never anybody, "White," I think a long time ago we would have questioned why we call ourselves "Black."

JIG: Yeah . . . that's the whole thing. The idea of "Whiteness" is really what creates every other racial term.

DPEL: Exactly. And with that being said, if you ask that so-called "White" man what his nationality is, he'll be able to tell you a real nationality. He'll be able to tell you Polish American. He'll be able to tell you Italian American. But if you ask that so called "Black" man what his nationality is, he can't tell you nothing. And then the funny thing about it is, when we see brothers who look just like us and don't even want to be considered "Black." They'll tell you, "I'm Nigerian American." "I'm Ethiopian American." You know, all of these different nationalities. They will identify themselves with the country they come from. But yet, it still doesn't click in our minds.

JIG: And this is when the question of nationality comes up when people are really open to asking and open to having what they believe unwrapped. So . . . in terms of people who say, "I'm kinda tired of this 'Black' shit. This doesn't represent me," tell me about the Moorish Science Temple of America's stance on nationality.

DPEL: Well, The Moorish Science Temple of America teaches only two things, [regardless of] what other people might tell you. All we teach at the Moorish Science Temple of America is nationality and divine creed. That's it. And so, speaking on the nationality aspect of it, when you look up the definition of nationality, it clearly just says "the state of belonging to a nation." . . . nationality . . . is how you're being recognized by the government in which you live and the nations of the earth. Because . . . we couldn't talk about history unless we were able to identify the people who were in history. If you can't identify them or recognize them, they have no value. So . . . it's so many layers to it. But the general problem is that between 1774 and 1779, there was a denationalizing process done for our people.[2] The famous analogy that can kind of give perspective to anybody is when Kunta Kinte in Roots was beaten to the point of accepting that his name was Toby. The [sad] fact [is] that he let go of Kunta Kinte, which connects him to his heritage. And a lot of times people miss the part where he talked about being Muslim . . . We overlook that part. He definitely recognized his Muslim roots. Because when you really look into the history, his ancestors were Muslim. They weren't Christian . . . But him giving up Kunta Kinte and becoming Toby is a perfect example of this denationalizing process . . . And so, in this denationalizing process, us being stripped of our nationality gave up our rights. And we were put in a position to seek privileges as opposed to holding on to our inalienable rights. This is the reason why the civil rights movement was so huge at its time, but yet it did nothing for us.

JIG: Say more about that.

DPEL: So, in the civil rights movement, you gotta take it back to the Naturalization Acts. You have to take it back to the Voting Rights Act and how [we were] considered 3/5 of a human. And if we wanted to have the privilege to vote, we had to go under a certain act. That is the reason why even when you look at the fifteenth amendment within Constitution, privileges were given to citizens of the U.S.A. But we [were] not US citizens. We are citizens of the U.S.A . . . . Which is on our nationality cards as Moorish Americans. So, when you understand who gets privileges, it starts to build more perspective on what are you really fighting for…Are you fighting for second class citizenship or are you fighting for first class citizenship? . . . So, swinging it back to nationality, nationality is a reflection of how the world operates and takes care of business. 'Cus if it wasn't, we wouldn't have a United Nations . . . "Black," "Negro," "Colored," and all these other terms that we use are not in the record book of history of a people that existed with those names. So, if that's true, then that means that you will never be recognized [as fully human, as humans have nationalities] and you will be considered an undesirable.

DPEL: Yeah. So [you can relate this] same concept to the Moroccan empire. Which [at one time stretched] from Egypt to South Africa, across to South America, all the way up to North America. That is the ancient Moroccan Empire, which Moorish Americans know as Northwestern AMEXEM, with "AMEXEM" being the divine name of Northwest Africa. And so, when we say "nationality," on your Nationality Card, it will say "Moorish American CPC." And it's because it covers a lot more than what you think. The Europeans know that we're Moors. But they ain't gon' tell you that. Because telling you helps you remember. Nobody wants to wake up the sleeping giant. No one. If you wake up the sleeping giant, you might not be able to put him back to sleep . . . So . . . we gotta understand that we've been divided and conquered. And the simplest way to put it is that even though you have so many tribes within this Moroccan empire, even though you have so many families or nationalities, we're all the same people.[3]

JIG: And this is what I think Pimienta-Bey's work in *Othello's Children in the 'New World'* [does]. He makes these links very clearly. And he really demonstrates that the people who have been called all of these things . . . can be traced back to the Moroccan Empire.[4] And it's not just him saying it. He actually pulls from several resources to make the argument.

DPEL: That's great. Great points. Dr. Pimienta-Bey definitely brought a lot of home academically. Which was needed to bring clarification. So, the Moroccan empire still exists, but it's been dormant for some generations because we've forgotten who we are. We've forgotten our connection to each other. And so, it plays a disservice in our development when we raise our children because when we raise our children, we cultivate them in the culture that we live in. But who's to say that Mexican culture doesn't have any connection to Taino people? Who's to say who you consider the "Black Olmecs" didn't bring knowledge and information from across the Atlantic Ocean . . . from Africa? . . . When you find pyramids in Peru, in Illinois, you know, it's no coincidence that if you connected all the puzzle pieces of the Mississippi River, it might most likely connect to the Niger River . . . Because at one point in time, we know that it [once was] a landmass that was considered "Asia."[5] Which we know is the reason why we consider our race "Asiatic" . . . According to Prophet Noble Drew Ali, there's only one race and that's the human race, right? But it's subdivided between Asiatic and European. But under those two umbrellas you have many, many nations. And these nations are recognized around the world. So, our people need to catch up to the program to see how the game is being played and why they're being played the way they're being played . . . They don't understand the value in nationality. And until they understand the value in it, they will always be considered undesirable. And so . . . When you walk through those doors [of an authorized[6] location of the Moorish Science Temple of America], nobody's saying that you're not a Moor. Because we [all humans other than those with ancestries tied to the region we now refer to as "Europe" and commonly classified as "White"] were all born Moors . . . It's just that it developed over time, but we're all the same people. "Moorish American" is a new concept brought by Prophet Noble Drew Ali that connects us to our old origin . . . And that's the reason why he states that the Moorish Science Temple of America is the sole foundation for ALL Asiatics in America . . . But that doesn't mean to stop practicing your culture. No. That means that your culture is every bit of it.

JIG: Didn't they change the [US religious corporation] laws after Noble Drew Ali created the Moorish Science Temple of America?

DPEL: They changed it after the Vatican Church [attained the status]. And this is the reason why Prophet Noble Drew Ali did so much moving in rapid speed before he changed form because he knew what he had to do before he left. Before they could even figure out what he did, it was already too late for them to stop him. The only thing that can do is join him . . . So that's what happened. And he created this religious organization. Religion, and me and you know it, has, you know, especially what we talk about in *ADVENT: A Modern Bible*[7] . . . You know, religion has become such a spookism thing. People fear being a part of religion because they think their religion is going to pigeonhole . . . But the way that Prophet Noble Drew Ali went about it, he approached it from the First Amendment of the Constitution [since] Congress can't pass a law against religion. So, it's our RELIGION to proclaim our nationality. It's our RELIGION to be ourselves. It's our RELIGION to practice our five divine principles. It's our RELIGION.

JIG: Amazing.

DPEL: So, he [Noble Drew Ali] created something that cannot be destroyed.

JIG: A clarifying question because this is something I had difficulty substantiating. The name "AMEXEM." How does the Temple back up that this was the name of the land mass of North America at one time or of northern Africa? Which [to the MSTA] was actually in North America?

DPEL: So, you know, a lot of this comes from research, obviously . . . Prophet Noble Drew Ali, being a prophet for us here in the United States of America. He had to speak our language, correct?

JIG: Yeah.

DPEL: So, if you're speaking our language, for example, Moslem [English]/Muslim[Arabic] . . . AMEXEM is the English way of saying what that is. What language were they speaking at a particular time and what was AMEXEM translated to, or what did it translate from? If you look up Al Morocco, now you're going back to Arabic. If you just look up Al Makhzen right now, you'll find something that sounds very familiar.

JIG: Okay. That makes sense.

DPEL: But then you think about AMEXEM, and I told you this a while ago, AMEXEM and Africa are uniquely put together. Because "America" is the old and the new. Because, you know, they like to tell you that Amerigo Vespucci . . . is where the name America came from, but that's a lie because we all know that if you name a place after you, it ain't gonna be your first name. It's gonna be your last . . . When you break down America, it's a mixture of old and the new. Take the "AME" out of "AMEXEM," which is the old, and then you take the new, the "rica" out of "Africa, and what do you get? "America." Because in essence, we are in Africa. We're in Northwest Africa right now, Because if you go back to when it was one land mass, New Jersey is knocking on Morocco's door. Yeah. And they have the evidence in a museum in New Jersey where they have a [map] that shows the evidence of Moroccan land meeting New Jersey land . . . So when you put that into perspective, it seemed so far away now because we're looking at the maps and how they look now. But our people already were in America before the Europeans even arrived.

JIG: That's the other part I think is very, very important. Which is how a lot of history programs in the United States, a lot of programs that you'll find in schools from kindergarten to graduate schools and doctoral programs locate the entrance of people that we now refer to as "Black" people . . . They basically refer to the entrance of people from the continent we now know is "Africa" happening during the Middle Passage and during the fifteenth century and they pretty much gloss over all the evidence pointing towards us being there long before that, you know? And this is one of them, you know? Would you assert that the Moorish Science Temple's view of nationality is the only way for non- Europeans in the Americas to gain adequate nationality? Or is it just one of many ways?.

DPEL: Let me read this and put it in perspective. [reading from frontside of the MSTA nationality card] "This is the nationality and identification card for the Moorish Science Temple of America, and birthrights for the Moorish Americans, etc. We honor all the divine prophets: Jesus, Mohammad, Buddha, and Confucius. May the blessings of the God of our Father, Allah, be upon YOU [emphasis DPEL] that carry this card. I do hereby declare that you are a Moslem under the Divine Laws of the Holy Koran of Mecca. Love, Truth, Peace, Freedom, and Justice. 'I AM A CITIZEN OF THE U.S.A.' Noble Drew Ali, The Prophet, Chicago, Illinois." There is actually a nationality card given out by Noble Drew Ali in Cuba. And the same words that I just read are in Spanish. I say that to say that those Asiatics in the UNITED STATES [emphasis] of America that claim to be "Black," "Negro," Colored," and currently "African American" . . . He [Noble Drew Ali] came directly for us to make sure that we got in tune with who we were by teaching us to be ourselves . . . We're such a powerful people. We just don't know our powers. You know, knowledge is power. So, if you don't have knowledge of self, you don't have power, but you are capable of it the moment you realize who you are . . . The Supreme Grand Council here in Chicago, IL is the Central Authority of the Moroccan Empire. And as these Moors live and grow amongst the United States of America, you need to build new temples. They are by all means in allegiance 'cus they're brothers and sisters of the Asiatics of ALL [emphasis DPEL] of America. So in my perspective, G7 (the MC name for Jon Ivan Gill) . . . The Moorish Science Temple of America is in the business of uplifting fallen humanity. And we've fallen because we've been divided and conquered and no longer look at each other as one people . . . One day, those flags are gonna switch where the United States of America flag is gonna switch over to the side of the Moorish flag and the Moorish flag is gonna switch over to where the United States of America flag was.[8] And what was once in the European's hands will now be in the Asiatic's hands. But it's all because the Asiatics [will have learned to] love instead of hate. That's all because the Asiatics learned to govern themselves . . . And that's where the nationality action comes into play . . . how could we have an allegiance if you don't recognize me and I don't recognize you?

JIG: One other question . . . Now we talked a little bit about reparations . . . now that the Moorish Science Temple has enabled a way for those without a nationality because of the atrocities of the Middle Passage, slavery, [or] what the Prophet might say is us renouncing our divine nature . . . What is the Moorish Science Temple of America's perspective on reparations?

DPEL: So while you've been saying this, I've been contemplating because I actually have footage of Pimienta-Bey speaking on reparations . . . I have several thoughts. The first thought that usually comes up a lot of times is a lot of brothers been coming to the temple proclaiming nationality, or try to proclaim their nationality—say that their name is Habbi Mufasa and [they] want to be Habbi Mufasa-Bey, right? But in order for you to get your Nationality Card, you have to show your ID. Because we're not just going to put any name that you made up on your Nationality Card. It's gonna be exactly what's on your ID. So, if your name is Todd Smith, you're gonna be Todd Smith-Bey. You're not gonna be Habbi Mufasa-Bey. I say that to say that Prophet Noble Drew Ali said don't get rid of your names. And I'm paraphrasing . . . Because there's value in that name . . . Because these names are evidence that our people have been through the plantation . . . So that's the reason why the Prophet tells us when you fill out your nationality card and we pick El or Bey, [it is] to correct your name as opposed to changing your name. Because you're gonna keep your name as Jon Ivan Gill. But that "Gill" carries value because it's evidence of what you've been through. But the "El" or "Bey" as Jon Ivan Gill-Bey or El is showing that you are now connecting yourself back to your ancestors . . . The second thing that I think that's gonna be more correlated to Pimienta-Bey's presentation in regards to what you even need to get reparations, which you already alluded to, that being "Black," "Negro," "Colored," you know, you're not going to be able to achieve anything because that's not in the record books as a people. Because you didn't go into bondage as "Black." You came out as "Black." So, what were you when you came in? And that's what you have to be connected to.

JIG: We were talking about Noble Drew Ali's understanding [that there is] one human race. But two types of humans: Europeans and non-Europeans . . . So this brings this brings the question . . . what is the definition of an "Asiatic?"

DPEL: Yeah. So, we have a questionnaire [called] "Questions for Moorish Americans." And it's 101 questions and 101 answers. And I think that in speaking about this . . . it would be important from the Prophet's point of view to speak on this and then I could just elaborate on it a little bit. You know what I'm saying?

JIG: Okay, cool.

DPEL: So, I'm gonna read a series of questions and let you see how it sinks into context. So, Question 52, and I'm probably gonna read different questions . . . So Question 52: "At what place on earth was the physical part of man formed?" The answer is "In the Garden of Eden." [Question]

53: Where is the Garden of Eden? The answer is "In the land of Canaan in the city of Mecca." Question 54: "What is the modern name for the Garden of Eden?" The answer is "Mecca." Now I'm gonna skip to 57. It says, "Who were Adam and Eve?" The answer is "They are the mothers and fathers of the human family." [Question] 58: "Where did they go?" The answer is, "They went into Asia." 59. What is the modern name given to their Children? The answer is "Asiatics." 60: "Who is guarding the holy city of Mecca? to keep the unbelievers away?" The answer is "Angels." 61: "What is the modern name of these angels?" The answer is "Asiatics." 62: "What is the shade of their skin?" The answer is "Olive." 63: Are the Moorish Americans any relation to those angels?" The answer is "Yes. We all have the same Father and mother." 64: Give five names that are given to the descendants of Adam and Eve." The answer is "Lucifer, Satan, Devil, Dragon and Beast. 65: "What is the devil sometimes called?" The answer is "The lower self." 66 says, "How many selves are there?" Answer is "Two." 67 says, "Name them." The answer is "Higher self and lower self." 68 says "What people represent the higher self?" The answer is "The angels, who protect the holy city of Mecca." 69 says "What people represent the lower self? [the answer is] "Those who were cast out of the Holy City and those who accept their teachers." And I'll stop right there . . . I just thought that that was important because you asked from a Moorish perspective how we look at that. And I think that just kind of puts a lot of things into context. But just with that last thing, who represents the lower self? And it says, "Those who were cast out of the Holy City and those who accept their teaching." You have a lot of stories out there, from the Yakub story to the Ice Age perspective.[9] Just to simplify it, Europeans used to be Asiatics. So, when they when they were cast out, they were still Asiatics at that time.

JIG: Because everybody's an Asiatic really.

DPEL: Right. In essence and origin, everybody stems from Asia, right? It's what that particular group of Asiatics did to make them be cast out and for what they did after they left. What you would call the holy city of Mecca, which carried the weight of a whole bunch of layers—But, you know, it's just an aspect of it if a group is radical within the civilization and we kicked them out . . . they ultimately are creating a culture . . . Because culture in its essence, and this is my drawing—culture in its essence is obviously based on certain rituals that you do, certain things that you eat, dance, talk, you know, the way you socialize amongst your group. There's a certain culture that's created . . . It's the same thing like, you know, one person might call you a nerd because that's all they know how to stereotype you as because they don't understand what your day to day is. And at the end of the day, you might be a nerd. But what they think of as a nerd doesn't encompass everything that you do. But you are part of multiple cultures that if they actually had a conversation with you or actually was around you and seeing how you move, they would be impacted by the culture that you are part of as much as you could be impacted by their culture, right? Just because somebody has a culture, it doesn't mean that it's a culture that has a good influence on you. There are bad cultures out there. Like as far as what we understand, gang cultures, right? They start off with good intentions of family and being recognized. But it can end as bad results for somebody else. And so, if a child is cultivated within a gang culture, their mentality [and] their reality ultimately becomes manifested tenfold every day. Just like us MCs, us being embedded in the culture, we're constantly eating, thinking and walking that. It's in us, right? Right. So, we know who's faking the funk and who's not. Just like somebody who's gang banging, and they know who's faking the funk and who's not. So, I [use] all of these different analogies to say that thoughts manifest reality, and the path that you take ultimately can be your demise or be positive in so many different ways . . . So, from my perspective, brother man, like when these particular Asiatics…were cast out, they were cast out for a reason.

DPEL: But what we do know is that when we speak about Asiatics, we're not just talking about . . . the immediate perception of someone proclaiming their nationality from the marks of a Black, Negro, and Colored. You know . . . "Asiatic" is Still a Mexican. "Asiatic" is still the Aboriginal people in Australia . . . "Asiatic" is still a Chinese man . . . I always use this as a perspective . . . But it's interesting to me that out of all of the [seven] continents, each continent [except for one] starts with the letter "A," which is Europe . . . And I would tell you that all of those individuals in those continents with the letter "A" is where you will find heavy origins of Asiatics . . . But if you have one original people, and one original people still means many nations . . . right? . . . It's not to say that it's just one thing, but they're still one people in essence . . . But all they were doing was starting you at the point of [the beginnings of a certain] people who started developing their own culture outside of the culture they were kicked out of . . . that's it from my perspective . . . but swinging it back to the point, "Asiatics" is our race because the first physical man, our Great Grandfather was the first to set foot is on the land mass of Asia. So basically, the whole land mass belongs to us . . . But that's before the [shifts of] tectonic plates… happened . . . That's before all of that. So, we as Asiatics are [directly connected] to the origin of the original man. But whatever it was, it took place over the course of time, that's where you get that subdivision [of lighter skinned inhabitants of Europe] . . . I was just trying to throw little things in there to kind of put perspective on why I would say that [and] why I would support that from my perspective.

JIG: I mentioned Aesop Rock[10] before and I'ma mention him again. If he were to go to Temple Number One and he were to say he wanted to proclaim his nationality and he would tell you that his ancestry is Moroccan, what do you think the response to that might be?

DPEL: Well, I understand the question you're asking.

JIG: And this is not anything he's coming up with. It's something that he can actually point to and say, "Well, these are my parents, and this is where they're from. What would you say?

DPEL: You're saying that he can say like, these are my parents. They are Moroccan. He could prove that . . . If we could see that he's Asiatic within that lineage of his parents, he could proclaim his nationality.

JIG: Okay, so And I guess that this this leads to the other thing . . . nationality in the MSTA is somewhat dependent upon appearance. Because would I be asked to prove my ancestry if I were to go there and claim my nationality the way that Aesop Rock may be asked to prove his, if he was asked to prove [his ancestry]? Maybe he wouldn't be asked to prove his ancestry.

DPEL: One thing I would say is this: when you're talking about appearance, there are certain phenotypes and different things that you can identify to tell that somebody's Asiatic. But there have been some individuals I came across, and I had to question like, "Are they European or are they Asiatic?" Someone that is not used to seeing an individual that might be a very light olive skin and have certain features they might say, "Oh, this dude is a White dude and y'all got him in the Temple?" But really, he's Peruvian. It's just that he has those type of features from his grandfather, His father . . . Now . . . a Sicilian is an Asiatic. But . . . if [someone] didn't know any better, [they] would say that a Sicilian is a "White dude."[11]

JIG: This does amaze certain people…not because they're dumb . . . but because they've never . . . been exposed to anything like that.

DPEL: We've been conditioned and taught to look at things in the wrong light, and that's the reason why we can never find a remedy to a situation. If we keep calling people "Spanish," and that's not even a nationality, that's a language.

JIG: Well, it is a nationality, but it's not the nationality of the folks who were called that.

DPEL: Exactly. It is a nationality in Spain. But when you're talking to somebody because they speak Spanish . . . because it's equivalent to calling a Mexican "Spanish," [is] calling us "English" because we speak English. We've just been conquered, and our native tongue has been misplaced. So, we speak in the language of the person who conquered us.

JIG: Like my grandparents and some of my family speak Spanish. But they're not from Spain. They're from Belize or Honduras. Either one of those places ... but you're right. All of those terminologies, man ... we were caught up and the colonizers have used them for their benefit.

It goes back to what we were talking about last time ... the nationality of Aesop Rock.

JIG: I don't know his nationality.

JIG: I think he's first generation Latvian.

DPEL: Got it. I'll give you example ... A lot of times you can know somebody's nationality by just a name ... The reason why, like a European, for example, will be denied membership [in the MSTA] is because, one, they already have a nationality. Two, [the MSTA] is the sole foundation for the salvation of all Asiatics in America. Because the reality is that the reason why we're divided and conquered is because we don't believe in the capacity of our group ... They [Europeans] never could solve our problems. We have to solve our problems. It starts with us believing in the capacity of our group. So, the Moorish Science Temple of America is not a hate group. The Moorish Science Temple of America is not against Europeans. The Moorish Science Temple of America is not against Christianity. We actually believe Christianity to be good for the European. It's just that WE (emphasis DPEL's) are letting go of Christianity ... So the Moorish Science Temple of America is in the business of uplifting fallen humanity ... and making an impact on proclaiming love, truth, peace, freedom and justice to everybody, and that includes the Europeans.

JIG: Understood ... Last question. And even along this wavelength of what you told me before and what I what I've read in my own my own research of the Moorish Science Temple of America ... the Prophet [Noble Drew Ali] as we know teaches us to love and not hate.

DPEL: I'm sorry. I gotta say this ... We do consider Europeans as sympathizers, though. So as a sympathizer, a European can come into the Temple, sit down and learn about Prophet Noble Drew Ali and the teachings of the Moorish Science Temple of America. They are not rejected at the door. They can come to as many meetings as they want. They just can't join.

JIG: That's great. With that being said, what is the relationship between the Moorish Science Temple of America and the Nation of Islam?

DPEL: That's a deep, deep history ... There was no Nation of Islam in 1925. There was no Nation of Islam in 1928. There was no Nation of Islam during the time of Prophet Noble Drew Ali starting this religious organization. In your book that I found in your room in Cali across the street from that library that you used to work at ... I don't know what book it is. If you could remember that book, I would love for you to tell me what that book is.

Do you remember when I woke up and I just happened to go through one of your books . . . I don't know if it was like African studies of religion or whatever like that, and I opened up that book, and the first page I opened that book up to . . . it was speaking about the first organizations in America that introduced Islam. Do you remember?

JIG: Yes. You're talking about the Amina Macleod text called *African American Islam*.[12]

DPEL: I would love for you to send me a link to that.

JIG: Yeah, for sure.

DPEL: That was a divine moment. Because here I am in your room, you got a whole bunch of books, and the one book I pick up . . . I opened up the book . . . don't even go through multiple pages. I just opened up the book, and that's the first page I see.

JIG: That's crazy.

DPEL: It's talking about first organizations that introduced Islam in America. What was the first one?

JIG: MSTA.

DPEL: Yeah. And that was when I was still green, and I'm still learning now. But I was really green at that time when it came to Moorish Science. So that was kind of a moment for me. And so, I bring that back to say that the Nation of Islam wasn't even thought of. And somebody would say, "What does that have to do with the Nation of Islam and the Moorish Science Temple of America?" Well, the brother that we know by the name of Elijah Muhammad . . . and also the brother that we know by Master Fard Muhammad, we're both members of the Moorish Science Temple of America. Not only were they members of the Moorish Science Temple of America, they were members in the same temple, which was Temple No. 4, located in Detroit, Michigan. [the temple in] Detroit, Michigan was run by the Supreme Grand Governor at that time, who was Lomax-Bey . . . I'm gonna send you a reference of what I'm talking about.

JIG: This is deep, man. This is deep.

DPEL: I just found it, too. It would be good for you to see this while I'm talking about it.

(DPEL texts me a document relating to the discussion at hand).

DPEL: So, this is primary. This is primary, right? So just to put things into context now, you see what date that is at the top of the right hand corner, right?

JIG: Yeah.

DPEL: What does it say?

JIG: July 3, 1928.

DPEL: Yeah. It says, "Temple No. 4." It has an address in Detroit, Michigan. And who was it written to?

JIG: This is written to Noble Drew Ali.

DPEL: This is written to Noble Drew Ali himself.

JIG: So, the monthly report is going to him, so he knows who's on the books.

DPEL: Exactly. So, every subordinate temple has per capita tax. And when you pay your dues or your per capita tax, that particular subordinate temple will send that money with a sheet verifying who paid their money as a member to be represented. Because it was also known as a "representation tax." That was sent to Noble Drew Ali himself during that time. If you look down, you're gonna see one where it says, "Brother Robert Poole-Bey." You see that?

JIG: Yep.

DPEL: And then under there, you see Sister Poole-Bey. Then you see another one that says, "Brother John Poole-Bey." Then you see another one that says, "Brother James Poole-Bey." Right? And then right under there, what do you see?

JIG: That's Master Fard.

DPEL: Brother David Fard-El.

JIG: Yeah. I couldn't read the David Fard-El. So, they're listed on the same role sheet. That's interesting.

DPEL: Robert Poole-Bey is Elijah Muhammad. Before he became Elijah Muhammad. The rest of those Poole-Beys are Elijah Muhammed, then Robert Poole-Bey's family.

JIG: Got it.

DPEL: With David Fard-El right there in the middle.

JIG: And he called himself David here, which is interesting.

DPEL: Now, this is in 1928. So, this is proof right here from the archives . . . because we have the archives that date all the way back to the first convention. Why? Because with any organization, for you to prove who you are, you have to have the minutes of every convention and annual convention when you're meeting with the board of directors, which the board of directors is the Supreme Grand Council. All the subordinate temples, every convention . . . makes their Hajj to Chicago . . . because the prophet had a national annual convention which I tell you about every time which Pimienta-Bey speaks at . . . The National Convention. We just had our 92nd annual Convention.

JIG: That's dope.

DPEL: [For] every day session that took place all the way back to the prophet, we have every single minute off what was said and what was done, what sheiks were made, what sheiks were taken out . . . all of that . . . And this right here is just a glimpse of the past . . . to a point in time when the Nation of Islam did not exist. Now, that's a heavy measure in itself. Let's now put things into context . . . Now, this is not me, for the record, bashing the Nation of Islam or hating the Nation of Islam. Islam, I'm only speaking Facts.

JIG: Right.

DPEL: To put things in perspective, there was a brother by the name of Kirkman-Bey.

Who is very famous in Moorish history. [the] Reason why he's famous is because when Prophet, Noble Drew Ali changed form, Brother E. Mealy-El, who was the first Supreme Grand Sheik was put in position to lead the movement, just like how Supreme Grand Sheik E. Braswell-Bey is in that position now. Kirkman-Bey influenced people to follow him instead of Brother E. Mealy-El, claiming that Prophet Noble Drew Ali picked him. This is the reason why that temple [in Chicago] on the north side on Milwaukee and Augusta is still operating in name of Kirkman-Bey . . . Brother E. Mealy-El during his time . . . was told by the Prophet to revoke certain charters and to change the charters from the Moorish Holy Temple of Science to the Moorish Science Temple of America.[13] And that was Temple No. 9 at that time. And they got their charter revoked. They still operate in their capacity as the Moorish Science Temple of America, Inc. Why are they "Inc.?" Because they not operating under the capacity of the Prophet. They filed under the state as a 501 c3. That's what all churches are. All churches are 501 c3s. They file under the state. That is not in the same capacity as the Moorish Science Temple of America, which is a religious corporation.

JIG: Right.

DPEL: So why did I bring that up? There was a split that took place after Prophet Noble Drew Ali changed form. You had those that stuck with the Prophet and who he appointed as leadership and Brother E. Mealy-El. You have brothers that left and followed Kirkman-Bey. You have other brothers claiming that they were the Prophet reincarnated. But nobody tried to follow that . . . But the thing is that Lomax-Bey . . . makes it very interesting. There was a particular meeting in Detroit and the Prophet was present. During this time, Detroit was about 1,500 strong in members. In the late twenties. That's a lot of members. And part of that membership was the names . . . on that document I sent to you. In front of Prophet Noble Drew Ali, he told the people to stop following the Prophet. Follow me.

JIG: Who's saying that?

DPEL: Lomax-Bey

JIG: Got it.

DPEL So, Lomax-Bey. Let me see if I could find a picture of him. It's one of the famous pictures you will see of Prophet Noble Drew Ali.

JIG: Is this the picture where it's like about 10 or 12 people sitting around a table?

DPEL: It's not that picture. It's the picture where they're standing in front of Unity Hall.[14]

JIG: Yeah, I've seen that before. If it's the one I think it is.

DPEL: You've seen it, but I'm about to do a close up to who Lomax-Bey is. You have to kind of blow it up. But you will know exactly who I'm talking about because he's dressed up just like the Prophet.

JIG: I see. Okay. Yeah, yeah, I'm looking at.

DPEL: So, you know, you see that sister that's in the middle sitting down?

JIG: Yeah. He's right next to her.

DPEL: Prophet Noble Drew Ali is on the left side. Lomax-Bey is on the right side, and he had the same sash just like Noble Drew Ali.

JIG: Got it.

DPEL: So, he was making a lot of money in Detroit and the power got to his head and he thought he didn't need the Prophet anymore. He basically proclaimed that he didn't need the Prophet, and whoever wants to go with him, come with him and leave the Prophet. Never heard of Lomax-Bey ever again. right? But Lomax-Bey, David Fard-El, and Robert Poole-Bey. That's the interesting question that comes up. What took place between that time to the time of the Nation of Islam hitting the scene?[15]

JIG: That's a very interesting question.

DPEL: It's a very interesting question, right? Because everything that they know all the way up to that point has been sparked by Prophet Noble Drew Ali. Because you gotta put it in perspective, man. They just got out of slavery in 1865. That ain't that long ago. You can't tell me people came out of slavery just knowing knowledge of self. You know what I'm saying? It don't work that way, man. You know, like it had to be something that was a grand event to spark, that type of energy. Even when we talk about Nat turner and Harriet Tubman, it wasn't necessarily like they were breaking down knowledge to them as much it was more like "I realized that we got played and this time to rebel. And I'm willing to die for this."

JIG: Yeah.

DPEL: And so, when Marcus Garvey hit the scene . . . when Prophet Nobel Drew Ali hit the scene, it was a certain type of shift that took place and consciousness when it came amongst our people. I say that all to say there are brothers that are in our temple now that went deep into the FOI[16] and they personally told me that when you go in the back of that podium behind the curtain,[17] you'll see the Holy Koran of Moorish Science Simple of America in one of the altars.

JIG: And Farrakhan even said this. I don't know if you saw that.

DPEL: I did. What he said is that noble Drew Ali was the forerunner to David Fard Muhammed and Elijah Muhammed.

JIG: I pointed that point out in my paper . . . I caught that too.

DPEL: Right. So, when you say that, that's really like a very convoluted statement. You're not really telling anybody the truth as much as you're just trying to say, "Oh, they played a part."

JIG: Right.

DPEL: But [according to] what I just sent you, how is he the forerunner? You were in his school of thought. You were in his class. You were in his sacred grove. Everything that you know was sparked from Prophet Noble Drew Ali. And so . . . I have to take into consideration that Farrakhan doesn't know. And when I say, "doesn't know," that doesn't mean that he doesn't know that the teachings are connected, but because of how he was introduced to it, it was probably taught him in such a way where he gets it honest but not in the right perspective.

JIG: Yeah, right. Because I don't see Minister Farrakhan as being disrespectful. I didn't read it like that at all . . . I just read it as him showing allegiance to his teacher. You know, his teacher was the Honorable Elijah Muhammed through the teachings of Master Fard Muhammed, which is a very interesting thing too… this person that we don't know anything much about, meaning Master Fard, is on the list [the aforementioned record of members of the MSTA]. Some of them consider him God.

DPEL: Right. So that that's a heavy measure, bro. Because I just sent you a list. If he's God, you know what I'm saying? If he's a prophet, why is he on that list? Why was he not made the Supreme Grand Sheikh of the Moorish Science Temple of America?

JIG: Master Fard Mohammed is one of the most interesting characters I've ever encountered in my life . . . No one knows where he came from. No one knows where he went . . . There are several stories about his history. And then there's this [information] that that you've just pointed out about him being on the list [the roll call of the MSTA] . . . I don't know what to say about Master Fard.

DPEL: Technically, G7[18] Every member of the Nation of Islam is a Moorish American. That's the connection and the origin of the nation of Islam. Every member of the Nation of Islam is technically a Moorish American and doesn't even know it. Well, I would say ["technically"] because of where their origin comes from. Technically, they're not, because they still have to proclaim that their Morrish American nationality in the Moorish Science Temple of America to be a Moorish American.

JIG: Oh, yeah, I get it totally.

DPEL: I was even shown some information from another Sheik [about] the brother who started the Hebrew Israelites.[19] He was a member. And he was a Bey.[20] So a lot of the quote unquote "Black" liberation movements didn't hit the scene until after The Moorish Science Temple of America.[21]

The Moorish Science Temple of America really brought forth that spark because the true forerunner was Marcus Garvey . . . what Marcus Garvey did was very similar to what John the Baptist did. He just galvanized the people. He got the people to hear the truth. He didn't care what religion you were. He didn't care where you came from. If you're a part of our people, be here. You know what I mean . . . He was just sparking that pride . . . that purity of who we were . . . After they were all galvanized, Prophet Noble Drew Ali hit the scene from a John the Baptist to Jesus analogy. That's when he hit the scene and gave them knowledge itself and brought them their nationality and Divine Creed. But they were already galvanized with pride to listen and be receptive.

JIG Yes, definitely. Yeah, that's heavy, man . . . Yeah, I think that's really all I needed, bro.

4 PERIOD, FULL STOP: THE OVERSIGHTS OF CANCEL CULTURE(S)

Introduction

In this chapter, I suggest that "cancel culture," or the boycotting of an individual or collective for holding positions and acting in ways seen to be oppressive by the entities now in active opposition to said individual or collective, is in many popular instances dependent on race and race-related language and based on the premise that race and race-related categories and the other categories with which they intersect are plausible means of identification in themselves.

The chapter critically explores whether the recent notable canceling of Rachel Dolezal (2015), Ye (2018), and Nick Cannon (2020) would be possible within a conceptual world in which race is recognized as a null set and abolished. I contend that cancel culture functions as a maintenance of the state-imposed[1] status quo of race/trauma and race/trauma-related language in its chastising of non-adherents to the rules of one's race/trauma caste by others who both voluntarily and/or involuntarily claim and accept membership. Cancel culture also subjects those who are considered as outsiders to a social group they happen to offend to conforming to colonial guidelines of identity.

Toward a Philosophical Definition of Cancel Culture

"Cancel culture," the ostracising of an individual or individuals from spheres in which they many times wield powerful influence due to some oppressive transgression offending voluntary and/or involuntary members of the set/social group, has its origins under this particular phrasing in the MeToo and Black Lives Matter movements and gained steam as a viable concept in the late 2010s.[2] In its popular usage, it has referred to a financial disciplinary action against notable figures. Further, cancel culture also renders said notable figures as social lepers. Also, cancelling is an instinctive "knee-jerk reaction" to certain types of infractions such as instances of perceived racial discrimination. Some have raised the issue of the impossibility of return for the cancelled even after steps are made in the direction of equity, and have argued that it is the same forms of bias the cancelled have been accused of.[3] For now, it suffices to say that cancel culture is founded on a clear either/or binary that requires an automatic and many times permanent separation from and defunding of (in various ways) the offender.

"Cancel culture" is a current name for similar castrations of offenders of perceived groups throughout history. This phenomenon of artificial boundaries that oscillates from conceptual to physical blockages has notable precursors spanning the length of documented time. The "monotheistic" Amenhotep IV, who renamed himself "Akhenaten" during the New Kingdom of Egypt, was cancelled when his name was removed from all iconography immediately after his reign. Another more modern example is that of charismatic-Pentecostal megachurch leader Carlton Pearson, who denounced the very types of monotheism that Akhenaten is thought by some to have invented.[4]

I call the aforementioned "active cancellation," or the intentional policing and erasure of those who were once either a part of or held in high esteem by those in the shadow of the offended group. There is also what I refer to as "subtle cancellation," or the more silent systemic removal of certain individuals from under the shadow of the social group while they may still technically remain. Michel-Rolph Trouillot posits the Haitian Revolution as a subtle cancellation in France's conceptual rendering of the Hatian revolutionary spirit as unjustifiably insolent, which by default can weaken the impetus for disobedience of the empire.[5] "Passive cancellation" refers to the rejection of heretical constructs that are just unthinkable due to their perceived impossibility.

Active, subtle, and passive regions of cancel culture function based on the presupposition that (1) the groups that are generally the subjects of cancel culture in some significant way exist. Further, (2) the types of groups involved in cancel culture, such as racial groups, are erected and defended by rigid boundaries that eliminate the possibility of anything (or anyone) existing outside of the realm of a clear definition. Therefore, the definitional existence of the set proceeds to automatically cancel anything that dares oppose it. The use of the N-word by any person perceived as exterior to the social group sanctioned to say it will receive a pre-reflective rebuke (at the least) by anyone convinced of the unwritten rules of dominant understandings of the social group "Black" in the United States.

A philosophical definition of cancel culture imprints the existential onto the categorical. It illustrates what Sartre would refer to as a modicum of experience ripe with infinite possibilities of appearance as opposed to some transcendent category that causes the "object" to be what it is and will become.[6] In cancel culture, Sartre's pre-reflective self of undetermined decision feigns as the Kantian self of eternal essences. The pre-reflective consciousness informed by and operating within the confines of the categories of its context as an agent is what automatically cancels.

The origin of Sartre's "indivisible, indissoluble being" cannot be located, as it does not exist.[7] The self is cancelled due to the assumption that the conscious experient referred to as the "self," "soul," or other related term is indeed able to be found within the logic of its racial social group definition, but the cancellation experienced cuts existentially deep on both the sides of the cancelled and the canceller.

I also identify a philosophically religious dimension within its ranks. Insofar as a sociological and anthropological definition of "religion" can refer to the lure of humans to make sense of a senseless world, we can think of racial social groups as religions in that they make sense of the world by constituting the very language game of cancel culture. Racial social groups can be adhered to as a fundamentalism. They are believed literally, enforced vehemently, and by deductive definition demonize transgressors. Religion scholar Catherine Albanese helpfully states,

> more than a form of belief, religion is a matter of practice, an *action system*. Body and emotions play as large a role in living religion as philosophical concepts. Perhaps in fact they play a larger role . . . mind and body are both necessary to human religious life, and they are always interconnected.[8]

We can observe how the racial sets under observation for our interrogation of cancel culture demand a certain conscious and/or unconscious allegiance to them. This gives somewhat of a different sense to Miller and Driscoll's statement that "religion is raced and race is religioned."[9] For Miller and Driscoll, religion is raced and vice versa because the categories as they are commonly defined imply each other. While my use of the InnerSection[10] between race and religion is conversant with and affirmative of Miller and Driscoll's statement, it is different in that I am more concerned with how racial categories are the very religions which are raced reflexively in what could be said is tautological. Race is a category which is inevitably believed in as a background assumption about the world and as an intentional reinforcement of this category. But it is as much of a tautology as Sartre's "self," which is its own ground and circular argument if understood epistemologically and not ontologically.[11] Therefore, if religion is defined sociologically as the function of humanity that manufactures meaning, and racial categories significantly influence individual and collective meaning, we are warranted to analyze racial categories and their relation to cancelling to the critical study of religion.

Finally, I conclude the architecture of a philosophical definition of cancel culture with the assertion of cancel culture as parallax. A parallax in my usage is the displacement of something due to a change in position. Cancel culture is powered by a displacement of the human *becoming* within the structures of a social group possessing boundaries of *being* that trigger disciplinary action when transgressed. In a conflation of the human with the racial category experiencing offence, the human loses sight of the fact that it is conceivable to think of them without thinking of the category. It is very possible to think of KRS-ONE as other than "Black" or any racial category, as this is not necessarily inconsistent. But the parallax of racial categories can cause us to behave as if it is a logical fallacy. Further, it might cancel anyone with the phenotype and history of KRS-ONE who would dare say "KRS-ONE isn't Black." A null set renders cancellation impossible since there is nothing to transgress that would trigger a cancellation.

Žižek's commentary on Kierkegaard's understanding of objectivity and subjectivity in relation to the ethically existing subject helps elucidate this perpetual holding at bay of identity performed through compliance with the accepted patterns of identity. He says,

> "The real subject is not the cognitive subject, since in knowing he moves the sphere of the possible; the real subject is the ethically existing subject." The idea is that, in a cognitive approach, every singular entity is reduced to an instance of some universality, to an arbitrary example of a universal law – to a *possible* instantiation of the law, while in the ethico-existential approach, it is my actual singular existence that matters.[12]

In the reduction of singular experience to a universal rubric occurring in racial language, Žizek reveals that the experient event is expected to be a singular example of the universal of the particular social group/set/trauma they most "normally" fit into. The hollow heart of stone acting under the mandate of the racial categories that have varying degrees of reality does not ethically act as itself but as the category, and therefore is not really acting at all. Conversely, what Unamuno refers to as "the man of flesh and bone"[13] is aware of the tendency to instinctively collapse the universal with the act of the particular. The [hu]man of flesh and bone has the potential to win in their own experience of the world. Compliance attempts to cancel the heart of flesh into submission through not only personal pressure to return to familiarity as "change is violent" to requote the Tunnel Rats,[14] but also by outside forces attempting to ensure that every individual experient is an instance of the universal.

Žižek extracts from Kierkegaard a very important distinction between the contingent and the arbitrary that emerges in a consideration of the universal and particular stances of ethically existing subjectivity. He says,

> that I (sort of) speak English is accidental with regard to the universal fact that, as a human being, I am a "being-of-language"; however, the fact that, in speaking English, I use language as a mere means of expression and/or instrumental manipulation, or that I use it poetically, in its world-opening capacity, is contingent. In short, "accidental" stands for a secondary specific

difference within the universal confines of genus, while "contingent" points toward the more radical level of deploying the potentials of the universal dimension itself. In this precise sense, the possibility that pertains to cognitive thought is the possibility of an arbitrary instantiation of the universal law, while the possibility that pertains to the ethico-existential approach concerns the thorough contingency of the decision about what to do with my singular life.[15]

Žižek reminds us that while the dichotomy regarding the action of the ethically existing subject may appear to be that dichotomy between the possible over the actual with the primacy falling to the former (similar to the Kantian postulate that "ought" implies "can"), the dichotomy of most importance is that of the contingent verses the accidental. Those under the linguistic jurisdiction of the racial category are plagued by a parallax, an unbridgeable impasse, preventing the experient from the realization that the possibilities of racial identification are not only actually arbitrary but potentially detrimental to the human.

In review, cancel culture in issues of race/trauma is founded on the presupposition that sets of categorical logic of which races can be a part exist in some necessary way. Secondly, racial sets/social groups are not only categorical but existential. Therefore, cancellation is chiefly exemplified and empowered by the hierarchical categorical logic of racial social groups. Thirdly, race/trauma is practiced as a way of life and of seeing the world and must be considered within the realm of the sociologically and quasi-religious. Finally, race is parallax: It obscures to the point of virtual invisibility through moving the unbridled experiential processes sometimes referred to as the "self" to a conceptual location where it confuses itself with the supposed controlled and determined essence of racial categories.

Cancel Culture as Categorical and Existential: Ye as Thought Experimental Case Study

Within the last eighteen years, the controversial actions and statements of rapper/producer/clothing company owner/record label owner Ye, formerly known as Kanye West, have placed him on a volatile spectrum between a horizontal maintenance of social group definition/expectation and outright cancellation. However, in another sense, it can be read as multidirectional. From his statements such as "George Bush don't care about Black people" in 2005 on national television in response to the former president's handling of Hurricane Katrina to the "slavery is a choice" refrain on TMZ in 2018 and his vocal support of the presidency of Donald Trump in large part due to his assertion that " Black" people actually have a better chance at advancement under this "pull yourselves up by the bootstraps" kind of "zero victim mentality," to borrow the phrasing of Chicagoland area pastor James Ward,[16] Ye is anything but linear.

NBC made it a point to distance itself from Ye's remarks on its station about the then president's neglect of victims suffering tremendous loss in New Orleans. Ye also found disdain to his statements against President Bush in the words of rapper 50 Cent, who said of the remark, "I don't know where that came from."[17] At the time of this statement, Ye was at the height of his initial stardom, and a statement such as this shot his artistic "approval ratings" through the proverbial roof with his core fans, many for whom maintenance and protection of the social group "Black" was synonymous with acting on the right side of the struggle for liberation.

Ye did not benefit from an immunity to cancellation by the many voluntary/involuntary members of the social group "Black." In 2017, the year of Ye's release *Yeezus*, he began to enter into ideological territory that would indeed offend large numbers of his fanbase.[18] Many of Ye's troubling philosophical musings were published on Twitter and aired through various radio and television interviews, some of which have been attributed to his bouts with bipolar disorder.[19] I will now briefly yet substantially turn to a part of the latter philosophy of Kanye as Ye that rely in some way on a classical/essentialist understanding of racial social groups for the possibility of and impetus for cancellation: (1) the "slavery was a choice" discussion and (2) the related support of a Donald Trump presidency.

Slavery Is a Choice: Cancel Culture's Categorical and Existential Dimensions

In May of 2018 during a TMZ interview, Ye provided an argument insisting that the descendants of the enslaved in the United States were in some ways responsible for their perpetual servitude. At TMZ, Ye offered, "When you hear about slavery for 400 years. For 400 years? That sounds like a choice." He also went on to say, "You were there for 400 years and it's all of y'all. It's like we're mentally imprisoned."[20] Is there any element of what Ye offered to TMZ about slavery important to a deeper understanding of the fissures of the categories that empower cancel culture?

In Ye's view, the United States has become a bastion of controlled opinions and actions, and he offers something that puts him at risk of losing good standing within the race/trauma set "Black" by both insiders and outsiders. Ye says,

> Well, it was really just my subconscious. It was just a feeling I had . . . People were taught how to think, how to feel; we don't know how to think for ourselves, we don't know how to feel for ourselves . . . people say "feel free" but they don't

really want us to feel free and I felt a freedom in first of all just doing something that everybody tells you not to do . . . I'm not coming up here to justify anything . . . you can't tell me nothing, I made the song (laughs) . . . You can't tell me what I'm supposed to do . . . I don't subscribe to icons. You take the Nazi symbol, if you go to India, it is all over the place, but it doesn't represent that. It represents something different. So to me to wear that [MAGA] hat means I want to make America great in my own way.[21]

One can reasonably conclude that the root of his use of MAGA apparel is less about supporting Trump and more about moving the general stream of decision-making toward heartfelt convictions. For the racial social group "Black," what follows in Ye's discussion with TMZ does not qualify as free thought because it moves in direct contradiction to the categorical imperatives of "Blackness," which imply under said interpretations that the absence of free thought is similar to Fanon's critique that the ingression of the occupations and ways of life of the colonizer post-independence from dress and governance to religion and social norms is a bondage that poses as freedom.[22]

Regarding the voluntary aspect of slavery, Ye says,

when you hear about slavery for 400 years. For 400 years? That sounds like a choice. Like, you were there for 400 years, and it is all of y'all?

It is like we are mentally in prison. I like the word prison because slavery goes too direct to the idea of blacks. It is like slavery/Holocaust, Holocaust is Jews, and slavery is Blacks. So prison is something that unites us as one race: Blacks and Whites being one race . . . we are human beings and stuff.[23]

This statement was, of course, a rock of offense to many within and without the social group "Black." Ye clarified,

Right now, we're choosing to be enslaved . . . okay so Ebro's [radio personality on NYC radio station Hot97] on FaceTime and I'm there with Candace Owens [right wing "Black" political commentator] . . . and Ebro starts bringing up his version of facts, right? And Candace starts bringing up her version of facts she's researched . . . and Candace just pulls out her Jedi lightsaber and just you know, chops Ebro's head off with facts. Then Ebro FaceTimes me the next day and he's talking . . . about music now. I said "Yeah, you're gonna have Candace on your show?" He's like "Nah man, she's mean." So you're gonna stifle her voice, Ebro? You're choosing to enslave people's minds? You're choosing not to let the truth be free?[24]

From Ye's response, one can make a strong case that the proposition "slavery is a choice" is not one that can be seen through the lens of a rigid analytic but must be considered for its symbolic reference, or that which is beyond the actual form of the sentence and dives into the felt content of what it communicates. The less-referenced Whitehead of the lectures included in *Symbolism: Its Meaning and Effect* argued that "Symbolic reference may be, in many respects, erroneous."[25] But Whitehead goes into adventurous realms with this in ways Kant would undoubtedly frown upon. One may ask what is the benefit of symbolic references' tendency to lure us away from the "truth" in matters of race, since beliefs about race have drastic "real" life consequences. Talib Kweli, rapper and long collaborator with Ye, referred to the use of the proposition in question to minimize countless years of oppression as "putting a target on our backs."[26]

Whitehead goes further into the erroneous nature of symbolic reference and says,

> By this I mean that some "direct recognition" disagrees, in its report of the actual world, with the conscious recognition of the fused product resulting from symbolic reference. Thus error is primarily the product of symbolic reference, and not of conceptual analysis. Also symbolic reference itself is not primarily the outcome of conceptual analysis, though it is greatly promoted by it. For symbolic reference is still dominant in experience when such mental analysis is at a low ebb.[27]

In terms of the perception of Ye's proposition by many outsiders, their "direct recognition," or their face value experience of the world, illustrates the antithesis of Ye's postulate: slavery is not a choice. Period, full stop. If the articulation of "Blackness" depends on slavery being totally involuntary, any adaptation of an idea different or incompatible with the premise "slavery is/was not a choice" jeopardizes the existence of the category of "Blackness" itself. But what would happen if the error of symbolic reference Whitehead mentions is the type of philosophical device Ye employs as the foundation for his fantastic proposition?

Both Ye and his dissenters believe slavery occurred. The disagreement is on whether or not it could be construed as voluntary. In many revisitations of this incident, commentators unfairly hold Ye accountable to the analytical literal consequences of the statement "slavery is a choice," thus missing the more synthetic allegorical implications he raises. Based on his reference to "400 years," which includes approximately 165 years after the abolishing of chattel slavery, it can be argued quite persuasively that the voluntary aspects of slavery Ye is referring to most do not include physical enslavement. Ye fissures the category of "Blackness" through perhaps unintentionally implying that the category cannot withstand such a redefinition of slavery. Whitehead says, "In the initial stages of mental progress, error in symbolic reference is the discipline which promotes imaginative freedom."[28] At the bare minimum, the exercise of imaginative freedom that Ye employs can potentially ground a more serious interrogation of how the core premises of racial categories expose critical flaws when examined.

To briefly account for what I have just presented, I will reformulate some of the many presuppositions and implications of Ye's interview in a somewhat linear form. This particular line of reasoning presented in this instance does not account for the ways in which we are forcefully raced. I do not deny that this is true. However, the focus of this stream of thought is to examine the identity-forming personal choices I read Ye to address in this provocative interview. They are as follows:

1. Slavery is the involuntary subjugation and commodification of a human for the purposes of creating other commodities. (P)
2. Slavery has both physical and mental aspects and consequences. (P)
3. "Blackness" emerged as one of many means of enforcing and justifying slavery through the reidentification of humans as property. (P)
4. Due to its origin, "Blackness" is by definition a condition of domination. (P)
5. After the abolishment of physical slavery in the United States in 1865, "Blackness" was not abolished and remained a key means of identifying and regulating who did and did not have full access to the society, namely "Blacks." (P)
6. Even though it's not common in the United States to conceive "Blackness" itself as oppression ("trauma"), the category can be said to mentally enslave those who are voluntarily and involuntarily associated with it. (P)
7. Various ideological shifts in the systemic framework of the country from the 1960s to the present such as the Civil Rights Movement, the Stonewall Riots, the Young Lords Party, Hip-Hop Culture, etc. uncover the preexistent[29] conceptual personal choice not to identify with "Blackness" or any other racial or race-related category, all inhibiting categories of race/trauma, which based on premises 3–6 is problematic in its conception and continuance of mental slavery. (P)
8. Those who identify as "Black" personally choose to be mentally enslaved. (C)

I suggest that what Ye offers in his interview includes the express premise that "slavery is a choice" and that it is equivalent to the suppressed proposition "'Blackness' is a choice." Therefore, choosing the category of "Blackness" as a means of identification is electing to remain in mental slavery. What happens to the power behind the cancellation that befell Ye if this were indeed a true proposition? Would the grounds for TMZ staff member Van Lathan's watershed cancellation of Ye have existed?

After following the "slavery is a choice" statement, Lathan says,

> I actually don't think you're thinking anything. I think what you're doing right now is actually the absence of thought. And the reason why I feel like that is because, Kanye [Ye's former artist name], you're entitled to your opinion. You're entitled to believe whatever you want. But there is fact and real-world, real-life consequence behind everything that you just said. And while you are making music and being an artist and living the life that you've earned by being a genius, the rest of us in society have to deal with these threats to our lives. We have to deal with the marginalization that's come from the four hundred years of slavery that you said for our people was a choice! Everyday, we have to walk into that truth while you choose to say things that to be honest with you dawg, are nonsensical! You wanna think freely, that's fine. I'll combat your free thought with my free thought because mine is grounded in a reality that I have been given, and the reality that I'm going to change. But I'm not gonna do it pretending that the enemies are on the same team as me. And frankly, I'm disappointed, I'm appalled, and brother, I am unbelievably hurt by the fact that you have morphed into something to me that's not real.[30]

What Lathan illustrates in this heated moment between him and Ye is the existential power of arbitrary racial categories taken as non-negotiable and necessarily existent by those socialized to be members of the categories. There is no "*If I become* a 'Black' man, I will potentially face systemic peril." There is only the "*Because I am* a 'Black' man, I face systemic peril." In Ye's fissure to the category of "Blackness," he opens the gateway of responsibility for one's own experience of the world in a way reminiscent of Sartre. Further, Sartre's assertion that the gap between the categorical and the existential is incapable of illustrating existential non-being emerges in an existential view of cancel culture. Sartre identifies that a categorical statement such as "the 'Black' race is the polar opposite of the 'White'" race in its part in "constituting Nothingness as a sort of geometrical place for unfulfilled projects" does not account for those entities within which being and non-being existentially share space.[31] Lathan exemplifies that this non-being is also paradoxically existent against its own categorical impossibility, as he vehemently argues against Ye as he attempts to maintain the existence of the chimera by identifying it as himself.

After Lathan gives his powerful treatise, Ye responds in kind with an admonition to have difficult conversations with those identifying with right-wing Republican and fundamentalist ideals as opposed to cancelling them. Lathan's facial countenance as Ye rebuts is arguably as poignant as the words that prompted his response.³² Whitehead offers that

> The human mind is functioning symbolically when some components of its experience elicit consciousness, beliefs, emotions, and usages, respecting other components of experience . . . the organic functioning whereby there is transition from the symbol to the meaning will be called "symbolic reference."³³

"Blackness" for Lathan symbolically references a mandatory existence (for him, at least) that is plagued with holistic existential peril, possessing what Whitehead calls "presentational immediacy," or sense experience that affects the percipient and becomes data for their continuance. "Presentational immediacy" for many who identify within the category of "Blackness" is by definition and experience not limited to but in large part consists of a pervading awareness of a perpetual struggle to be recognized by self and society as human.³⁴ For Lathan, the category of "Blackness," encoded with its various structures of cancellation, is his only option, very similar to Whitehead's critique of both Hume and Kant's understanding of "causal efficacy," or the "why" of how one modicum of experience affects and makes subsequent experience possible. Whitehead dismisses both Hume's and Kant's conclusions that causal efficacy is not directly perceived by the faculties of reason of the percipient (Hume) or the pre-reflective structure by which we perceive the world (Kant).³⁵ For Ye, suppressed in his discourse at TMZ is the premise that there is nothing apparent in the causal efficacy of "Blackness." Hence referring to oneself within the definitional confines of the category should not by necessity include an "apparent" cancellable contradiction.

This admittedly non-comprehensive re-viewing of a key segment of Ye's trajectory from praised icon to cancelled pariah intends to not absolve him of any charges of harmful rhetoric but to raise to the fore largely ignored underlying currents within his thought that must be reckoned with if any fair analysis is to be done on his move to sympathy with the right. If the cancellation impetus encoded in the category of the racial social group "Blackness" was not caretaken but critiqued, to pull from the provocative title of critical theorist of religion Russell McCutcheon's text *Critics Not Caretakers: Redescribing the Public Study of Religion*, a different dialogue might have ensued between Ye and Lathan. Such a dialogue may have possibly maintained the involuntary historical reality of slavery while also offering a deconstructive rereading of Lathan's valid existential concerns. Or the question could be rephrased more directly (and perhaps more provocatively) in an interpolation of and addition to the Philippian jailer's statement in the book of Acts, "what must I do to renounce 'Blackness?'"

Rachel Dolezal: An Instance of the Rigid Religion of Cancel Culture

In 2015, Rachel Dolezal, former president of the NAACP Spokane Chapter, was cancelled for stating that she was "Black" while understood by her parents and other onlookers as not having membership in this racial social group due to a lack of assumed biological connection to the category. Dolezal posits an interesting case for the religiosity of cancel culture. In this instance, race is religioned not in the sense of a presupposed notion of certain racial groups as having higher or lower ratios of favor to transcendent deities. Rather, race is religioned in that its practice not only shapes beliefs but is a major ground of possibility for foundational beliefs themselves. In other words, race/trauma as religion generates what is and is not conceivable about human personhood.

Rachel Dolezal was born to Lawrence and Ruthanne Dolezal, both of whom personally identify and are generally identified by the "common" structures the society as members of the set/category "White." Dolezal raises a type of radical skepticism about whether Lawrence and Ruthanne are her biological parents. As a good empiricist, she argues that not only does she not have any substantial proof confirming that they are as she stated, "I haven't had a DNA test. There's been no biological proof that Larry and Ruthanne are my biological parents."[36] Throughout her early life, she followed the path of her parents and phenotypically demonstrated the non-augmented characteristics common to many people voluntarily and involuntarily placed within the social group "White," such as pale skin, straight brunette hair, etc. However, early on, she demonstrated an affinity to the social group "Black," and displayed this through not only high school art projects, but portraits of herself in the color brown, a proposition that Larry and Ruthanne deny.[37] In the application for her college years at Howard University, there was no request for a racial distinction. Therefore, due to the history of the institution and her interests, Dolezal was thought to have been someone who, many if not most members, within her context would accept as "Black."[38] Interestingly enough, while at Howard, Dolezal unsuccessfully sued the university for discrimination due to alleged unfair treatment because she was considered to be "White" by the administration.[39]

Dolezal's situation came to a head when she was asked point-blank during a television interview, "Are you African American?" She responded that she did not know how to answer the question and abruptly ended the interview.[40] Soon after, she was asked to resign from her position as president of the NAACP Spokane Chapter, removed from the website of Spokane's Eastern Washington University, where she taught Africana Studies,[41] and basically cancelled. I approach Doelzal through the thought of writer and theater critic Hilton Als, philosopher/theologian James Cone, and critical theorist of religion Monica R. Miller. Als causes us to think through the possibilities of racial identity that Dolezal embodies, Cone provides a philosophico-theological basis for Dolezal's embodiment of the category of race/trauma known as "Blackness," and Miller provides an explicit defense for Dolezal through an appeal to critical theory.

Hilton Als' Philosophical Construct of the "White Girl" and Dolezal's Understanding of Identity

In an interview with Reihan Salam of Vice Magazine, Hilton Als states that the symbol of the "White Girl" used in Als' book of the same name is a status that a gay "Black" man aspires to because it symbolizes a historical comradery between "Black" gay men and "White" feminists, those who also experience holistic oppression due being on the underside of the system of patriarchy but do not experience the racial oppression of a "Black" man. In this comradery with and acceptance from "White" feminists, the gay "Black" man enters a philosophical space in which he is theoretically synonymous with "White Girl," the category the former is most comfortably identified with in the US society. In this conceptual identification, the gay "Black" man as a "White Girl" moves closer to a position of power in some instances.[42]

Of the concept of the "White Girl," Als offers,

> I think people always aspire to the thing that they think has more freedom or more privilege . . . and if you read people like Shulamith Firestone who talks about the White woman's identification with Black men . . . these sort of 70s ideas were very interesting to me about feminism. How do you pass in the world of feminism if you're a man and how do you pass in the world of Black maleness if you're a White woman? So I wanted to mix those genres up while using that idea that Shulamith Firestone had laid out in her book and that Eldridge Cleaver . . . attacks in his book . . . all of these ideas that I had actually grown up with as a kid because of my sisters who were politically involved . . . it was really important for me to sort of . . . extricate or at least kind of go deeper into those ideas about identification and mirroring. How do you become or how are you someone else's mirror? I don't think it's really possible, but it's very moving to me when people seek to identify with someone not of their race or class but based on emotion and narrative.[43]

While Als states that it is impossible to become someone's mirror in the ways that critics say Dolezal is attempting in her supposed ingression of "Blackness," what he gives as an answer to the definition of the concept of "White" girl leads us to ask what methods we could use to determine whether or not Dolezal is attempting to be a mirror at all. If the structures of the concept "White Girl" were to be enacted by Dolezal with the only difference being that the category is "Black Woman," is she absolved from any fair cancellation?

In Rich Benjamin's review of *White Girls*, he says,

> A gay black man, Als portrays gay black men's longing to cherish what they cannot sexually love, the putative opposite of themselves, yet the emblem with which they deeply identify: white girls. Als admires and loathes white girls, mocks and mimics white girls, is ignored by white girls, is depended on by white girls, is perceived to be a white girl. "White girls," he shows, is not just literal people. It's a state of mind, an art of being.[44]

There is arguably a discrepancy between how Als works out the plausibility of this mirroring of the other that he calls the "White Girl" in its various conceptual forms in the interview and how it is aesthetically presented in the text, perhaps due to the satirical and allegorical nature of the text. In the Vice Magazine interview, he says that this sort of mirroring is impossible. However, he sees it as admirable and "moving." In the case of Dolezal, she fulfills the role of Als friend whom he names "Mrs. Vreeland" who, like Dolezal, can move in the world as a "White Girl" since she possesses the phenotype and historical contexts associated with "Whiteness" but ostensibly rejects it. However, are we able to substantially support Als' claim in the Vice interview that what some might refer to as "mirroring" in the concept of the "White Girl" cannot happen?

Perhaps we could argue that for Als the "White Girl" of the text and not the interview is mirroring because in their authentic occurrences, two categories thought to be not only distinct but also contradictory by many are identical. This is the other type of "White Girl": an individual who identifies with but fails to exemplify most of the so-called "common" characteristics of the category, thus giving those within and without the category loyal to its definition just cause for cancellation. Als says of his lover SL, which stands for "Sir or Lady,"

> In 1975, he [SL] returned to America on his own, ostensibly to attend college, although he never went. Instead, he fell in with New York-based feminists, some of whom roamed the Berkshire woods naked with bow and arrow, looking for men to kill, while others stepped on the accelerator when they saw men crossing the road. In this world, SL became a wife, supporting a number of friends' and lovers' work while his own work took a backseat; it was the least he could do: he had a father, and he would have no further truck with that. By the time I met him and longed to be his wife, SL sometimes described himself as a lesbian separatist. No man could have him.[45]

While one could argue that Als' description of SL as a "White Girl" in this section is tongue in cheek and conclude that he never was one, I see a subtle shadow looming behind his literary lure. We could see how SL's feminist friends may have categorically understood SL as a member of the social group. Their feminism was close enough to SL's that he as a man was allowed within their ranks. What leaks out here is Sartre's notion that bad faith is not only the disregard for the world as it actually is when creating one's own reality, but also appears when one takes the physical situation of things as the only determining factor of what one can become.[46] The "White Girl" in Als conveys this kind of unsettled oscillation involving a spectrum of "Whiteness," "Blackness," and "Girlness" that illuminates the instability of racial and gender categories. Als is right to say that mirroring is impossible, but what could also be said is that its impossibility is due to there being nothing essential in the definitional nature of the "White Girl" since its arbitrariness has been described as the core of identity. If the "White Girl" and "Blackness" are less about meeting a set of prerequisites but more about what one shows commitment to as ways of life through the quasi-religious InnerSectional practices of race and gender, what prevents anyone from being whatever they want to be? As cancel culture's defense against such free identification, neither SL or Dolezal is widely accepted as a full-fledged member of the categories they experience the world within. In the moment of Kierkegaardian absurdity, the religion of race becomes untenable, and its devotees can either admit its Nietzschean death or continue to uphold it in the face of blatant contradiction. However, Dolezal seems to do both.

Dolezal on *The Real* and the Strict Maintenance of Racial Religion

In an interview with the television show *The Real* in 2015 with hosts Tamera Mowry, Adrienne Bailon-Houghton, Tamar Braxton, Loni Love, and Jeannie Mai, Dolezal was taken to task for the ways in which she identifies racially. The hosts executed a series of questions based largely on an essentialist understanding of race. First, when asked by Loni Love if she was ashamed of being "White," Dolezal responds, "Well, like Dick Gregory said, White isn't a race, is a state of mind." Love retorted that this was inaccurate, as Dolezal's phenotype is closer to a common conception of "Whiteness" than her own. Therefore, according to Love, Dolezal is afforded the option of existing within and without the expectations of the category of "Blackness."[47] In the claim that race is a state of mind, Dolezal affirms a dislodging of the category from an essentialist understanding and thus kills the concept of race that the hosts are under the jurisdiction of. Of course, the hosts don't acknowledge this death, and the concept still exists in its classical construction for them. The "failure to communicate" results in the continued use of the word "Black" by both Dolezal and the hosts to refer to two different experiential realities. Loni Love and Dolezal continued a futile debate about

"Blackness" in terms of what Monica R. Miller says "is through the discourse of what it cannot be."[48]

In elaborating on racial categorizations on various forms, Dolezal said,

> I think when it comes out to filling out forms . . . that the form in particular usually defines things . . . so for example, one of the forms I filled out that was called into question this summer, it said "White" in parentheses "having European ancestry," "Black" in parentheses "humans originating from the continent of Africa" . . . I checked "White" and "Black" because we all have origins in the continent of Africa. I mean that's true, right? Human populations originating in the continent of Africa is everybody.[49]

Als' "White Girl" as lived out by Mrs. Vreeland in "Tristes Tropiques" serves as a literary account of the critical gaze which cancelled Dolezal. Mrs. Vreeland serves as a counter-narrative to that of Dolezal's "Blackness" as an act for selfish gain. As a very related sidenote, there were some critiques leveled by those who maintain the category of "Blackness," asserting that individuals who suggested Dolezal was acting irrationally in wanting to subject herself to the derogatory status of "Blackness" were actually unearthing their own presuppositions about "Blackness." Als' champions women such as Mrs. Vreeland and Jane Fonda, women who he argues were more comfortable outside of privilege than within it, and became "Black" sans being forced into the category and aided the cause of liberation for those who the society gives no choice but to be "Black" in the ways that Dolezal claims to have done with the NAACP.[50]

Theologian James Cone offers something explicitly relevant to how Dolezal conjures the practice of race as religion in her life and work. In his seminal 1969 text entitled *Black Theology and Black Power*, Cone forecasts exactly the type of being in the world a person the society readily calls "White" should embody. For Cone, God is on the side of the oppressed, and regardless of what one may claim about their Christianity, a "White" person is not really a Christian unless they identify with the oppressed. For Cone, being a Christian means that "Whites" must be transformed to their core by and identify with the "Black" experience and become "Black." At the end of *Black Theology and Black Power*, Cone says,

> It is to be expected that many white people will ask: "How can I, a white man, become black? My skin is white and there is nothing I can do." Being black in America has very little to do with your skin color. To be black means that your heart, your soul, your mind, and your body are where the dispossessed are. We all know that a racist structure will threaten a black man in white skin as quickly as a black man in black skin. It accepts and rewards whites in black skins nearly as well as blacks in black skin. Therefore, being reconciled to God does not mean that one's skin is physically black. It essentially depends on the

color of your heart, soul, and mind. Some may want to argue that persons with skin physically black will have a running start on others; but there seems to be enough evidence that though one's skin is black the heart may be lily white. The real questions are: Where is your identity? Where is your being? Does it lie with the oppressed blacks or the white oppressors? Let us hope that there are enough to answer this question correctly so that America will not be compelled to acknowledge a common humanity only by seeing that blood is only one color.[51]

There is a grossly overlooked unique theological philosophy of race embedded within in Cone's philosophy of religion in the final pages of *Black Theology and Black Power*, not surprisingly reminiscent of Dolezal's mention in The Voice interview of activist Dick Gregory's assertion that "White" is a state of mind and not a race. To quote him verbatim, he says, "I always say white is not a color, white is an attitude, and if you haven't got trillions of dollars in the bank, then you can't be white."[52] For Gregory, "White" is merely a placeholder representing access to power. When one subjects oneself and/or is subjected to the category of "Whiteness," one conforms/ is made to conform to the constraints that accompany privilege. In Cone's religious redefinition of race, the possibility of the transformation of identity within the concept becomes its focal point as a crucial way of enacting one's religion. If one accepts Cone's philosophy of race on this point, they will have several questions to answer if they also were to cancel Dolezal for her "Blackness."

Finally, Monica R. Miller, in her talk with Mark Anthony Neal on the *Left of Black* series in 2015, remarked in a stream of extemporaneous comments on some of her upcoming publications that Dolezal was being treated unfairly due to conceptual double standards commonly accessed and applied within the marketplace of ideas. Miller says,

> there's something about that conversation that really, really, really disturbed me on social media. The Dolezal piece . . . Because here's what I saw: I saw . . . people who I thought to be and who I knew were your social constructionists, your postmodernists, your Black feminists, you know, your Latina feminists, your nihilists . . . so many other categories, right . . . and . . . on all other points of social difference and identity-based differences, we're social constructionists . . . But . . . when people want it both ways . . . and we need to be intellectually honest about that . . . I'm not saying she should be Black, I'm not saying she should or should not have talked about her own . . . reinvention of herself, but there is something wrong within the digital space when . . . in rhetoric we're going to embrace the slippage over here and here and here and we know that identity's fluid and we know that movements are fluid and leaders are fluid, but when it comes to this one individual, we're essentialists . . . And as someone who is okay with social categories and identity categories being fluid and moving and that agency . . . it's

important to be able to name for yourself. So why am I going to advocate for the slippage over here and the flexibility and the fluidity and the queerness of politics over here, but over here, I'm disciplining a White person [for being politically Black]? ... What does it mean to be politically Black in a digital moment?[53]

Miller shines an uncomfortably revealing spotlight on the publicly private allowance of some identities exterior to "normative" understandings and the forbiddance of others. If the postmodern, existentialist, and poststructuralist renderings of the human that many accepted liberation movements such as Black Lives Matter find foundations in are valid, the grounds on which many within their ranks have canceled Dolezal become increasingly shaky. If many of the "Black" people who cancelled Dolezal did so based on the premise that Dolezal's was not being authentic, they would also have to cancel themselves, as "Blackness" could be said to be equally inauthentic for anyone identifying as such.

Nick Canon and the Parallax of Cancel Culture

We conclude this section on cancel culture with a look at the 2020 firing and subsequent backlash of rapper/TV show host Nick Cannon's recent cancellation by Viacom for remarks perceived to be antisemitic made by both Cannon legendary 1990s rapper Professor Griff on his YouTube TV program "Cannon's Class." This novel treatment of Cannon's cancellation will consider this situation as an example of parallax, the obstruction of vision by a change in position. As aforementioned, this look at cancel culture as parallax takes as its point of departure the ways in which Žižek utilizes the idea in relation to various strands of transcendental and existential thought. Here, I suggest the largely unexplored possibility that the incident reveals less about Cannon's supposed antisemitism and more about the structural marginalization inherent in certain articulations of the race-related category "Jew."[54]

Nick Cannon, Professor Griff, and the Cancellation of Antisemitism

The context for Cannon's cancellation that stemmed from the June 23, 2020 episode of Cannon's Class starts with Griff challenging a certain idea of "Jew" that creates a parallax which by definition obstructs the idea that those labeled as "Black" can be included within the category. I say "obstructing" as opposed to "prohibiting" because the notion of a "Black" "Jew" is an intersection that can be thought without contradiction. A "Black" "Jew" is not *inconceivable* in concept.

However, several Ashkenazi Jews have participated in active cancellation by stating that many "Black" Jews are guilty of cultural appropriation.

Griff inaugurates this stream of thought by offering a definition of "Semitic." He says,

> Let's look up the word "antisemitic." Who are the Semitic people? . . . and there's a list of Semitic people [ancient people hailing from the parts of the world now referred to as the "Middle East" and "Northern Africa" from the 2nd millennium BCE], and anyone can do this right now. You can look up "Who are the Semitic people" "What are the Semitic languages?" Has absolutely nothing to do with any White people. So in order for me to be antisemitic, I'd have to be anti-Black man, anti-Black woman, anti-Black people, anti-Africa, anti-all of the people.[55]

In this revisiting of the rhetorical move that got him into a lot of trouble "back in the day," Griff demonstrates on Canon's Class that to charge as antisemitic his infamous proposition that Ashkenazi Jews in the music industry benefit from "White" privilege is logically inconceivable, as "Jew" and "White" are incompatible categories for him. This is of course the very position many refer to as "antisemitic."

Furthermore, Griff also argued that his claims about people who identify as "Jewish" who are leaders in the music industry were not from a place of hate but simply a "stating of the facts."[56] Griff would also assert that his reference to the leaders mentioned was in no way connected to the fact that they are identified and/or identify as "Jewish." For Griff, there is a strong connection between these individuals' positionality in racial hierarchies and their influence in the music industry. But perhaps "antisemitism" is not the right term to snapshot Griff's statements. "Antisemitism" has been defined by the Oxford Dictionary as "hatred or prejudice against Jewish people."[57] In Griff's previous history in discussion on this comment, he does not seem to harbor hate or prejudice. Griff says,

> It wasn't a Jewish conversation. It was about the music industry. The first twenty minutes of the conversation, we was laughing, joking, dapping each other up, talking. His girlfriend walked in. We talking about David Mills, who dropped dead on a movie set. His [the interviewer's] girlfriend walks in, and his girlfriend's White and Jewish . . . [When] she came and set down, complexion of the conversation changed. It became more [finger pointing gesture] . . . and I'm like [ease back and relax hand gestures] . . . couple of times he even pressed the pause button on the cassette recorder . . . So now he had to change his tone because now the White Jewish girlfriend is sitting next to him. And she's getting offended by me calling out [Lyor] Cohen, the Moskowitz, and the Blacks. And I'm like, "Okay, but [pause] still no hatred involved, just laying the history out." When he finished the interview, he admitted and said to himself, "You know something: this is the kinda stuff that can get you in a lot of trouble."[58]

Griff continues this stream of thought after Cannon asks,

> If the true children of Israel, if we're speaking of the Jewish community, if we're speaking of the Abrahamic faiths that Islam comes from, that Judaism comes from, that Christianity comes from . . . all comes from Abraham, and we are speaking of brotherhood and unity, why . . . is it such a problem, why is there so much fear specifically in the Black community and the Jewish community . . . why is it such a problem to speak the truth?[59]

Griff responds,

> it became a problem for us because of the propaganda machine. But it's more of a problem for them [so-called "White" Jews]. They've taken our birthright . . . they don't want us to be us. They don't want you wrapping your head . . . now because you recognize and now they identified you, "Oh man, Nick knows who he is." And now the flipside of that [is] you know who they are.[60]

To this statement, Cannon offers,

> when we talk about the six corporations [GE, Time Warner, Disney, News-Corp, Viacom, and CBS] . . . when we go as deep as the Rothschilds, centralized banking, the thirteen families, the bloodlines that control everything even outside of America . . . we're talking about the people who if we were the children of Israel and we're defining who the Jewish people are . . . because I feel like if we can actually understand that construct, then we could see that there is no hate involved. When we talk about the lies, the deceit . . . how the fake dollar controls all of this, maybe we can get to the reason why they wanted to silence you [Professor Griff], why they wanted to silence Minister Farrakhan [current head of the Nation of Islam], and they want to throw the "we are having hate speech" when it's never hate speech . . . you can't be antisemitic when we are the Semitic people, when we are the same people who they [European Jews] want to be. That's our birthright.[61]

The referenced segments do not showcase Cannon and Griff promoting hate of Ashkenazi Jews. Rather, they embark on a quest to uncover the ways in which so-called "Black" people have been denied full and rightful access to "Jewish" identities through racism. The parallax generated from perceiving at the position of a Euro-dominated notion of "Jewishness" does not by logical necessity require that "Jews" must have the physical features and lineages commonly associated with the Jews of Europe, but in many instances, for example, the so-called "Black" "Jew" is asked when they converted to Judaism, indicating a parallax that obscures viewing them as full-fledged members of the set.

Renowned Egyptologist and anthropologist Ben Yosef Jochannan, also known as "Dr. Ben," engaged in a heated debate with Rabbi Joseph Seltzer, in which the latter's words arguably indicated a suppressed premise—that Jochannan, a person who identified as an "Ethiopian Jew," had appropriated cultures not his own. In Dr. Ben's responses throughout the program, he argues that European Jews have shaped the definitions of "Jewish" on reflexive presuppositions. As examples of the parallax preventing a forced intersection of the category "Black" with the category "Jew," Dr. Ben cites the prerequisite of Ethiopian Jews such as himself to "reconvert" and undergo circumcision when emigrating to the State of Israel.[62] Almost forty years after the airing of this broadcast in 1985, Ethiopian Jewish Israeli activists such as Shula Mola are still fighting against the oppression of Ethiopian Jews in Israel outlined by Dr. Ben and not addressed by Rabbi Seltzer. While Seltzer charges Dr. Ben with a contradiction of arguing that there is no Jewish race while basing his points on the existence of "Black Jews" as foregrounding the lineage of all Jews, Mola states from experience that "If we were not Black people, if we would come from other white countries, even not European, even Asian,—the whole dynamic could be different."[63] This double standard for non-European Jews is also buttressed by Lewis Gordon's work in the essay "Rarely Kosher: Studying Jews of Color in North America."[64]

Another instance of the parallax placing volatile enmity between the category "Jew" and the category "Black" (or perhaps its reverse in some ways) is the clever Marc Levin production *Brooklyn Babylon*, starring Black Thought, lead MC of The Jimmy Fallon Show backing band The Roots. Here, Levin crafts a romance narrative between a Hasidic European Jewish woman and Black Thought, a first-generation "Caribbean" "Black" man and MC amid Brooklyn's Crown Heights Riots of 1991. Black Thought's character, Solomon, meets Sarah, the co-protagonist and eventually his love interest, through a car accident in which they are both involved. Throughout the movie, Sarah and Solomon's relationship gradually moves into the spotlight and becomes a source of tension between many of the descendants of "Caribbean" countries and many descendants of the "Middle East." Solomon is named after the biblical king Solomon, and his name is interpreted through Rastafarian lenses. On Sarah and Solomon's second chance meeting in a park, they both share elements of Orthodox Judaism and Rastafari, respectively. The similarities between their religious philosophies such as belief in arguably the same God (Jah and Yahweh) and references to the Hebrew Bible are striking though interpreted differently by both. While there is never a moment in which either Solomon or Sarah (or anyone else outside of their chosen and involuntary communities) verbally affirm an understanding of any sort of shared belief system, I read Levin to leave this deductive conclusion to the audience to potentially realize.[65]

Gordon perfectly articulates this mirage, or this parallax, of the "Black" "Jew." He says,

> To begin, there is already difficulty in talking about Jews because of the presumed universality of local manifestations of Jewish people. As Jews traveled through all parts of the globe, nearly every country developed some notion of Jews on the basis of its local Jewish population. This did not pose much of a problem in the past, since international, intercultural, and global communication was limited. But today, "local" versus "global" influence each other to the point of creating hegemonic forms of symbolic life. What is often lost, however, is an understanding of the history of how such dominant representations came into being. Jewish people are thus often studied without the important additions of how particular groups of Jewish people became representatives of all Jewish people.[66]

This clear identification of the "dominant representations" of Jewish identity—so everywhere they are nowhere—plays into the difficulty of viewing Cannon as a member of the social group. In an episode immediately following his program with Griff on a subsequent installment of the series, Cannon offers an apology to the "Jewish community" in a talk with Rabbi Abraham Cooper, Associate Dean of the Simon Wiesenthal Center. In this discussion, Rabbi Cooper and Cannon addressed several issues concerning antisemitism.[67] The parallax maintaining enmity between the categories "Black" and "Jew" comes into full play when Cannon reveals facts about his own ancestry in another interview with Rabbi Noam Marans representing the American Jewish Committee.

In the interview with Rabbi Marans in March of 2021, Cannon says,

> I told Rabbi Noam this before and it's actually something that I never really wanted to share in the public because I didn't want to seem like I was using it as an excuse . . . and I'm still even nervous talking about it . . . my great grandfather was a Spanish rabbi and he [was] a Sephardic Jewish man . . . so as much heat as I've been catching from the public and the outside, this hit home for my family in a real way because I come from a Black and Jewish family on my mother's side . . . in this weird mixed up world . . . [there are] men and women in the Jewish community who speak Spanish . . . who have Black [phenotypes that cause society to easily place them in the category of "Blackness"] . . . it's so fascinating . . . even in that, those [Jews without physical features that easily allow them to have varying levels of membership in the social category "White"] are the people that we need to step up and be a part of these conversations more than ever.[68]

I hold that the racial and race-related parallax at play in not only the perception of Nick Cannon but also the ways in which others are perceived is a metaphysic of thought through which one intuitively (in a Kantian sense of "anschauung," or "looking upon," which does not indicate feeling but a presentation of the world in a clear way, i.e., automatically resistant of other interpretations such as a person who "looks" "Black" as anything other than "Black") excludes someone from a race or race-related category they claim membership in.[69] Nick Cannon is not metaphysically comfortable in the position of "Black" and "Jewish." Therefore, the parallax of incongruity between the two categories renders Cannon never fully visible to himself or others on his "own" terms. If the intrinsically dehumanizing racial category "Black" was understood as a null set, Cannon's cancellation could have possibly occurred sans the premise of Cannon offending the social group from the outside, or perhaps not at all.

Conclusion

Cancel culture and its relation to the linguistic metaphysics of racial categories has yet to be explored in depth in philosophy of race, philosophy of religion, linguistics, and metaphysics. This chapter was a small step in that direction but is by no means intended to be exhaustive. After outlining active (intentional), passive (unintentional and instinctive rejection of an idea antithetical to the order of accepted understanding such as 1+1=3), and subtle (a sneakier means of implementing the active mode in methods like redlining) forms of cancellation, I moved toward a description of cancel culture as (1) categorical (exerting the power of definition), (2) existential (the lived effects that emerge from taking race/trauma categories as "real" and necessary, hence policing their transgression, such as Ye), (3) religious (as that which one becomes invested in via ritualistic quotidian experiences of practicing racial categories through a "belief" in the rules of particular racial sets that include some and exclude others from "following" by sheer definition, such as Rachel Dolezal), and (4) parallax (the obstruction of certain possibilities of identifying and being identified as relative to one's proximity or the lack thereof to categories in question, such as Cannon). I attempted to illustrate how the arbitrary existence of and the adherence to racial categories empowers and informs cancellation and bring to the fore the potentially hidden "who" or "what" is being cancelled. This is intended to stimulate a progressively intense interrogation into whether race/trauma as distributed and caretaken (McCutcheon) via cancel culture reifies types of identities toxic to the idea of "humanity." In a word, is cancel culture another way in which race/trauma distracts us from the *becomings* we could approach through holding us in a snapshot of a "fallacy of misplaced concreteness," keeping us what we've been told must *be*? We turn to a deeper look at this shroud in the following chapter.

5 THE LURE OF THE SHROUD: THE QUESTION OF THE "MATTERING" OF THE CONCEPTUAL HUMAN ILLUSION

Introduction

We start with a musing of sorts. What would a world in which race was not the metaphysic of said world be like? How would things look, smell, feel, taste? What possibilities would such a context open and constrict? Can we imagine how the more or less "tangible" structures around which the world is organized (e.g., governments, education, media, social interactions) would function? If the answer to such a query is "No," it wouldn't at all be surprising. Honestly, an overly eager embrace of a post-racial world would and perhaps should be cautioned for various reasons, namely because doing so potentially obscures and prevents critical attention toward the ways in which the metaphysic of race/trauma is so ingrained into the fabric of many modern societies even when it is not referred to as "race." Therefore, an ahistorical turning of a blind eye to its significance could arguably be harmfully irresponsible. The racial and race-related linguistic structuring of the world are the impossibility of thought to think the circular square: human *being* must be racialized; if not, humans are rendered invisible. We've already looked at the invisibility of the "Mixed Race" individual in Vest and will return to it again for different purposes in the next *capitulo*, but the implications of said invisibility apply further in that the absence of race as a category adds not only obscurity but a type of absolute loss of ground. In other words, the obscurity that befalls those who are identified and identify as "Mixed Race" is akin to the clarity that would befall everyone if the foundation of the metaphysic of race was erased. And that string of words is exactly why Pharoahe Monch is one of the ancestors of all my writing styles.

Anyway . . .

The work engaged here is an outflowing of the inquiry into cancel culture from the previous chapter. The pit stop conclusion is this: racial language encodes within it faultily founded and, in many cases, unnecessary and (hence) oppressive rules and norms of societal engagement upheld by cancel culture. Stated differently, racial language creates and maintains lines of scrimmage between categories that involuntary and voluntary group members organize to defend. What is not implied by the intrinsic antagonism of the category is an interrogation around whether the human identity the category represents should actually be invested in and/or is identical to the category itself. To say this even another way, the query in Chapter 4 was concerned with whether or not racial language creates the very conflicts that people are cancelled for. Therefore, it calls into question the plausibility of widely accepted cancellations such as that of Ye, Rachel Dolezal, and Nick Cannon since said cancellations emerge from a caretaking and defense of certain arbitrary and potentially oppressive categorizations of humanity.

Here, I aim to build off this fluid foundation and interrogate an underrepresented consequence that emerges from such a line of thinking. My suggestion in the previous essay was that race/trauma unnecessarily creates the very categories cancel culture defends against. I now step behind racial language from the vantage point of asking another question (a question that scholars such as Kerry Rockemore and Sheena Michelle Mason have posed in their own prevocative ways): can there be any hope of a non-racist world without the abolishment of race? The critical reflection in the previous section on cancel culture's relation to race/trauma is metaphilosophical in that it operates from the vantage point of race as an intrinsically antagonistic and arbitrary assumption. Similarly, the explorations of this chapter metaphilosophically target the arbitrariness of race (root cause) through a novel and thorough examination of racism (symptom). Similar strategies employed in Chapter 4 will return here to examine racism itself and the possibility or impossibility of eliminating it without eliminating its cause, race/trauma, or race *as* trauma. This, of course, is grounded on the proposition I have been advancing in this work, like Naomi Zack, namely that race is incapable of being/representing authentic identity due to its definitional, existential, and traumatic creation out of the "othering" projects starting in the late-fifteenth-century colonization efforts of Spain, Britain, France, and others. A point of distinction between Zack and myself is that I add that race is not only racist but also primordially traumatic when structures are set, and it is applied to humans. Race is not simply a hierarchical categorization in the sense of ruler and their subjects that may or may not turn oppressive. In my view, race is trauma inflicted onto the human that shatters previous awareness and possibilities of InnerSection.

This question of whether or not antiracism has a real chance of any substantial success without an elimination of the metaphysic of race not only in practice but in thought has of course been asked and answered within and without the discourse of philosophy of race. But for various reasons, the idea of race being something that can actually be abolished has so far had its greatest purchase in the theoretical realm (e.g., Zack). The purpose of this section is not only to put forth a case for an abolishment of race as a means of eliminating racism but also to lure current theory and praxis toward a heightened sense of comfortability with thinking and thinking about this notion and demonstrate that not all post-racial concepts and adjacent ideas are dismissive of the "real" impact of race/trauma on human experience. Another related aim is to consider thinkers who come close to outright stating that race itself *is* racism but do not. They continue to reify race as a valuable if not authentic and the best means of identity formation and negotiation in some sense. I am suspicious that such an oversight hinders the progressive impact of their work.

The chapter is outlined as follows: I will start with my own brief account of race as a "shroud" and the "myths" that "lure" us into a perpetuation of them as an attempt to ground what I observe as the context and contours of the provocative issue at hand. Next, I move toward a look at what I refer to as the "And/As Dichotomy," something I raised in *Underground Rap as Religion* in relation to Hip-Hop and its relation to religion. Here, it applies to pole (1) the compartmentalization of race and racism (the inability or unwillingness to see race and racism as interchangeable) and pole (2) the conflation of race and racism (the inability or unwillingness to not see race and racism as interchangeable). I consider Ibram X. Kendi, Mahzarin R. Banaji, Cornel West, Judith Butler, and Ania Loomba as thinker/actors somewhere in between or on either side of the spectrum. Lastly, I reintroduce multi/race/less/ness substantially as a potential alternative to the "And/As Dichotomy" in relation to the progressive quest/ion of maintaining race without racism. This reset of multi/race/less/ness gives context for an updated employment that will extend throughout the remainder of the text.

The Shroud, the Myth, and the Lure

The Prolegomena of this text starts with a conflation: that of race and trauma, which becomes race/trauma. This idea of race as trauma grounds this thought experiment and serves as a core reason for abolishing it. If race is indeed trauma, and one goes to therapy for trauma to get rid of it as opposed to caretaking it, the motion to get rid of race is one that many would assent to. The barrier to this is that race is not considered traumatic or not just purely trauma, but a complex system of identity formation, symbolism, and maintenance to which trauma occurs. In the same way, "race" as being interchangeable with "racism" is not self-evident to "common" collective theoretical renderings and practices of the idea. Some work must be done to demonstrate why this is so, and some of the thinkers covered in the next section who appear in conversations associated with racial eliminativism craft substantial arguments as to why. The main proposition of the argument I advance comes from the same stream of thought as many eliminativist positions. My conclusions with and qualifications of racial eliminativism make this particular project a novel and hopefully beneficial InnerSection into philosophy of race. I call the widely practiced tendency and background assumption of race and racism having related but separate conceptual existences "The Shroud." Shrouds can cover that which they are placed over, but in many instances that which is concealed is also revealed (Heidegger).[1]

What I am referring to as "The Shroud" is perfectly laid out by Larry L.W. Miles. He says,

> So, what visions do IAFW[2] (Indigenous Autochthonous First World) people have of themselves? Are we too busy attempting to reassert our humanity while being bombarded by other people's visions of who we are? Are we too busy attempting to function within someone else's world view? Can we envision ourselves as more than the machinations of a post 1492 narrative? Have we become content with saying that "this is the first Black/African American" to accomplish something in someone else's cultural milieu? If this is our vision of humanity, then we are suggesting that we are functioning in someone else's reality.[3]

The Shroud interrupts a truly in-depth encounter with the ancestral information it wears just enough to fool us into believing it is who we are. We are our race, and as those who are warriors for justice, it is our responsibility to struggle with hegemonic power until our race is accepted. But we fail to remember (or be aware) that any racial or race-related category other than or not benefitting from the impossible to locate but ubiquitous category of "Whiteness" is doomed to never find justice within the category. In addition to concealing the confluence between race and racism, The Shroud could also be thought of as a forced border between the two, suspending the ability of thought to clearly conceive them as identical and without contradiction.

"The Myth" concerns the stories told to cement race as an authentic identity in "normal" "everyday" and academic discourse. As Miles mentions, championing the first of "insert any category other than 'White'" person to accomplish a task is a narrative structure many have accepted as progressive. This is merely sneaking a victory past a system not designed for the success of anyone under the jurisdiction of the category in question. These and similar "myths" are all emerging from the root Myth: that there is a possible world where race exists without racism. Of course, significant gains can be made against treacherous odds while identity is wrapped up within the racial category. But stories fashioned as "myths" of capturing the horizon of race with the race itself can serve as dangerous roadblocks to a serious critical analysis of race as racism.

"The Lure" refers to the strong gravitational pull The Myth of the Shroud exerts on how we see and can potentially see the world. Thinking race and racism as separate entities is conceivable, even intuitive. As we were reminded in the last chapter, thinking outside the borders of racial categories means that one relinquishes one of the most spendable linguistic currencies available, and doing so can cause one to be ostracized not only by intention but by default. One can be kicked out of social circles but one also may lose relevance based on how they do and do not interact with society. The aim here is to examine whether putting a microscope to the metaphysical separation of race and racism will uncover a counterintuitive process of thinking The Shroud and The Myth mystically make opaque.

This chapter is intended to be a lure toward a serious examination of the less than commonly addressed confluence of race and racism, which could potentially offer another case for the dissolution of race. Pimienta-Bey states that trying to use pejorative racial labels positively is "like pushing an elephant up a hill with roller skates."[4]

Race and/as Racism: A Deeper Consideration

When a genius of the art of rap writes a mind-blowing treatise packed with plays on words, metaphors, hyperbole, and strong propositions sometimes referred to as a "hot 16" or something of the sort, many times what occurs is not really writing at all. Rather, in these moments of stretching the language in question to perform highly acclaimed acrobatics, what's really happening is more akin to an organic realization or sublimation as opposed to authorship. In other words, the MC does not "write" in these moments but brings to fruition dormant possibilities of the language others may not notice. The superior MC emerges into the entity that erases any scrimmage lines between them and the language itself. It is the distinction between Samprajnāta (focusing on a particular object) and Asamprajnāta (the complete absence of contemplation) in the Yoga system, with the latter being a type of sublimation of thought into becoming. The related but distinct sort of conflating of the self with the metaphysics of thought displayed in Cartesian and Kantian strands of the "I think" must be treated with caution when dealing with human identity, as it has the tendency to lose a type of individuated and embodied self that Thandeka argues is resolved through Schleiermacher's appeal to feeling as a basis for authentic (read enfleshed and existential as opposed to deontological) human experience in the *Dialektik*.[5] However, this enlightenment brand of a collapsing of the divide between reason and the human which manifests when writing is perceived as realization of the metaphysics of language as opposed to actual authorship is a useful analogue alongside which we might consider race as racism. Similarly, what would it mean to seriously reconceptualize racism *as* the structural implications of race? Would the grounds upon which we base the myths of race still be justified?

Ibram X Kendi: "Antiracist," Not "Not Racist"

Ibram X Kendi, author of the influential bestseller *How to be an Antiracist*, released during the last half of the Trump administration and shortly before the height of BLM efforts reinforced due to the death of George Floyd, finds himself within what I refer to as the "Spectrum of Race And/As Racism." One side of the Spectrum represents the notion that race and racism are related but separate concerns while the other asserts that they are synonymous. Kendi's articulation of the position of antiracism finds itself nearly in the middle but slightly favoring the "race and racism are separate" side. Or perhaps his work oscillates closer to various ends of the Spectrum depending on what part is being discussed. Parts of the text shows him affirming much of history of the social construction of the category of race covered in Chapter 1. In the chapter entitled "Power," Kendi defines race as "a power construct of blended difference that lives socially."[6] But earlier in the text in a footnote, he "shrouds" the intuition of the interchangeability of race and racism with "myths" illustrating both the alternating between struggle and victory of those identified and identifying as any non-"White" racial label. To this point, he offers an updated definition of "racism" and "racist," which identify different functions in them but connect them to power.[7] Because of this, the reader is given the option of not taking race itself *as* power, because "racism" and "racist" become the locus for relational multiplicities reduced to parallel singularities. I hold that if the critique Kendi levels on racism is applied to race, the dichotomy of "not racist and "antiracist" he trades for "racist" and "not racist" would have to be rethought.

With no argument for why race/trauma, a contentious category in perhaps virtually all theoretical and "common," "everyday" discourses, is presupposed as a quasi-essential[8] foundation for the rest of the book, there lacks a substantial metaphysical account of why race matters. Kendi tells us it matters, and we (at least I) don't need much convincing that it certainly does. But what we don't have is a justification for why we should continue to perceive the world through this arbitrary lens. In a TED interview with Whitney Pennington Rodgers and Cloe Shasha, Kendi defines being "racist" as actively and/or passively upholding hegemonic systems that are founded on the idea of one racial group's superiority over another.[9] Kendi fails to at least seriously consider the definition of racial groups as intrinsically racist due to their roots in colonial hierarchy. He also states in the interview that racial categories are made to be hierarchical, missing the tautology, as race is a category that arguably is *always* hierarchical by definition. In *How to Be an Antiracist*, cancer is a metaphor Kendi offers for racism, but race itself is never seen as a cancer that needs to be made obsolete.[10]

In the context of a discussion with Eliseo J. Perez-Stable on racial and ethnic equality in relation to scientific definitions of race and structural racism in light of the National Institutes of Health's strides in human genome mapping and discarding of race as biological, Kendi says, "it could be said definitively that race is a fiction and racism is a fact."[11] Since Kendi's work generally thinks race is related to but separable from racism, his statement is passable. But not without some difficulty. If Kendi actually thinks that race is fiction, then are the racial metaphysics he echoes by ingressing those society deems most suited for him ("Black") and spreading others to those whom they "fit" also fictitious? If they are, one must ask why he never mentions imagining a world without them considering they seem to perpetually structure the world hierarchically wherever they appear. If he means to say they are not merely fictions but rather quasi-essential, then one would be well within their rights to ask what their "real" utility is and whether or not our use of them is more problematic than progressive, as Pimienta-Bey suggests.[12]

Kendi's watershed text and articulation of antiracism is commendable in the deconstructive work he does on racism, which produces the novel dichotomy of "not racist" vs. "antiracist." The lived scholarship he presents provides a critical closer look at the mechanism of race and/as racism. However, his "pump fakes" toward race as racism and return to regressive quasi-essentialist applications of race are in my view insufficient since racism is analyzed critically while race is allowed to harmfully run free unscathed. In a reassessment of Kendi's place on the And/As Spectrum, he charts as residing mostly on the "And" side with unpredictable and fleeting jumps within the realm of the "As."

Mahzarin R. Banaji and "Mind Bugs"

Before leaving Kendi, it must be noted that *How to Be an Antiracist* "gets straight to the point" about the topics covered in depth by critical race theorists such as Eduardo Bonilla-Silva and Kimberlé Williams Crenshaw's work on "color-blind racism" and Richard Delgado and Jean Stefancic's critique of rewriting histories with stories that diminish the seriousness of structural racism. Because it offers these important ideas on structural racism to the reader without steeping them in "ivory tower" jargon but rather through compelling and relatable narratives, it commanded attention to these important ideas for a very large readership outside of academia.

But is antiracism as conceptually simple as Kendi presents it? We must consider what Harvard professor of psychology Mazharin R Banaji refers to as "mind bugs." Pimienta-Bey draws attention to Banaji's work when arguing for an Alian (as in "of the teachings of Noble Drew Ali") poststructuralist approach to racial language. In a TED Talk, Banaji defines a "mind bug" as a type of parallax that constricts one to perceive an idea in the world from either one or a limited set of conceptual standpoints. In the talk, Banaji begins with an example of two two-dimensional tables drawn by psychologist and illusion theorist Roger Shepard that initially seem different in size but are actually demonstrated to be the exact same dimensions when a copy of the images are placed on top of each other with the help of an "old school" projector.[13] The mind bug is then used as a way to talk about gender and racial biases as ideas that restrict a more organic human contrast (what some might refer to as "interaction"). Banaji says about the table example/error in judgment,

> "all I can tell you today is that it [your brain] made this mistake because your brain learned to get messages from your eye in a very old-world thousands and thousands of years ago, millions of years ago. And in that world, the natural world was always three dimensional, so your brain learned to make some computations that it is making even today even though you know that this is not a 3D image. This is a two-dimensional image and your brain can't cope with that new world."[14]

Toward the end of the TED Talk, Banaji does an experiment with the audience where she asks them to rapidly associate names and professions with their "appropriate" gender roles. What was discovered is that while the audience was probably one who lived out progressive thoughts about the possibilities of humans professionally *after reflection*, they affirmed possible underlying gender and occupational norms in their "off the cuff" responses *before reflection*.[15] Names thought of to be traditionally those of women were instinctively applied to occupations traditionally associated with the category "woman," such as "mother," for example. Mind bugs are about conditioning, and we are conditioned to perceive several things that are not actually "there." Race is a type of what Banaji refers to as the culture leaving "its thumbprint on your brain."[16] Racial and race-related language is not only conditioned by expectation but *is* the condition of expectation itself. Therefore, through the lens of race/trauma, the mind bug sets a foundation for a reductive and restrictive perception of one's existence. It is at the point of the separation of race and bias that my project parts ways with Dr. Banaji. Banaji holds that with conscious effort and admission through her appeal to Rumi that we all are jackasses, we can overcome the mind bugs by adjusting how we think about categories such as race and gender; the mind bugs are not synonymous with race and gender. For Pimienta-Bey, one cannot de-mind bug race. In his use of Banaji, mind bugs are taken further than Banaji and for him, race *is* a mind bug.

In *Blindspot: Hidden Biases of Good People*, Banaji and Anthony G. Greenwald provide a definition of "hidden biases" as "*bits of knowledge* about social groups.[17] They go on to say,

> These bits of knowledge are stored in our brains because we encounter them so frequently in our cultural environment. Once lodged in our minds, hidden biases can influence our behavior toward certain members of a social group, but we remain oblivious to their influence. In talking with others about hidden biases, we have discovered that most people find it unbelievable that their behavior can be guided by a mental context of which they are unaware.[18]

Banaji and Greenwald's quasi-essentialism allows the hidden bias of the category of race/trauma to perpetually escape any serious deconstruction. Hidden biases are not race to Banaji and Greenwald. They are the unfortunate judgments and following actions that befall those who identify/are identified as a racial social group. If the category of race/trauma is indeed a mind bug, then race/trauma would qualify as a hidden bias that societies must take initiative to responsibly eliminate.[19] Based on this, race would not be salvageable. What is salvageable is how we perceive the person the racial category represents, and I argue that this is only possible when the category of race/trauma is understood to literally be the mind bugs and hidden biases Banaji skillfully explains and illustrates.

In light of the Spectrum between race as/and racism, I find Banaji mostly in the middle. Unlike Kendi who occasionally slides into "race as racism" while residing mostly in the "race and racism side," she provides a clear and persuasive theoretical justification of the mind bug. But after presenting the thesis on how we must consciously resist biased ancient ways of perceiving that persist in the present, she fails to consider race itself as a clear and valid example of the biased ways of perception she addresses. But what we must keep from Banaji is exactly what Pimienta-Bey keeps: *the equivalence of the mind bug with race/trauma.* This equivalence allows us to talk about race as not an actual identity but a pre-reflective and arbitrary epistemology that deontologically reads onto rather than authentically discloses.

Cornel West: The Lure of Racial Reasoning

In *Race Matters* on the topic of the race betrayal and convenient claiming of racial categories in the Anita Hill/Clarence Thomas debacle, Cornel West argues that "racial reasoning" needs to be replaced with "moral reasoning" in such a way that enforces that "the black freedom struggle is not an affair of skin pigmentation and racial phenotype but rather as a matter of ethical principles and wise politics" while maintaining race as a quasi-essential means of identity.[20] West poignantly pinpoints the difficulties and inconsistencies in actions that accompany working within the paradigm of racial reasoning. West states that "Black" "male" leaders couldn't openly state that they weren't in support of Thomas' appointment to Supreme Court justice because to do so would be a betrayal of the category of race/trauma and gender they identify/are identified as and are loyal to.[21] This is a key example of The Shroud separating race and racism and the "myths" perpetuating the fallacy of misplaced concreteness. West is able to do the deconstructive work on the category of race while infusing it with a folk power that in my estimation redoes what he undoes. His twofold definition of "Blackness" in this chapter is "either the perennial possibility of white supremacist abuse or the distinct styles and dominant modes of expression found in black cultures and communities."[22] West locates the kernel of what it means to be "Black" in commitment to the struggle against "White" supremacy, the preservation of various cultural manifestations of the descendants of US chattel slavery and related tragedies (since "Blackness" as West discusses it is mostly about the United States context) in relation to the fight against oppression, distinct religious traditions developed amid people of many nations forced together, etc.[23] To be "Black" for West is to have a moral commitment to the social group, which, would exclude Thomas.

But if "Blackness" for West is defined here as this sort of descriptive definition that safeguards against it suggesting that there is "a black essence and that all black people share nor one black perspective to which all black people should adhere," how does it become robust enough to contain the image in the popular imagination of something more unified? If I take it at the word of the ostensible definition West provides, is the only thing I can say about race with certainty is that it is a team I choose or choose not to play on? How do I reconcile West's dismissing of a "Black" monolith with his assertion that "Blackness" in some ways should have a moral trajectory that by default determines whether one is an authentic member?

West draws attention to a very important and detrimental underlying mind bug prevalent in racial reasoning: the sense of obligation to stick by the side of those you identify as/are identified by when you would choose otherwise. West highlights the ways in which Thomas and Hill supported policies detrimental to those on the underside of economic oppression, many of whom identified and are identified as "Black," just as they do.[24] But what fails to occur here or anywhere else in West's impeccable body of work is an interrogation into how it may be impossible to think race without a type of racial reasoning, as the metaphysical logic of race foregrounds the racial reasoning he is critical of.

Further, there is a "spirit" emanating beyond the intensional definition of "Blackness" in West that is evident to me in lines such as "The nihilistic threat to black America is inseparable from a crisis in black leadership."[25] "Black leadership" means more than just "leadership" by "Black" people for West. But the question is whether or not it *can* really mean anything more on his own terms. The very thing he attempts to modify in the twofold definition of race lifted here and in even more technical definitions in *Prophesy Deliverance* is mitigated by a quasi-essentialism that goes on as if the ghost of race is a universal objective reality. West speaks as if he believes in race as an adequate means of identity even in light of statements such as "The Black American Struggle for self-identity has always contributed constructively to the American struggle for self-identity, though the latter has only exacerbated and complicated it in return," arguably implying that either "Black" and "American" identities are unstable or that they haven't and perhaps cannot be fully realized.[26] The sort of reductive statements West makes about race in his work cause one to wonder why there is more on the reification or race and less interrogating of the metaphysics of race itself.

What might an application of West's critique of racial reasoning as employed by leaders during the trial of Clarence Thomas look like if we considered how thinking of Thomas and Hill as "Black" people presupposes the actions of "Black" leaders in relation to the affair, going back to mind bugs? It could be said that thinking through the lens of race in any capacity made some of their responses virtually inevitable since race could be thought of *as* racism, and that can negatively or positively affect one's "own." If they were to speak on the issue solely from a moral vantage point contra the racial reasoning West persuasively argues against, and since a definition for his more intuitive read of "Blackness" is never given, what solid ground is available for race to rest on? Noticing how the world racially constructs people is obviously important, as this aids us in pinpointing motivating factors in structural injustices and addressing them. But this cognizance is possible without the more than merely descriptive reification of race West engages in.

On the And/As Spectrum, West is constantly and equally moving back and forth. His theory of racial reasoning and observant identification of its problems is never turned onto the subject that provides the possibility of the query: race itself. As in Banaji, everything is present in the line of thinking to at least enter into a serious consideration of the quasi-essentialist equating of the self with race and the simultaneous separation of race from racism. But this never occurs. The Shroud is extended indefinitely by the Myth of race/trauma as a category of identity worth maintaining.

Judith Butler: Categories as Power Dynamic of Performance

As I continue to reflect on the category of race/trauma, I always return to the compelling and groundbreaking work of theorist Judith Butler. While Butler's work has centered on the category of a deconstruction of gender, (1) there is no critique of the category of race/trauma that cannot include the category of gender and (2) much, if not all, of Butler's analysis of gender can be applied to a deconstruction and poststructuralism of race/trauma. I will take the time here to say that an absence of an elongated "intersection" of race and gender (as categories developed by assertions of antagonistic difference, they do not "InnerSect") has not occurred up to this point in the text because I am most concerned with the category of race and an authentic, responsible transcendence of it. However, where I aim to go with multi/race/less/ness affirms that such a move involves a related and simultaneous destabilization of the essentialism of gender and gender norms. Human identity after a responsible and careful postracialism will have emerged into a becoming energy that exceeds the categories of a related gender identity. It is not the task of this text to elaborate on this in any detail, but gender as InnerSected in multi/race/less/ness is an important concern I and hopefully others will take up in future projects.

A few things about Butler's interrogation of gender must be briefly stated here, as their method of gender deconstruction was highly influential on the texture of multi/race/less/ness and their train of thought on gender allows us to place them on the And/As Spectrum on race. Butler offers a more preliminary account of gender than West does of race. The very beginning quote of the first chapter of Butler's classic text *Gender Trouble: Feminism and the Subversion of Identity* is from Beauvoir: "One is not born a woman, but rather becomes one."[27] This is a contrast in methodology from not only West's and Banaji's application of methods to trick race/trauma and race-related categories into being capable of justice but by addressing gender identities themselves as potential problems. One can choose to become or not to become a woman, but very often, society is the "one" that chooses. They state,

> Recently, this prevailing conception of the relation between feminist theory and politics has come under challenge from within feminist discourse. The very subject of women is no longer understood in stable or abiding terms. There is a great deal of material that not only questions the viability of "the subject" as the ultimate candidate for representation or, indeed, liberation, but there is very little agreement after all on what it is that constitutes, or ought to constitute, the category of women. The domains of political and linguistic "representation" set out in advance the criterion by which subjects themselves are formed, with the result that representation is extended only to what can be acknowledged as a subject. In other words, the qualifications for being a subject must first be met before representation can be extended.[28]

This question of who is being represented in the political function of feminism is brought to the fore when Butler tells us that there is no agreement on said subject's identity. Therefore, without a consensus, there is not enough information to assert that said subject exists outside of subjective constructions of a classic kind that many buy into. But the clincher of utmost importance to our work in a philosophy of multi/race/less/ness is this: political and linguistic representation is what creates the subject in question, not the converse. There is no woman outside of context of patriarchal hegemony that decides what "woman" is. In reference to Foucault, Butler says,

> juridical systems of power *produce* the subjects they come to represent. Juridical notions of power appear to regulate political life in purely negative terms—that is, through the limitation, prohibition, regulation, control, and even "protection" of individuals related to that political structure through the contingent and retractable operation of choice. But the subjects regulated by such structures are, by virtue of being subjected to them, formed, defined, and reproduced in accordance with the requirements of those structures. If this analysis is right, then the juridical formation of language and politics that represents women as "the subject" of feminism is itself a discursive formation and effect of a given version of representational politics. And the feminist subject turns out to be discursively constituted by the very political system that is supposed to facilitate its emancipation.[29]

As a thought experiment, what if we were to replace every appearance of "woman" and "subject" in the previous quote with the race-related category "Asian" and "feminism" with "antiracism (we could insert any race or race-related category)? Would we come to a statement that gives a substantial foundation for an argument asserting that race *is* racism? Let's see.

> juridical systems of power *produce* the Asians they come to represent. Juridical notions of power appear to regulate political life in purely negative terms—that is, through the limitation, prohibition, regulation, control, and even "protection" of individuals related to that political structure through the contingent and retractable operation of choice. But the Asians regulated by such structures are, by virtue of being subjected to them, formed, defined, and reproduced in accordance with the requirements of those structures. If this analysis is right, then the juridical formation of language and politics that represents Asians as "the subject" of antiracism *(such as the popular phrase "Stop Asian Hate")* is itself a discursive formation and effect of a given version of representational politics. And the *Asian* subject turns out to be discursively constituted by the very political system that is supposed to facilitate its emancipation.[30]

Are there "Asians" outside of the juridical systems Butler speaks of that produce the category? In a postcolonial world where racial and race-related categories are shadowy reductions of pre-colonial InnerSections of enfolding and unfolding identities, we could persuasively argue there are not. But we continue to use this type of language in service of liberation. Because of the work of Judith Butler,

Julia Kristeva, Monique Whittig, Gloria Anzaldúa, and countless others, we've been ushered into shifts of thought where queerness, non-gender-conforming identities, and non-heterosexual orientations are more conceivable in the common imagination to where even those who may not agree have had to seriously consider identities and orientations other than their own.

On the spectrum, we can plausibly conclude that Butler, when the rubric of their theories on gender are applied to race/trauma, would be fully on the side of "race as racism." There may be pushback from some who say that gender and race are both constructions but grant the former a fluidity they deny the latter because of the inability to change phenotype (e.g., a "White" "woman" can change genders, but a "Black" "man" can never become "White"). However, I hold that while this takes into account the *difficulty* of a "Black" "man" being accepted as "White" "woman" in various parts of the world, it does not consider the *possibility* that they *could* be accepted as such. It also overlooks the fact that those who reject conforming to gender binaries and norms aren't accepted by everyone. If one's identity needed validation by the majority of a society in order to be taken as authentic, then gender non-conformity might be found wanting in many contexts. Butler's work is an outstanding example of the category of "woman" as definitionally hence structurally subordinate that "lures" the trajectory of multi/race/less/ness I aim to put forth in the remainder of the text. Their work is inspiration that there may be a day when "non-race-conforming" is not as counterintuitive for many as it is now.

Ania Loomba: Race as Caste

Literary scholar Ania Loomba discusses race and/as caste in her chapter "Racism in India," found in the 2018 edition of the *Routledge Companion to the Philosophy of Race*. In this chapter, Loomba not only identifies how caste fuels racism against those who emigrate to India from countries in the "African" continent but also pulls out the underlying mechanisms revealing how race and caste are in many critical ways synonymous. The work is rooted in Stuart Hall's statement that racial categories (such as "Blackness" for him) are constructed, told, and found and are not that which preexist or emerge aside from their construction. This is of course comparable to the move Butler makes about gender as a "performance," a performance that society bullies one into in many if not most instances. This has been said many times, and will continue to be said as a "lure" toward a perpetual skepticism of quasi-essentialisms such as race.[31] However, Loomba's reasons for employing the all-too-well-known concept of race as a social construction take a different turn than many of the thinkers we've previously encountered when she concretizes in no uncertain terms a conflation of race and caste opposed by many, which gives a clear basis for the proposition that race *is* racism.

The arguments against considering race as synonymous with class are steeped in claims that Portuguese, British, and Dutch colonizers placed their ideas of race and/as onto caste, a concept of culture and not necessarily bound to the phenotypical descriptions of race. Caste is also said to not be inextricably linked to capitalism, is founded in a religious as opposed to a racial or even economic system, etc.[32] But Loomba counters by stating that (1) the colonizers' ideas of race were mapped systems of creating/negotiating difference already in practice for thousands of years prior, (2) the cultural/ritual aspects of caste are not purely caste but are in fact inseparable from class and hence employed in service of a type of economy, and (3) religious compartmentalization of caste doesn't exempt it from acting as an agent in creating and maintaining hierarchies.[33] Throughout the chapter, Loomba thoroughly argues for a conflation of race and caste. How she does this is by an assertion that race is not identity but a system of hegemonic world organizations not under which humans *fall naturally* but under which they are *placed hierarchically* and *arbitrarily*. Since Loomba exposes the logic of caste as internally biased by using race as an analytical too, she by default legitimizes its abolishment.

In another echoing of Stuart Hall in reference to his understanding of race, Loomba says that caste is "the modality in which class is 'lived,' the medium through which class relations are experienced, the form in which it is appropriated and 'fought through.'"[34] To truly think of race as purely a "medium" is something counterintuitive to the thought process of many. But those same people may see caste as exactly this. Loomba is telling is us that while race and caste are indeed different concepts and manifest distinctively in the world, they are similar in the comparability of their effects. Therefore, we can conclude for Loomba that they are both oppressive.

Caste is a useful cipher through which one can decode and illuminate the metaphysic of race/trauma due to its lack of reliance on phenotype, even though it may in several instances include it. This can be used as a mechanism to mitigate the mind bugs that cause race, a non-empirical conceptual framework, to be "seen," "heard," lived, etc. Dalit leader B.R. Ambedkar is cited in the chapter as an example of someone who affirms the social construction of caste but follows much of the thought of his time on race by denying that caste could be race precisely because caste is not biological, but race is.[35] Therefore, Ambedkar reinforces race in ways that allow all of the hierarchies represented in the caste system to compose people of the same race who are superior to Indians with origin in countries such as China or Nigeria.[36]

Considering the And/As Spectrum, Loomba, like Butler, perhaps inadvertently offers a clearer way to consider how a conflation of race and racism might be warranted. While this occurred in very imperfect ways, as its "alive and well" status in Indian society indicates in no uncertain terms, caste was "abolished" in 1950. The fact caste still determines the possibilities of life for India is important to note.

But what is more important to note is that it was considered something in need of abolishing. Because Loomba's article never (in my estimation) reifies race after relegating it to caste unlike West, Kendi, and Banaji after their deconstructions, Loomba is all the way to the side of "race as racism." When one thinks race as caste, one relinquishes background assumptions that undergird the category of race's essentialist and quasi-essentialist composition and activity in the world

Interlude: The "Lure:" Racism as the "Shroud" and the "Myth" of the Ring

> And some things that should not have been forgotten were lost. History became legend. Legend became myth. And for two and a half thousand years, the ring passed out of all knowledge.[37]
> **GALADRIEL** in *Lord of the Rings: The Return of the King*

In the spirit of expanding the possibilities of how race can be understood, the concept of the ring in J.R.R. Tolkien's epic fantasy Lord of the Rings occurred to me as another novel lens through which we could experiment with our perception of it. As we (possibly) know, the story centers on a limited number of rings created by the dark lord Sauron which were given to the leaders of the elves, dwarves, and humans. Within these rings were "the strength and will to govern each *race*" (emphasis mine).[38] What the rulers where not told was that Sauron created a master ring that could control all other rings, centralizing his lust for domination over all the people of the realm known as "Middle Earth," thus using said rulers as proxies for his project of magical domination. Without going into detail about the rest of the plot, the narrative follows Frodo, a member of a simple "idyllic" race known as "Hobbits" that was immersed within what Paul Tillich might refer to as "dreaming innocence." The Shire, the realm from which he originates, is so removed from the power relations that structure the world beyond it, as Frodo and his closest companion discover when the former comes into possession of the master ring and is commissioned to destroy it and return it to where Sauron created it, the realm of Mordor. The Shire enfolds and unfolds in beautiful pastures of the most organic nature, the backdrop upon which peaceful community amid its various families and a "general" naivete about the world occur. Note that the Shire has no prescribed set of governance and Sauron never created any ring to control it. It was somehow outside of the system of domination and subordination attractive to Sauron. The Hobbits, especially Frodo's unusually well-travelled uncle, Bilbo Baggins, are to some degree familiar with the demarcations that create people groups outside of the Shire and the assumptions that come with being viewed as a member of one of them. But the context of the Shire operates on what Gilbert Simondon might refer to as a "technical object," or "the convergence of functions into a structural unit, rather than one of seeking a compromise between conflicting requirements."[39] The technical object, like the Shire, is an organism composed of a synergy between various elements in generative reciprocal relationships. On the outside of the Shire where kingdom struggles against kingdom and tenuous agreements between them are made to ensure shallow peace, the quest for power becomes solidified and Sauron has a field day.

So, where the hell does race/trauma come into this, other than its mention in the quoted words of Galadriel starting this section, which just MUST mean something different in that context than in the ones we are most interested in here? In *Lord of the Rings*, it appears that although different, there are some similarities to how we have been discussing race. First, race is a method that indicates a fundamental difference between one "group" and "another." Elves are fundamentally other than humans (men), humans are fundamentally other than "Hobbits," etc., Wizards are akin to humans but are actually Maiar, or primordial spirits sent by the fourteen Valar or demigods to assist the inhabitants of Middle-Earth in their war against Sauron, etc.[40] Secondly, race in LOTR inscribes assumptions about various so-called "groups," many of which are antagonistic (e.g., Dwarves are said to be greedy and humans to be weak in moral fortitude).[41] Thirdly, race is hierarchical. We were (not) surprised that humans are casted as superior while the Hobbits (halflings) are quite low on the scale of most sophisticated. Race in LOTR is appropriate for analogy to race/trauma. Like Loomba reminds us about the comparison of caste and race, race in LOTR and the category of race/trauma cannot be identically mapped upon each other, but the fact that they produce similar effects of disenfranchisement that determine how bodies can live and die (necropolitics) warrants us to consider how one might serve as invaluable insight into the other.

However, the ways in which LOTR negotiates race is not totally central to the ring as/and race/trauma, though it is connected to its fate. If race in LOTR is an "arbitrary" (I put this in quotes because it is not at all clear to me whether Tolkien's understanding of race is or has to be biological) demarcating of "groups" more akin to race/trauma as we've previously discussed it, race as the ring itself refers figuratively to the irresistible metaphysical "lure" of perceiving human identity solely through the lens of race/trauma. The ring didn't have to exist but now it does, and it transforms *becomings* with InnerSectional agency into intersected *beings* defined by how they can serve the ruler/rubric, Sauron.

If we know anything about the saga, we will remember that Isildur, ancient king of the legendary land of Gondor, could have destroyed the ring after he defeated a powerful Sauron by cutting off his fingers amid a massive war, which in turn stripped him and his minions of their coercive power over the people "groups" of Middle-Earth. But Isildur was drawn to the power of the ring, knowing full well the evil "trauma" that comes with it. Instead of destroying it, he kept it and was killed by another who desired it as he did. Tolkien reveals in his creative writing a vicious side of humanity when they encounter the ring. This tendency is shown to lie latent in even the most altruistic people: the desire for power is insatiable. Some characters in the saga, such as Gollum (formerly the hobbit Smiegel), are just obsessed with the ring and hide in caves admiring it. Others want to use it to dominate the same ways Sauron did. Others want to use it to do good, a naïveté to which, Aragorn, heir of Isildur, says "no one can wield its power."[42] Due to the weakness of various figures to destroy the ring, it existed for 2,000 years after the previous full-scale battle for Middle-Earth, harboring the strength for Sauron to regain the human form he lost after his defeat.

Does the thought experiment of the ring as race capture the lure it has on our collective unconscious? Race is the kind of power Sauron was interested in. It is a metaphysic grounding our possibilities for perceiving identities and our identities being perceived by the contexts within which we find ourselves. It determines and dominates the psyche, as Sauron does that of the rogue wizard Saruman. It creates "us" and "them." The nine kings who were given rings by Sauron eventually lost their organic identities due to the witchcraft of the ring and became invisible, only seen to those of and/or attuned to the spirit word. They eventually became known as "Nazgûl," fully sold out to the thirst for the power of the ring.[43] Does something like this happen to us when we follow the "lure" of the "shroud" separating race from racism and engage the "myths" that we can reform race/trauma by "wielding its power?" Smiegel loses his identity through the power of the ring and becomes Gollum. The ring creates a split personality within him, and he doesn't know which one is "really" him in many instances. Even Frodo is created by the ring. He's still called "Frodo," but after several conflicts with both Sauron and the Nazgûl, he is formed into that which is beyond what he was before this encounter. If race is indeed the ring because it is inherently racist not only by definition but in practice, we have presented another solid case for why it should be abolished.

Should race/trauma be returned to Mordor and destroyed in the fires of Mount Doom? As Isildur's "heirs" ancestrally bound to the metaphysics of race/trauma, what novel adventures of the processes of human identities might shoot forth in the hopeful shadows of its wake?

Multi/race/less/ness: A Preliminary (Re)Definition

It is at this point I will introduce what I have been developing as alternative to race/trauma and race-related categories of identification, categories that all too easily consume us. Everything up to this point including not only this chapter but previous chapters have been an attempt to reset how we see, hear, taste, smell, think, and enact identity. Perhaps we usher in a new age as Aragorn does with his accession to the throne of Gondor, a context within which humans bow to Hobbits as a sign of reverence for their invaluable part in the unforeseen victory of the people of Middle-Earth against Sauron and the forces of Mordor. Before Aragorn's inauguration, something like this would seem far-fetched at best and absolutely inconceivable at worst. But here, something different is breathed.

Perhaps this sort of escape of the programmed subconsciousness of racial thinking is what multi/race/less/ness can offer us. But first of all, what is multi/race/less/ness?

In *Underground Rap as Religion*, I coined the term "multi/race/less/ness" to describe the politics of the networks of reciprocal relations among people in the microverse of underground Hip-Hop, relations that did not center on race/trauma as a primary means of understanding and demarcating humans within the Culture. Since becoming a member of these global communities in my teens, I've been immersed in a cross-continental nation of individuals who theoretically and more often than not practically view Hip-Hop as what legendary MC and philosopher KRS would call a "collective consciousness." In this collective consciousness, one's identity becomes their own unique engagement with the five core elements/concepts of Hip-Hop, which are (1) Graffiti, (2) B-girlin'/B-Boyin' (known to many as "breakdancing"), (3) Deejayin', (4) Emceein', and (5) Knowledge and Understanding. For many living in the underground "place" of Hip-Hop, which to the dynamic battle duo LPG is more mental than physical in a Kantian sense of the noumena of Hip-Hop forms reading themselves upon the phenomena of the elements as enacted by practitioners and experienced by adherents to the culture in various geographical locations, the place is not structured on race/trauma. It never really mattered much. It wasn't a fundamental arbiter of authenticity within an artform that "above ground" representations have a-priori generally defined as the cultural property of people with considerable amounts of ancestry in the region commonly referred to as "Africa," and more particularly and persuasively in the "common" imagination (or "common tongue" since we've been riffing off of Lord of the Rings) referring to descendants of "Africa" with ancestries shaped by the brutal histories of the United States (e.g., slavery, segregation, the Blues, Jazz, free "Negroes," Moors, etc.). The underground in very significant ways sublated race/trauma in its systems of "seeing" the world. While it did not vanish, it took a back seat in how large numbers perceived other humans within and without the Culture. We stumbled on a world that wasn't so bridling to our senses, and we became thinkers of expansion, where a fundamental valuing of our counterparts was rooted in not race/trauma identities but by their creative transformation through Hip-Hop's core principles of peace, love, unity, and having fun. As KRS-ONE says, "All people on the planet are Hip-Hop . . . Some know it and some don't know it. That's the only difference."[44]

The focus of this text is an elaborating and unpacking of what I not only relegate to merely just one chapter of URAR but also discuss solely in terms of underground Hip-Hop. In URAR, multi/race/less/ness was merely *prescriptive*, as I felt it was needed to address a looming elephant in the room in contrast with other theoretical work in Hip-Hop studies: I wanted to provide a robust case for why a reification of "Blackness" as intrinsic to Hip-Hop common to large amounts of the scholarship was absent in mine. When I presented this idea in Anthony

B. Pinn's Hip-Hop and Religion class at Rice University in the fall of 2018, some students pushed against it. This was a year before URAR was released, and perhaps this and other currents I was swimming upstream against in the discourse was why I added this chapter to the monograph. I wanted to put voice to our (meaning mine and considerable others') method/ology of living in the world, a method/ology that in praxis renders race/trauma and race-related categories emanations an insufficient metaphysic for perceiving humans. Multi/race/less/ness hints at more novel and intense possibilities that process beyond what we've known and thought before.

In the service of manufacturing a new way of seeing that will hopefully become a metaphysic ingressed and lived as background assumption until it needs to be unearthed and deconstructed and even abolished in the future, multi/race/less/ness moves from its stance as *descriptive* in URAR to *prescriptive* in this project in relation to how it can transform itself and build anew novel possibilities to underlie thinking itself. In a brief, thorough, and exceptional introduction to deconstruction, Mark C. Taylor states that,

> Western philosophy points toward the constructive subject that is always remaking the world in its own image. As such, philosophy transforms remaking the world in its own image. As such, philosophy transforms theology into anthropology. The implications of ontotheology become explicit in Hegel's identification of man with God. By attempting to de-construct both the constructive subject and the horrifying world it has created, Derrida points beyond the certainty of absolute knowledge to the uncertainty of postmodernity. Always arriving late, forever coming second, and never returning on time, deconstruction repeatedly demonstrates the impossibility of modernity by soliciting the other, which, though never present, "always already" haunts presence.[45]

This "logic of the one" Laurel Schneider identifies as a feigned theological origin determining the metaphysics of what is possible to be thought secularizes through the cross-pollination of a myriad of confluences in the space of time and the time of space into philosophy, science, religion, politics, art etc. and demands an implicit rubric which would bring all that exists under the domination of a singular overarching concept. "One ring to rule them all, one ring to find them, one ring to bring them all, and in the darkness bind them"[46] This is the true target attribute of the analogue of the ring as a cypher for race: singularity. In its light, there is only one way identity can be thought and that is through the singularity of race/trauma with the category of "Whiteness" taking the role of Sauron, and all other categories are dominated to varying degrees. In Derrida's deconstruction of the history of "Western" philosophy, he argues that philosophy has attempted in various ways to discover and articulate a perceived preexistent order that it fails to realize is its own creation. From this creation of a type of order of all things comes this order of humans known as "race" and known to readers of this work as "race/trauma." Its singular constriction of human events existing beyond and before the colonial technologies that confined how they could identify to laws of the excluded middle is held to be intrinsically racist.

Multi/race/less/ness as *prescriptive* relinquishes not only monolithic and singular cubicles of identity in name but also in thought. The attempt is for the reader to visualize the possibility that there is really a future beyond a reduction of the multiplicities converging within our rich human events other than coercion into racialized methods of identity, difference, and perception. In an attempt to explore Derrida's "uncertainty of modernity" as an alternative to identities fashioned by race/trauma, identities that are intrinsically racist, we now turn to multi/race/less/ness as *prescriptive* for alternative ways of becoming humans.

6 MULTI/RACE/LESS/NESS: A NEW NAME FOR TIMELESS WAYS OF HUMAN BECOMING

This is a revolution of the mind.[1]

JAMES BROWN

Introduction

In this chapter, I attempt to explore that which philosophy has difficulty thinking coherently: that irreducibility of human becoming and the identities that serve as what Whitehead referred to as "useful abstractions." These useful abstractions are intermittent "snapshots" that collect a multiplicity of influences, sometimes known as the "self," into a diversified unity. They give the guise of singularity and allow us to feel, think, and communicate the phenomena we find ourselves enmeshed within and thrown into but are not to be confused with the *noumena* from whence the appearance emerges and can never be reduced to. The category of race is just this confusion.

The plan in this section is this: I will expand the etymological basis of "multi," "race," "less," and "ness" I gave in URAR to bring to the fore the undercurrents of what it has always been: a mode of becoming that deeply engages and *prescribes* contrasts grounded in a lived acknowledgement that multiplicity permeates. Next, I will offer a broader definition of multi/race/less/ness in *Underground Rap as Religion*. The section ends with a schematic showing how multi/race/less/ness can be thought of as a philosophical practice.

Multi/race/less/ness as a way of thinking, "a revolution of the mind," takes its initial cues in this section from Brian Massumi, Alfred North Whitehead, and James Brown, all multi/race/less philosophers in their own right/write. What would it mean to reconceptualize identity not as the appearance of race/trauma but the inevitability of *vanishing*, or a mode of thinking that sees the "self" as that which always dissolves and/or slips away when it's thought to be captured? What is the value of an appeal to Whitehead's notion of returning to the essence of energy before symbolization is confused for the event in question? What does multi/race/less/ness offer us that the category of race/trauma does not?

Well, what are you waiting for? Let's enter the process and find out.

Multi/race/less/ness: Fine-Tuning for Optimal Processual Performance

I think it is worthwhile to inaugurate this section by offering the definition of multi/race/less/ness given in URAR. It is as follows:

1. Multi

The "multi" portion of "multi/race/less/ness" speaks to the difficulty and (impossibility) to talk about anything in the universe as a singularity. Every entity in the universe is perpetually composed of an infinite number of influences and decisions. To talk about any entity is to talk about not a thing but an event that includes many things. "Multi" avoids Whitehead's "fallacy of misplaced concreteness" by admitting the processual nature of the universe.

2. Race

In the category of "race," we encounter a very constrained confluence of social constructions that are treated as a fixed idea(s) by which we box people who look a certain way, are from a certain part of the world, etc. In many ways, this category, while inevitably being a multiplicity, is in direct opposition to the fluid of the "multi" in its push to reduce the processual "many" of the universe into a static "one." In "multi/race/less/ness," "race," like "multi," also serves as an admission. "Race" admits an authentic existence of both the category and the effects. This is why I utilize the word and do not turn a blind eye to it. It is not posited to ask the question "Does race exist?" It is poised in the multi/race/less/ness question to ask "How does race exist," and from there excavate the results of its existence.

3. Less

"Less" is about rejecting the category of race in favor of a "multi" understanding of self. In such a formulation of identity, the experiencing subject may become concerned with nationality and ethnicity (things that could be argued to be defined more by the individuals and collectives who partake in said nationalities and ethnicities than by an outsider desirous of reducing multiplicity to something more line[a]r and easier for them to understand) as opposed to race. In the "less," race is rejected either subtly or overtly through ways of life that defy playing the idea of identity by the rules of the racial categories. To combine the two words, "race/less" is the acting against racial categories by acknowledging their existence and enacting recalcitrance. I would argue that in regard to the underlying ways of being that compose underground hip-hop, these means of resistance are so much a part of the organism of the culture that they may evade conscious choice in many ways.

4. Ness

This is simple. The "ness" is merely the act or state of being multi/race/less.[2]

In looking at this elongated definition, we can see that nothing about it makes it distinct to underground Hip-Hop. Underground Hip-Hop is thought of in URAR as one of many possible temporal accidents of multi/race/less/ness. The previous chapter attempted to show antiracial (in contrast with Kendi's "antiracist") tendencies in the projects and concepts of various thinkers who have appealed to but not sufficiently explored the implications of multi/race/less un/logic. Derrida might refer to this as the end of the philosophy of formulaic resolution and the beginning of philosophy as writing/thinking that which cannot or is extremely difficult to be written/thought (Dis/solution).[3] Multi/race/less/ness oozes from the orgiastic experience of identity processing unbridled, and this transcends categorization. It is lived and thought as the fluid underlying activity of both experience and conceptual epistemologies of perceiving and inscribing our ideas of "ourselves" and "others."

In this work, the "multi" aspect of "multi/race/less/ness" maintains its use in URAR as focusing on events in contrast to separate and distinct pockets of reality. The problems of racial and race-related identities we've examined in this book so far have been the seeming inevitability of racism if the category of race stays a live option for perceiving the processual human. Here, the "multi" is updated to remove the use of the word "things." Instead of saying "To talk about an entity is to talk about not a thing but an event that includes many things," I could have said "To talk about an entity is not to talk about a thing but an infinite event with contrasting related characteristics. In this project, the "multi" is taken to a radical level, luring a destabilizing whenever a seemingly solid understanding of a particular human comes to the fore. "Event" is a word skilfully used by Whitehead to alert us to the fluidity and instability of all.

In an articulation of a future after racial and race-related categories, I must reiterate the position articulated in URAR that multi/race/less/ness is not what some refer to as "color-blindness," or the assertion that race is somehow magically a thing of the past. While multi/race/less/ness does indeed assert forwardly that race/trauma is not a plausible method of constructing human identities in process, it does so, in Sankofa fashion, while maintaining a focused eye on race/trauma's past and present as it moves imperfectly toward its abolishment. We have not beaten race/trauma. Multi/race/less/ness ventures into temporary "virtual realities" as prescriptions (such as underground Hip-Hop Culture) while perpetually maintaining awareness and lived critique of how race/trauma presently impacts lived realities.

On this idea of a reckoning with the reality of the function (not of an objective existence) of race, I state,

> It would be inaccurate to say this anti-Euro supremacist way of identifying people in underground hip-hop does away with race. What it can be said to do is *displace* race as the primary factor of identification, for a multiethnic community of people in many instances is the norm for underground hip-hop. The differences that people are described by in terms of hip-hop's artists are their respective crafts, the essence of which links the practitioners back to the larger body of hip-hop, since all elements are understood to be segments that compose a larger unified situation. To explain this complexity shortly, it could be said that in underground hip-hop as a theory, a person's humanity is valued before their race, if they subscribe to racial categories at all.[4]

In an extraction of multi/race/less/ness from the entanglement in Hip-Hop that birthed my *articulation*, not *creation*, of it, we see that multi/race/less/ness is a *displacement*, not an erasure. This displacement of race, sliding it to the peripheral and observing how identity formation carries on with it relegated there, serves as a way of remembering and pinpointing when and where oppression due to a belief in the category of race occurs and allows us to address it. However, this present articulation of multi/race/less/ness is skeptical of the language "multiethnic" due to a subtle reinscription of racial categories the word implies. This is for at least two reasons. The first is that the term "multiethnic" is now a "buzzword" tamed by the hegemonic systems conditioning its potency. Secondly, I hold that "multiethnic" could possibly imply something I wish not to assert with the prescription of multi/race/less/ness: that the ethnic groups I referred to are fundamentally or necessarily different from one another. All in all, an updated concept of "race" in multi/race/less/ness is still aware of the real issues cause by a belief in race while simultaneously displacing it and guarding against its reintroduction.

Considering the "less," it is the relinquishing of the category of race/trauma; the act of the displacement just mentioned. Here, I would want to return to this deconstructive antagonism and locate progressive identities post-race/trauma specifically amid this acknowledgement of race and its deconstruction. As soon as race is reinforced, the right side of the backslash abolishes it until its sublation becomes that which has the possibility of being thought as second nature. "Abolish" is key language in this part of multi/race/less/ness, for to abolish an idea, a law, a practice, etc., does not mean said practice magically goes out of memory in the way that a theory of racial utopia might suggest and desire (Wouldn't that be nice?). Multi/race/less/ness is hard and conscious work, and in that way is quite similar to what Kendi defines as "antiracism." A calculated struggle relies on a keen awareness and knowledge of that which is struggled against.

Also, I would add that the initial combining of the abolishing of race and the taking on of nationality and ethnicity as post-racial[5] move in the "less" is slightly premature. In this articulation of multi/race/less/ness, the creation of new post-racial identities is not in the "less," as the volatile struggle occurring in the "less" is too much of tropical *huracán* to locate the more constructive than deconstructive ideas of ethnicity, nationality, and culture within. While affirming that ethnicity and nationality are indeed abstractions and unbridled, they are useful abstractions and need the *image* of a pronounced character to hold effective sway on the individual and collective imaginations. Therefore, I locate them in the "ness," where the more constructive epistemological and metaphysical poststructures take shape.

The Phases of Multi/race/less/ness

I will provide a map of sorts for how I currently understand multi/race/less/ness to function. Multi/race/less/ness is not an "out there" philosophy of post-race. It is not articulating the purely transcendental work of the mind imposed on temporal experience as in Kantian deontology. It is also not searching for a multi/race/less structure of the universe and attempting to apply it to human understandings of race. It is, however, the emergence of novel faculties of reason and experience in reciprocal relations undefined and impossible to chart. If multi/race/less/ness is a type of primordial and progressive fluid grounding of how human identity can be rethought and rethought of, concepts of the understanding are involved as the world writes on the "self" and the "self" in turn writes on the world presented to it.

I utilize the term "contrast" in place of "contradiction" to indicate a noticeable change or changes within a context of *relation*. This stance implies that modicums of experience seemingly opposed as contradictions are actually contents of the same event formally known as the racialized human being but now referred to as the multi/race/less human becoming. Taking a cue from the Whitehead of *Adventures of Ideas*, contrasts, not contradictions, are the most beneficial presentations of the multiplicity we inevitably live within. We can do more with contrasts, the embrace of the harmony of divergent events, than with contradictions, the continued struggle against opposites of various kinds (fundamental, ideological, mathematical, analytic philosophical, etc.). The former processes. The latter for all intents and purposes stands still. Multi/race/less/ness is a philosophy that founds human identities in process on contrasts, for when human identity is reconceived as an ongoing event composed of smaller phases of events reciprocally related or InnerSected, a fuller post-racial collective conscious experience can potentially emerge.

So, multi/race/less/ness, "a revolution of the mind," is a shift not discovered as a universal reality but a perpetual co-creation which shapes how what was once thought of as contradiction is a contrast. The proposition "Blacks are fundamentally different than Whites" is no longer self-evident, if tenable at all. Rather, humans previously thought of as "Blacks" and "Whites" are not different in the ways our background assumptions coerced us into thinking they were, and the contrasting harmony of all humans in reciprocal relations becomes a primordial phase from which the metaphysic of race/trauma is displaced. What happens when we take off the glasses of race/trauma?

Muti/race/less/ness' four cyclical phases are as follows: (1) Creativity, or the untamed energy birthing the possibility of a fresh type of human identity, (2) Useful Lived Abstraction, or the manifesting of fluid concepts by which the post-racial human co-manufactures identity with/in their contexts, (3) Dis/solution, or the perpetual challenging and revisiting of lived abstractions so that they do not become ossified categories of identity similar to race/trauma, and (4) Repetition, or the continual practice and perpetual "remixing" of (1)–(3).

Creativity

"Creativity" in the context of multi/race/less/ness is the act of selecting and realizing the multiplicity of "transcendent" possibilities of human identities available to be actualized. The work of the painter, sculptor, playwright, etc. is the intentional and unintentional assembly of elements in a context into an event in which said elements are set alongside each other and indefinitely contrasted. Oftentimes, we are not aware of the event nature of works of art that appear to be still, such as a portrait, but Massumi via Susanne Langer's notion of the "*occurrent arts*," or the aesthetic productions which trigger processual motion on the observing event (the human in this case), ask us to see the perpetual flux in what is deceivingly stagnant. He says, "All arts are occurrent arts because any and every perception, artifactual or 'natural,' is just that, an experiential event. It's an event both in the sense that when it happens something new transpires."[6] A painting abstracts concepts and ideas prevalent in a context and presents them for the viewer to interact with. Here, I use the term "abstract" in a Whiteheadian sense: to provide a "clear" presentation of an entity is to really provide a misleading presentation insofar as said "concrete" presentation is thought to virtually be the end all of the entity.[7]

Of Creativity, Whitehead says,

> Creativity is without a character of its own in exactly the same sense in which the Aristotelian "matter" is without a character of its own. It is that ultimate notion

of the highest generality at* the base of actuality. It cannot be characterized, since all characters are more special than itself. But creativity is always found under conditions and described as conditioned. The nontemporal act of all-inclusive unfettered valuation is at once a creature of creativity and a condition of creativity. It shares this double character with all creatures. By reason of its character as a creature, always in concrescence and never in the past, it receives a reaction from the world; this reaction is its consequent nature.[8]

For Whitehead, Creativity is the *process* by which entities develop defining character. It's grasped precisely by its elusiveness. But Creativity has no character of its own since clearly conceptualizing the act of perpetual energy fusing a plethora of entities into a diverse unity is difficult if not impossible. It is like that unrealized, raw potential for the characterization of uncharacterized material that describes Aristotelian matter. This is something like what I referred to when I named Boricua Sandy's and my VirgoTwins' record "*ArtSpace*." The ArtSpace itself, whether physical or conceptual, is never clearly defined, for its equivalence with procesual bringing into becoming is exterior to the very idea of definition. Creativity is not an entity in process. Creativity is a fleeting image of the epitome of process itself.

Do babies come into the world with racial, cultural, religious, philosophical, gender, and other identities? Or are these identities created on their consciousnesses after they are born? To apply Beauvoir's axiom about one *becoming* and not being born a woman to race/trauma identities, we (like countless others) have already asserted that race, like many other identities, is that which is not innate but that which one is led/pressured/structured into by one's family, society, religion, and more. We must interrogate the types of racial and race-related identities we have co-created on/with young children in their formative years, implying that they *are* a particular racial or race-related identity and are not and cannot *be/become* anything but this. In the phase of Creativity, multi/race/less/ness *prescribes* a side-stepping of a perpetuating of race/trauma categories on newly born humans and an ushering in of novel possibilities for identity formation rooted in other sources. Instead of coercing the child into colonial and postcolonial identities essentially and quasi-essentially viewed as inevitable and even mandatory (e.g., You are Latinx and you should be proud of that), what would occur if societies allowed the child to co-create their individual identities with said societies in ways that seem most equitable and liberating to them? In keeping with the "race" of muti/race/less/ness, this would still include ensuring the child confronts how race/trauma is a lived reality but multi/race/less Creativity would ensure the child is not predetermined to ingress racial and race-related traumatic identities.

In speaking of a kind of Creativity relevant to our inquiry, Fanon says,

> The colonist and the colonized are old acquaintances. And consequently, the colonist is right when he says he "knows" them. It is the colonist who *fabricated*

and continues to *fabricate* the colonized subject. The colonist derives his validity, i.e. his wealth, from the colonial system.[9] (italics author's)

We could replace the word "fabricated" and "fabricate" with the words "created" and "create" in this quote respectively and still communicate the brunt of this: even though we understand theoretically the elements of social construction constituting the category of race/trauma, it doesn't always "click" that race itself might be the real enemy. Is it easy to regress into a quasi-essentialism of race/trauma. For Fanon, "Decolonization is truly the *creation* of [a] new [hu]m[a]n."[10] (emphasis mine) For multi/race/less/ness, this creation implies a struggle against and an abolishment of race/trauma, a fundamental fabrication of the colonists, as race/trauma is key in the metaphysics of colonization. Multi/race/less/ness in the phase of Creativity, like decolonization, enacts "the urgent need to challenge the colonial situation" by authoring new and fluid structures of thought and becoming through which humans can reimagine themselves.[11] [12]

Creativity primordially transforms the metaphysics of human identity formation by positing as a premise (1): the live option to reject racial and race-related categories. Following from (1), we can posit as a premise (2): the conceptualization of post-racial identities as not unrealistic but actualizable possibilities. After (1) is accepted as the ground for post-racial identities, we can then begin to organically and intentionally come to them through the multi/race/less unstable synthesis of Creativity. At this phase, we open ourselves to not merely ingressing what race/trauma has said we *are*, but what our ancestors, traditions, and more unmediated by race/trauma imply we can *become* as we co-create our own "dwelling" in a Heideggerian sense of living authentically as opposed to mechanically.[13]

For Whitehead and multi/race/less/ness, Creativity is the most ultimate, or foundational, force in the universe. It is not external to the world and manifested within as is a demiurge or deontological and/or deistic philosophy of a classical creator/first cause. Creativity is the very *process* of many entities converging into one, as in the Aztec idea of "nepantla," the in-between that Anzaldúa described herself as.[14] Creativity is the force responsible for every existing event often referred to as "things" but is also only evident in "things." It is never exterior to the entities of experience, whether physical or conceptual.[15] Creativity's indeterminacy due to numerous possibilities alongside each other before they converge is also akin to what Simondon calls "negativity," or an absence of content that lures multiplicity toward beneficial reciprocal relation by creators calling it forth (there isn't a hospital in a town so we need to build one).[16] It indicates that the world doesn't have to continue to be what it seems to persist to be, and that seemingly fixed systems are malleable through the introduction of interesting propositions, which Whitehead holds are better than true ones because they present novelty to the world.[17]

Useful Lived Abstractions

After Creativity takes its course, novel "things" emerge. Creativity has created characters with defining characteristics. In this case, we are concerned with the characters of post-racial identity Creativity introduces through co-creation between humans and their possibilities, unrealized passive co-created concepts which Whitehead refers to as "eternal objects." According to John B. Cobb, Jr., eternal objects are "objects" and not Platonic forms because for Whitehead, they must refer to an experiencing subject. The eternal object is an eternal object for me, and since they are passive, they depend upon me and others to coalesce them by Creativity into useful forms. The "eternal" in eternal object does not refer to anything preexistent such as the forms, but merely the status of something as nontemporal, like an idea.[18] The symbolism of "black" as a racial concept and legal term started as an eternal object during the colonial period. Initially, it wasn't necessarily a reference to skin color. As time went on, the brown skin of the people mostly referred to under the category "negro" shifted to the point in the present where "Blackness" as a racial descriptor and identity causes us to perceive brown skin as "black" skin. How is it possible to "see" a color on your skin that is not there?

It's possible because Creativity births what Massumi calls *lived abstractions*.

A *lived abstraction* according to Massumi is the "semblance" of all experience that, though seemingly concrete, is "abstract."[19] Once again, we're reversing the "conventional" use of the word "abstract." In process philosophies, there are no fixed "things." All is in motion always. This includes human formations of identities. With the absence of the concrete, there is only that which *becomes*. There is nothing more precisely because there is perpetually all the more. Therefore, it is only possible to live in abstraction: in process. Racial "Blackness" is seen on bodies because it is *abstracted* onto them, not because it is actually "there" or is required to be "there." It could be argued in a racial sense that "Black" is understood to mean brown and not literally black skin. Notwithstanding, it is intriguing that when it comes to racial categorization, some would instinctively compare their complexion to a black crayon and not a brown one. We experience not objects but images etched in flux which move beyond us the instant we enjoy them. To live is to engage without ever grasping the nothing that's "there." Racial reasoning is the type of *lived abstraction* multi/race/less/ness hopes to provide an alternative to.

Massumi says,

> What we call objects, considered in the ontogenetic fullness of process, are lived relations between subjective and objective forms occasionally abstractly nesting themselves in each other as passed-on potentials. They are the inter-given: the systematic form in which potential is relayed from one experience to another. "Objectification itself is abstraction"[20]

Whitehead understood eternal objects to have more of a fixed nature than the flux of the temporal world, since the reason we can even somewhat concretize the perpetual motion of the universe is through the impressions eternal objects leave in indefinite lines of process. The rotating clay on the potter's wheel eventually gives the abstraction of pure solidity when the pot is made through the eternal objects not only converging in its presentation to the senses as data but also being used by the potter to lure the lump into the idea of the "pot." However, I want to suggest and pay attention to the potential flux of post-racial eternal objects, as they (and all eternal objects) change with changing contexts. I hold that if multi/race/less/ness is to ever conquer the hierarchies and ossification of race/trauma, the concepts emerging from it must resist ossification by being attuned to the process of Creativity intrinsic in all. That resistance is done by ensuring that *lived abstractions* of post-racial identity are *useful*.

Where does the "useful" of Useful Lived Abstraction" come from? This is directly from the Whitehead of *Process and Reality*, who preceded Massumi in his skepticism of taking experience as singular, solid, nonrelational, and simple. For Whitehead, the complexities of what appears to be very basic encounters with sense data, concepts, etc. need to be accounted for by close attention to the ways in which experience really happens. Clockwize of La Puente, CA Hip-Hop collective Crop Circles720 and Echoes of Oratory Muzik confirms in the song "The Listener" that "This is how we live."[21] Since we live in process, and human identity thought in process takes intermittent forms as *lived abstractions*, what types of forms can be created to be most equitable for the passing phases of human identity? Whitehead says,

> Primitive men were not metaphysicians, nor were they interested in the expression of concrete experience. Their language merely expressed <u>useful abstractions</u>, such as "greyness of the stone." But like Columbus who never visited America, Descartes missed the full sweep of his own discovery, and he and his successors, Locke and Hume, continued to construe the functionings of the subjective enjoyment of experience according to the substance-quality categories. Yet if the enjoyment of experience be the constitutive subjective fact, these categories have lost all claim to any fundamental character in metaphysics.[22] (emphasis mine)

The problem Whitehead picks up on here is evident: if things in themselves are said to have a type of reality existing outside a perception of them, then the human center of a subject that Descartes also asserts is a preexistent soul and serves as "the primary data of philosophy" runs the risk of feigning an objectivity (clear ideas) which is actually a starting point of subjectivity.[23] This is why Whitehead argues that once such an *individual* move is made, a philosophical system can no longer claim to disclose any *universal* metaphysical truth.

In this section of the 1929 Gifford Lectures where the words "useful abstractions" are uttered, Whitehead is making a case for process philosophy, or what he refers to specifically as the "philosophy of organism," by contrasting it with both what he calls "the subjectivist principle" (the "stuff" in the world can be accounted for by universal concepts of which they are types and are disclosed in reflection, as in Descartes) and the "sensationalist principle" (there is nothing but the empirical and localized experience of the senses from which to know the world, as in Hume and Locke). The former is flawed because it asserts the existence of pure conceptual "things" but cannot completely confirm their existence. The latter misses the mark in its reduction of our knowledge to the senses. Whitehead counters with the "reformed subjectivist principle," which maintains the focus on the human "self" as a mainframe through which epistemological information is organized through analysis (subjectivist principle). It also holds that only that which is experienced should be allowed as a part of a philosophical system (sensationalist principle). For Whitehead, abstractions permeate all. The reformed subjectivist principle allows us to come to terms with the abstractions in the world of sensory experience while simultaneously acknowledging the reciprocal relation between concepts, here not thought of as classically transcendent but embodied within and influencing actual entities. Rafael Reyes says,

> All things are abstractions, science included. Our lives are the culmination of the finite and infinite, the finite fact with the deriving value of the infinite. Thus, when one begins to analyze this finite event, the actual object, one does not know all things objectively, but rather what it portrays to us in its "superjection," its letting out its satisfaction or decision, or what we might say is your efficient cause. So when we analyze it, we are analyzing its feelings of the satisfaction, as well as our own feelings of what we have prehended. Not only are we abstracting the event from the whole, but we may also be abstracting a portion of the event from the event, which is a whole of a larger event. Thus we have at best is a partial knowledge of the reality of the cosmos. All things, therefore, are impartial.[24]

To return to our example of the color "black" concrescing (becoming) into the race/trauma category of "Black," the reformed subjectivist principle can explain why we "see" brown skin as black in ways neither the subjectivist nor the sensationalist principle can. In the sensationalist view, it is impossible to see brown skin as black provided your physical eyes aren't obstructed and working correctly. It could also be said that under the subjectivist principle it would be impossible to perceive the *lived abstraction* of brown and perceive black since the universal "black" is a clear idea that can't be confused by the "thing that thinks." Under both accounts, an experience we know happens because we experience it often if not everyday has little validity. By contrast, the reformed subjectivist principle acknowledges the essential nature of experience in philosophical thought while affirming the InnerSectional communion between ideas and the empirical world. What is being felt (experienced) can't be reduced to what is being perceived, as the retina is not "seeing" the universal color black but the mind is referencing the color to the skin in ways that restrict this phenotype from readily being referred to as the shade of brown it more closely corresponds to.

This process repeats itself *ad infinitum*. "Useful abstractions" is a phrase I am extracting from a series of thoughts Whitehead conveyed in this section of the Gifford Lectures recorded in Part Two of *Process and Reality*. It was somewhat buried within. Useful abstractions rise up from a more basic situation of an admission of flux and a subsequent "freeze framing" of it. The "primitive men" Whitehead mentions were not implying universal truths with the proposition "the stone is grey." They were abstracting the perception of "greyness" and "stoneness" as a guide to what the grey stone is useful for, such as building dwelling places or fire pits. Useful abstractions are means of understanding while not overstating the characterized phases of process. Multi/race/less/ness asserts that race/trauma is a "useless abstraction," or that which by nature commits the fallacy of misplaced concreteness: race/trauma essentially implies that race is a universal non-negotiable. If we have sufficient grounds to claim that race/trauma is indeed a useless abstraction, what would useful abstraction of multi/race/less identity look like?

Multi/race/less/ness initially takes steps towards the nexus (core) of one's identity emerging from their particular context (family heritage, place of birth, customs of heritage and birth deemed most important to implement, etc.) and not being restricted by and reduced to the definitional deductive sum of race/trauma. This involves a letting go of expected norms of identity. The foundation of the useful abstraction of multi/race/less/ness identity is the "uncarved wood" mentioned in the Tao Te Ching. While the image of "wood" as such emanates from the matter to the mind, the wood in a sense is not tailored (e.g., telling the child they are "Native American" and moving them toward an adaptation of "Native Americanness") but is left to *become* (e.g., the child is afforded the metaphysical and social space to organically come into processions of identity in flux perpetually, and this becoming may very well be antithetical and deconstructive of the category of race/trauma).[25]

I notice a certain fluidity in identity formations of culture as defined here that I hold is absent in the categories of race/trauma. Furthermore, cultural usages of racial and race-related terms are caught up within the flux of ever-transforming structures of perception and understanding. Therefore, what racial and race-related terms could mean 150 years ago may symbolize completely contrasting eternal objects today. However, race/trauma gives off the illusion that racial identities are fixed. But what maintains them is a quasi-religious belief that they are. On the flip (contrastingly), culture, nationality, and genealogy are series of enfolding and unfolding of elements of experience which converge and diverge in unpredictable relation. This is akin to the "emic" pole of what Victor Montejo refers to as the "interactionist theory of indigenous cultures," or emergents (members) of the culture perceiving the indefinite event threading the ensemble of their process of becoming. Montejo primarily locates exegesis within the "etic," which, converse to the emic, is the vantage point of the outside researcher.[26] I take this to imply that what occurs in the perspective of the person invested in a complex reciprocal relation of a nexus of particles of experience we might refer to as "culture" is more lived than reduced. Its flux flows within and beyond without ever really being "understood." Montejo talks of the need for "Indigenous" people to "'present' themselves and their own cultures"[27] The fluid multiplicity evident in that which composes any given culture defined as we have here might be the reason why some elements of this mode of becoming are difficult to describe to outsiders: the process never actually concretizes for those born into the event of a culture. Hence, the element in question never became a "thing" for them to describe. Rather, they are constituted by the process of their culture(s), and infinitely co-create their ever-changing identity within its events.

Useful Lived Abstractions are temporary investments in a particular picture of the reciprocally related human until said picture passes out of relevance and is replaced by others. For example, "They/them" in its lack of hierarchy ("they/them" is outside of/beyond the structures of male/female, which are arguably intrinsically dominant and subordinate respectively) passes from useless to useful in its shift from a stagnant gender binary to a fluidity not bound to the contested concepts of "man/woman." There may be an "after" for those who identify as "they/them," and if such a time comes, what humanity can become must be reimagined. More importantly, since change is inevitable, one must come to terms with the impermanence of Useful Lived Abstractions, and guard against them becoming useless postulates of race/trauma.

I've mentioned post-race identities "emerging" throughout this chapter. But a bit more should be said about this in relation to process philosophy before we move forward. Of Creativity, Whitehead says,

> In all philosophic theory there is an ultimate which is actual in virtue of its accidents. It is only then capable of characterization through its accidental embodiments, and apart from these accidents is devoid of actuality. In the philosophy of organism this ultimate is termed "creativity"; and God is its nontemporal accident. In monistic philosophies, Spinoza or absolute idealism, this ultimate is God, who is also equivalently termed "The Absolute." In such monistic schemes, the ultimate is allowed a final "eminent" reality, beyond that ascribed to any of its accidents. In this general position, the philosophy of organism seems to approximate to some strands of Indian, or Chinese thought,

than to Western Aziatic or European thought. One side makes process ultimate; the other side makes fact ultimate.[28]

From Whitehead's notion of pure Creativity, the lure within (not exterior to) all by which contrasting entities coalesce into one, comes a nontemporal "image" of this universal process of fusion. From the ultimate activity of the universe comes God, the means by which the by-products of Creativity, or what Whitehead calls "actual entities (every event in the universe partaking in experience)," are evaluated. This is because eternal objects are in the actual entity of God for Whitehead and can only influence the world if they are triggered by an actual entity.[29,30] God is also the ground of Creativity, that which calls forth novelty appearing when the "many" become "one." This separates the act of creativity from God, making Whitehead's philosophy of religion quite distinct from the omnipotent Gods of classical theisms, "theological mistakes" according to Whitehead's student Charles Hartshorne. Contrastingly, Whitehead's God seems to "emerge" from the sheer possibility that many entities can become one, not the converse. There have been various positions within Whitehead scholarship on the plausibility of separating God from Creativity, such as John B. Cobb, Jr.'s notion that the philosophy of organism has difficulty locating the "why" of the existence of the world we know if God is divorced from Creativity,[31] and Robert Neville's caution that Whitehead's ontological principle (actual entities are the only reasons for what occurs in the universe) makes it impossible for Creativity to do anything since it doesn't "exist" and is therefore not an actual entity.[32,33]

In a Whiteheadian framework, cultures, just like underground rappers, emerge to assume the function of Gods in that they set the terms for how the world can be experienced by those within them without being exempt from metaphysical laws unlike supernaturalist claims about the divine.[34] For all intents and purposes, culture is the God of its context in its orchestrating, valuing, and distributing of components by which the humans within the culture "dwell" and find their place in the world.[35] Phillip Clayton defines "emergence" as the appearance of new communities of organization in the physical world that have laws distinctly different from their predecessors. He says that "Emergence means a sort of dynamic that exists in systems with a certain level of complexity that does not exist in systems of less complexity."[36] An example of this in the scientific world is the appearance of quantum physics out of physics. Clayton's defense of "strong emergence," or the doctrine of different levels of the evolutionary chain being governed by different laws, though intended by him to explore a compatibility between science and the idea of God, is foundational for multi/race/less Useful Lived Abstractions of identities in process.[37]

Clayton utilizes strong emergence as opposed to "weak emergence" (the idea that when new evolutionary levels appear, they are regulated by the laws of the previous levels) to arrive at the possibility of a God that corresponds to Whitehead's

God as well as what I have defined here as "culture," which, according to KRS-ONE, is when entities gather around one or more common purposes.[38] The progression from which God flows involves previous natural stages establishing the grounds for subsequent stages conducive to God's concretizing. Clayton says, "God was at one time merely potential and only gradually becomes actual over the course of history."[39] From the intuition of the possibility of the existence of something more than just the bare empirical data of the universe emerges philosophical questions that postulate the possibility of the Useful Lived Abstraction of God, which only by necessity needs to refer to an orchestrating principle, similar to our definition of culture. In contrast to the questions asked of more classical notions of God around why the world is as it is, metaphysical questions that can be asked of multi/race/less understandings of culture start with an assumption of flux and ask "How long will the group name and understanding I assent to presently reflect who I am becoming?" and "How should I co-create my identity with my context when the time comes to move beyond the post-race Useful Lived Abstraction I currently use to abstract my human process of identity formation?"

Dis/solution

All of the phases in multi/race/less/ness are permeated by Creativity. It could be said that they emanate and return to Creativity because they are its formless form. Dis/solution refers to the intentional impulse applied to Useful Lived Abstractions to ensure that no particular "solution" of identity is given the status of metaphysical exemption. When individual Useful Lived Abstractions (ULAs) cease to be exemplifications of the nexus of the context, they need to be "dis/soluted," or thoroughly scrutinized. If a ULA is or has become incompatible with its context, another Useful Lived Abstraction should be co-created in its place. Dis/solution has two poles, "Forward" and "Reverse." The aforementioned refers to the Reverse pole: this pole *actively* works backward in its analysis of the ULA.

Dis/solution is also the *passive* mode of becoming all actual entities experience at some time or another within the duration of their reciprocally related event: what "is" will not always "be." Events lose the energetic vibrance they once had. They dis/solute. This is the Forward pole. The Anti-Shorthand works automatically in this pole. While the Reverse pole focuses specifically on the ULA and its deconstruction, the Forward pole illuminates the tragic "fact" of the eventual loss of the event which the ULA was co-created to participate in. Whitehead says, "The ultimate evil in the temporal world is deeper than any specific evil. It lies in the fact that the past faces, that time is a 'perpetual perishing.'"[40] Dis/solution in the passive tragic sense is another way of saying with Lamon Manuel, "Sh*t. Everything We Have Together Is Falling Apart."[41]

The Dis/solution poles of Forward and Reverse find a cool analogue in the deity Shiva. First, the active/Reverse region. Among a variety of characteristics in the tradition, Shiva is the deity of the Trimurti (trinity) associated with *acts* of chaos.[42] It could be said that if Shiva was to look at sheet of thick metal instead of an old wooden ship (a ship that The Jefferson Starship might want to sail on and take berry-flavored drugs during the voyage), there wouldn't be a regressive transformation from wood to ash, but a process of malleability in which the melted metal is still useful. Think of the old wooden ship in the third eye of Shiva as the multi/race/less ULA that has run its course. It could not survive the flame. Also, think of the sheet of metal as a ULA that still has purchase in its particular context. While Shiva might be able to melt the metal at hot temperatures with fire, he won't be able convert it to uselessness, since heated metal is still good for making things. ULAs remaining relevant throughout the passage of time in some sense might survive active Dis/solution because something about them still has relevance and influence.[43] Dis/solution asks whether the ULA in question is still "useful" after Dis/solution is enacted.

The passive/Forward pole ushers us directly into the tangible fluidity of process itself. We experience the aim of an allegory largely through the mind's eye, but we are within and co-create the flux of the universe and perceive this with not only the mind but also the senses. The context of Shiva's destructive work also implies that the stories of Shiva are not about a transcendent deity breaking the laws of and intervening in the natural world. Shiva symbolizes the passive/Forward Dis/solution that characterizes the world of actual entities. We all move toward Dis/solution. Daykeeper Hunbatz Men illuminates this perfectly in his statement about the Pre-Columbian philosophical systems of the regions of the lands currently referred to as southwest "Mexico," "Belize," "Guatemala," "Honduras," and El Salvador when he says,

> The Maya did not have a mythical concept of deities, but instead maintained that lords represented the forces of nature, with a sense of symmetry, a redundancy of plurality in unity and unity in plurality. Thus, the Mayan thinker maintained that lords, humans, and numbers were one in the same. And all, without exception, were dependent on the Absolute Being, Hunab K'u, whose symbolic representation is found on the pyramids as the Giver of Movement and Measure, in the geometric form of a square within a circle.[44,45]

From an emphasis on the tendency of many narratives of deities to have both mythical and natural interpretations, we can see how Shiva represents both poles of Dis/solution. While Dis/solution is not invested in questions of literal and figurative renderings of religions, it draws from the *active* character of Shiva as destroyer in the mythology as well as the *passive* character of the mythology interpreted in a largely cosmological way to clearly illustrate both poles.

In the discourse of philosophy of race, one the places in which the *passive* and *active* characteristics of Dis/solution show up is in Jennifer Lisa Vest's notion

"Mixed Race." In an employment of "Mixed Race" in a multiplicity of negotiations of identity and identity formation utilizing ULAs, we are forced to rethink what the categories mean. Further, we now must determine whether or not they are logically consistent. In the discourse of essential race, racial categories are virtually exclusive. They are defined *antagonistically*. What Vest does with "Mixed Race" is Dis/solution in that it connects categories thought only to be capable of exclusivity *relationally*.[46] Vest says,

> What people think they know about race precludes the possibility of Mixed race. In order to know that Mixed people exist, self-identified monoracials would have to give up knowing what race to assign people they see or meet. They would have to give up their concept of race. They would have to give up the urge to monoracialize, the need to assign a *true race* to Mixed persons. They may have to give up their own identity as a member of a race. They would have to admit that they don't know. They would have to abandon the hostile refusal to know Mixedness as a real thing. And giving all of that up is just asking too much. Giving that up would require white people give up all of their unearned privilege. Giving that up would require that Blacks give up their political solidarity movements, so essential in the face of institutional and individual racist violence. It might require that indigenous people give up their treaty rights, their nationhood or their sovereignty, or redefine them in the absence of Indianness as racial/based [ancestral or current dominations of] blood quantum.[47]

Vest argues that despite the definitional inconsistencies that should render "Mixed Race" people nonexistent, "Mixed Race" people indeed exist. "Mixed Race" is actually another category of race/trauma and is deployed in a battle for liberation where it subtly becomes a tool in service of the side Vest is fighting against. However, Dis/solution permeates this quote. What Vest offers here as a possibility for the creation of Useful Lived Abstractions may serve as substantially progressive if thought and practiced. In Dis/solution, multi/race/less/ness willingly takes the risk of losing political solidarity movements inseparable from race as an identity, treaty rights, etc., as confusing these potentially useless abstractions with ULAs might regress more than progress human collective liberation. Dis/solution is the leap that Vest and other indicate but never fully make. However, Vest demonstrates with impeccable clarity what Dis/solution could look like in the aforementioned quote.

Multi/race/less/ness promotes the challenging of ULAs through daring yet careful means. Responsible Dis/solution directly corresponds to the "less" segment of multi/race/less/ness in that it requires an attunement to the ways in which the ULAs under scrutiny operate within the context in question. Irresponsible Dis/solution is the exact opposite. Race/trauma has been a knife many philosophers of race and critical race theorists have attempted to treat instead of set the groundwork for a responsible gradual extraction. After some deconstructive work, Cornel West, Ibram Kendi, and Vest find themselves partaking in varying degrees in the treatment of race/trauma categories from nearly total reification to near extraction and serve as inspirations for us to proceed with caution in our challenging of deep symbols of human identification, such as race/trauma. Responsible Dis/solution is akin to Noel Ignatiev's statement/title of article "Treason to Whiteness is Loyalty to Humanity."[48] Ignatiev was known to call for the abolishment of "Whiteness." But his abolishment of the race/trauma category of "Whiteness" is by no means Irresponsible Dis/solution. In his deconstruction, Ignatiev holds that even when you renounce "Whiteness," it can always find a way to return, as the category is embedded in the very structures regulating thought and practice.[49] Responsible Dis/solution (RD), unlike Irresponsible Dis/solution (ID), is never a claim that one is beyond a prevalent and influential ULA in their context. In this particular moment, it is the Dis/solution, or differently stated, it is the "dissing" of the "solution" (that which is perceived as a unity of diversity in the Whiteheadian sense) with the potential to introduce novelty by a cautious taking apart of a ULA and considering whether or not the ULA in that form should remain as a useful a technology of identity.

Dis/solution is a sort of thought experiment phase of multi/race/less/ness. For example, the category "Indigenous" starts as more *descriptive* (e.g., "indigenous" refers to the original inhabitants of a geographical region not brought or arriving from another geographical region) eternal object. With movements of social justice, the term began to gradually emerge into a *prescriptive* and *descriptive* ULA, importing the "descriptive" meaning of "indigenous" into "Indigenous," the "prescriptive" foundation of a type of human identification and expectation. Whitehead refers to this emergent reciprocal relation between the lexical and experiential (read existential) use of words when he says, "Often the written word suggests both the spoken word and also the meaning, and the symbolic reference is made clearer and more definite by the additional reference of the spoken word to the same meaning."[50] People who were indigenous by *description* emerged by a tenuous relation between *description* and *prescription* into "Indigenous" people by conscious and unconscious conformation to the definition. The need for Dis/solution becomes evident when hegemonic institutions such as the legal system, academia, and the news media latch onto the word "Indigenous." This generalizes instead of relationally individuating within multiplicity.[51] It is as this point the potential of such a promising ULA is restricted to and considered a category more or less equivalent to the racial and race/related "Black" or "People of Color," as evidenced in its inclusion in the acronym "BIPOC." A possible approach of Dis/solution in an instance like this might be in the spirit of what Kwame Anthony Appiah calls "a moving from the realm of moral obligation to the realm of ethical flourishing."[52] The alternative is to push against the "*identities*: genders and sexual orientations, ethnicities and nationalities, professions and vocations" with the reverse engineering of Dis/solution.[53] With Dis/solution, we might reveal the engine, perhaps better than the previous model ("Native American"), is still releasing a bit too much pollution in the environment. Dis/solution, as Appiah asserts about his idea of "ethical flourishing," returns "to questions that absorbed the ancients: questions about what lives we should lead, defining the well-lived life as something more than a life to which our preferences are well-satisfied."[54] We may be comfortable identifying ourselves by racial and race-related terms. But comfortability is not only an enemy of progress. It is also the friend of oppression in its various forms. Dis/solution awakens us from "dogmatic slumber."

Dis/solution is a type of Derridean deferring in two ways: (1) its reverse engineering of presently influential ULAs and (2) the tension generated from the act of RD toward existing post-racial ULAs is always susceptible to "new takes."[55] The motion of Dis/solution is similar to Caputuo's rendering of Derrida's philosophy of the messianic. Of Derrida, Caputo says,

> Once the messianic is given determinate context, it is restricted within a determinable and determining horizon, but the very idea of the messianic, of messianicity, is to shatter horizons, to let the promise of something *tout autre* shock the horizon of the same and foreseeable.[56]

Dis/solution is an attunement to the deferring that organically occurs within the ingression (application to a situation) of post-racial ULAs as well as the process of conscious deliberation on whether or not said ULAs have run their course and need to be relegated to a less immediate position in the chain of influence.

Repetition

After the phase of Dis/solution determines that some ULAs are unfit to continue their status as prominent influences for the formation of post-racial identities, the process starts again. Phases 1–3 are now "repeated." Process philosopher and theologian Monica A. Coleman, in an extemporaneous discussion on Third Wave Womanism, succinctly articulated that the term "Black" means different things in different eras and/or different geographical regions, including and excluding different elements based on the context in question. Coleman's comments are rooted in a sense of Dis/solution. The process in the category of race/trauma over time is clearly evident.[57] But what is not evident is that racial categories only allow process to go so far. Under Coleman's articulation of a Third Wave Womanist understanding of "Blackness" as stated in the panel discussion referenced, in any epoch, one could reasonably conclude that a "Black" person is and may always be still "Black." However, as with the word "Indigenous," the tendency to commit the fallacy of misplaced concreteness with multi/race/less ULAs requires the need to return to the cycle and enact phases 1–3 indefinitely. Even if the metaphysics of post-racial linguistics are not hierarchical by the logical constraints of their definition like race/trauma, they still run the risk of confusing human identity with post-race ULAs.

Therefore, "Repetition" refers to not the reproduction of the same idea, but to the perpetual conscious enactment of process. Repetition is the loop in various strands of electronic and sample-based music. Are you really hearing the same thing over and over again, or is the sound of the consecutive cymbal (symbol) each four bars identical in its every appearance in the song? Where can we find this novelty of repetition I speak of? Doesn't that seem impossible? With every revolution, every breath that seems to have the exact same structure, something that wasn't there before bursts onto the scene. Each revolution of that cymbal adds something not there before. For the Deleuze of *Difference and Repetition*, both possibility of difference[58] itself and the perpetual re-presentation of the world are the backdrop from which identity emerge.[59] In Deleuze's own words, "To repeat is to behave in a certain manner, but in relation to something unique or similar which has no equal or equivalent."[60]

Repetition is also the lure for expansion. After the opening of the phase of Creativity to the fluid concretization of Useful Lived Abstractions to the thoughtful and cautious scrutiny of Dis/solution's deconstruction, the desire for more is craved. After the "liquicity" (a Drum and Bass term) of the world is realized and flux is accepted, one's eyes are open and focused on what they could *become* as opposed to what they've been quasi-naturally[61] mandated to *be*. James Brown kicked us off with "a revolution of the mind." Multi/race/less/ness is largely about our responses to a shift in thinking that reveals the inescapable impermanence of all. I argue that when this shift occurs, a sort of unlocking of Freeemasonic (or perhaps more accurately "Moorish") secrets about the illusion of "things," occurs. For José Francisco Morales Torres' phenomenologically based theological anthropology,

> Wonder is always a focused moment, whether it is the stable field, whether it is the whole "field" giving itself (e.g. a romantic dinner with the white tablecloths, the candles, the dimmed lighting, the beloved awaiting one's embrace) or a singular pixel within that field (e.g. the lover's twinkling eyes within the field of that romantic dinner). In either case, the initial gripping of the wonder-filled moment is a focused perceptual and sensuous (as in the senses) event prior to the subject's act of bracketing. Indeed, it can be said that is the distinct contours given pre-reflectively that pull or draw – or grip – one's attention away from all else.[62]

Repetition as an "initial gripping of the wonder-filled moment" comes yet again as the recurrent lure for the novel that draws us away from existing combinations of multiplicity and orients us toward a remixing of available eternal objects or "samples" toward a "sound" of post-racial human identity we've never heard before.

In this way, the same elements are prehended, whether from the background or the fore. They never go anywhere, for there is nowhere to go but the "here." They pass back cyclically from conceptual potentiality to physical actuality in the experiential event of the temporal world. But the uniqueness of "bracketing" *ex materia* and not *ex nihilo* is the newness that is characteristic of this definition of Repetition. Selves long to be recreated more equitably. And this recreation occurs within and because of an emergent and progressive "focused moment" of wonder, calling forth a human identity in process that is new through its reminiscent countenance as a mode of *becoming*.

Conclusion

This chapter is a drastic extension of multi/race/less/ness from its more succinct articulation in *Underground Rap as Religion* and aims to be a type of base from which a lived philosophy of responsible post-race can develop. To summarize shortly, the basic etymology of multi/race/less/ness as offered in URAR was updated. Since the more robust etymological genealogy offered in this sector of the work should not be taken to strictly indicate a *linear* motion from "multi" to "race" to "less" to "ness," the phases of Creativity, Useful Lived Abstraction, Dis/solution, and Repetition offer a *cyclical* schematic as to how multi/race/less/ness' expansion/action *could be* thought of in the world of post-race identity in motion. Creativity, as in Whitehead, is the "ultimate" activity, and is the act of converting the potentials of post-race/trauma identity formation into viable and equitable actualities. Useful Lived Abstractions are blocks of ice in the sun; in process but giving off the impression that they are (mostly) at rest. Dis/solution is a type of deconstruction intended to safeguard against any ULA committing Whitehead's fallacy of misplaced concreteness. Repetition is the impetus luring us to repeat and "remix" the cycle of multi/race/less/ness once more.

The following chapters will serve to represent how multi/race/less/ness is lived and/or can potentially be lived. The suggested more tangible instances of multi/race/less/ness we will now turn to less technically are culture, nationality, and genealogy. These three facets are the manifestations of multi/race/less/ness which, if successful, render race/trauma an unnecessary and potentially obsolete category of identity.

7 BIODIGITAL JAZZ: REFLECTIONS ON EMERGENT MULTI/RACE/LESS/NESS IN HIP-HOP AND BELIZE

Kevin Flynn: "Something unexpected happened."
Sam Flynn: "The Miracle."
Kevin Flynn: "The Miracle!" You remember. (laughs). ISOs. Isomorphic Algorithms. A whole new life form.
Sam Flynn: "And you created them?"
Kevin Flynn: (laughs). No. They manifested. Like a flame. They weren't really ... really from anywhere. The conditions were right, and they came into being. For centuries, we've dreamed of gods, spirits, aliens, intelligence beyond our own. I found them in here. Like flowers in a wasteland. Profoundly naïve. Unimaginably wise. (laughs) They were spectacular. Everything I'd hoped to find in the system, order, control, perfection ... none of it meant a thing. [We've] been living in a hall of mirrors. The ISOs ... shattered it. The possibilities of their root code, their digital DNA ... disease?! History! Science, philosophy, every idea [hu]man[ity] has had about the universe up for grabs. *BioDigital jazz, man.* (emphasis mine)[1]

A scene from Tron: Legacy

An Opening

Tron: Legacy dropped during my second year as a doctoral student in Claremont Graduate University's Philosophy of Religion program. The movie always stood out to me as a creative playing field for questions of metaphysics, God, creativity, and unexplored futures for the universe. When I began to teach philosophy, I continually offered it as required material for my fellow-learners (to the dismay of a few students who think the movie is total shit). Kevin Flynn, the tech genius protagonist played by Jeff Bridges, states in a speech toward the movie's beginning that he's creating a digital world known as "The Grid," "a digital frontier to reshape the human condition,"[2] fraught with various regressive structures of oppression.[3] Kevin Flynn found an answer to the world's ills: to systematize a virtual world where divisive and oppressive tendencies plaguing this world aren't possibilities. He strove to "create the perfect system."

But he was deceived. And the ISOs revealed this critical mistake.

This chapter is a more "technologically earthy" engagement of multi/race/less/ness than the last episode. Now that a fluid philosophical schema has been offered to theoretically explain multi/race/less/ness in relation to various strands of process, deconstructive, emergent, and poststructural approaches, I'd like to illustrate "on the ground" what a more technical description can never fully convey. Where multi/race/less/ness "lives" is not in a description of the theory, although as a theorist I acknowledge its potency. However, multi/race/less/ness literally "lives" within the *experience* of the fluidity of identity in process, a resounding harmony between the InnerSection of ideas and the world.

As an alternative to identities steeped in race/trauma, I move in this section to illustrate ways in which a post-race philosophy fueled by Responsible Dis/solution (RD) can create new and more expansive canvases upon which more equitable and progressive identities can be written. Three regions of thought were suggested in the previous chapter as being capable of more equitable multi/race/less identities never knowing definitive destination: culture, nationality, and genealogy. The foci of this chapter are culture and nationality. Underground Hip-Hop will be utilized as an instance of a multi/race/less culture, and Belize will serve as an instance of a multi/race/less nationality.

Without *descriptions* of multi/race/less/ness, one might reasonably conclude it is prescriptive. Whitehead, in his classic "airplane example," stated,

> The true method of discovery is like the flight of an aeroplane. It starts from the ground of particular observation; it makes a flight in the thin air of imaginative generalization; and it again lands for renewed observation rendered acute by rational interpretation.[4]

It is important to be cognizant of the fact that muti/race/less/ness in the corpus of my work started with my "particular observation" of identities in perpetual process in underground Hip-Hop culture and Belizean nationality but moves to the careful "imaginative generalization" of calling both of these regions "multi/race/less/." And as we return to the sites themselves, we will be looking at how the theory as it has been presented holds up.

This text starts in a type of "aura" articulated by Benjamin: the aesthetic quality of human identity as indefinitely co-creative and the process by which it gains and loses said identity as particular relations emerge and submerge.[5] Multi/race/

less identity formation/reformation in both Belize and underground Hip-Hop are viewed as sources of basic connection to the world for the human and are manifested in the aesthetic creations of food, music, historical narrative, moldings of the human self amid community, etc. Flynn is an artist of sorts in *Tron: Legacy*: he creates digital sentient entities and a background, from which emerge the ISOs, who impact the trajectory of humans outside The Grid. Multi/race/less/ness as "BioDigital" illustrates an Aesthetic Religion which makes never-ending significant meaning in/with the body, similar to what Mayra Rivera Rivera would refer to as "poetics of the flesh." The "jazz" is the spontaneity I argue manifests in both underground Hip-Hop culture and Belizean nationality.

Definitions

Culture

To refresh, I previously defined "culture" as "identity-shaping practices and ways of becoming." Culture is the Repetition and passing on of modes of life which have proved useful for human flourishing. Culture is always in a perpetual process. Culture in this work, unlike strict rubrics for behavior and thought as in the form of a rule spelled out in a legal document, performs a subliminal and underlying function of perpetually conditioning and valuing the eternal objects (conceptual historical artifacts) of periods in space-time. Culture doesn't necessarily determine what we see. Rather, culture sets the very stage for possibilities of perceiving our world(s).

So, culture is not only just (1) the *process* of the practice and perpetual revision of modes of becoming but also (2) the *embedded propositions* fueling said practice and perpetual revision. We can think of examples such as the *process* of harmonious[6] living with all entities in the universe, found in the *embedded proposition* of a type of identity formation becoming in community with all events. Victor Montejo calls this a "process of reciprocity," occurrent in his definition of "culture," which is,

> a forceful[7] relationship among the three fundamental categories: humans, nature, and the supernatural world, which are generative of life and existence. Each part or element individually affects the other and vice versa. So, to have some harmony, we must observe and comply with the rules and the norms of conduct established by the ancestors as we live and experience life in our communities.[8]

Another significant example of the *embedded propositions* and the *process* of our updated definition of "culture" here is that of Rastafari's "I and I." Trading a separatist notion of the universe being composed of individual "things" for a doctrine of all as instances of the diversely unified divine, I and I symbolizes a type of dynamic monism. This move, which could be compared to the infinite substance of Spinoza, does not reduce distinctions and individual experience but does shatter the metaphysical difference between "this" and "that." Such an *embedded proposition* of the I and I, a presupposition for individual and distinct practices of *process*, can take different forms in culture, such as the Italian-born Reggae singer Alborosie's practice of Rastafari, something some on the exterior of the practice find unthinkable, being that he would be categorized as "White" within the arbitrary hierarchy of race/trauma, and this *category* is antithetical to the teachings.[9] What must be understood is that in the philosophical schematic of Rastafari (the literal language of the tradition does not always reflect this), any practitioner renounces the categories of race/trauma by default, as to affirm them would be to deny I and I.

Closely related to my research definition of "culture" is ethnicity. In the previous section, "ethnicity" was defined as "those who share such identity-shaping practices [from culture] and perhaps other characteristics (e.g. common ancestral lineage)." Ethnicity has also been referred to as whatever social "group" one is a part of, and membership in said social "groups" is generally determined by factors such as country of birth, race, diet, religious beliefs, etc.[10] Ethnicity is modified here to only refer to the data, not its interpretation. Culture and nationality both prehend the data of ethnicity, but what they do with it through enacting the phase of Creativity is what gives it its character. In a multi/race/less framework, I would be amiss to conclude anything quasi-essential about an individual based on the raw data of their ethnicity, which perhaps tells me that people who have amalgamated said data within themselves have been referred to as "Asian," "Indigenous," "White," etc. in the past. Ethnicity without culture or nationality is virtually empty. We could also define "ethnicity" in this project as "the 'pure' "Creative" *potential* for the processual identity formations of nationality and culture."

Nationality

Nationality is that which places one under the jurisdiction and protection of governmental structures of any given country. Nationality is gained by being born within the borders of a particular country, being naturalized by gaining citizenship in the country, or some other means such as descent from a national. Nationality situates all who have it within the nation's historical and bureaucratic narrative. Nationality theoretically foregrounds a legal assurance that the human rights and privileges of citizens will be protected. Understanding and using the rights and privileges of nationality doesn't totally prevent one from abuse by hegemonic systems at play in a particular context, but it does offer a type of identity more legally substantial than race/trauma in its rootedness in the attempt to ensure the rights and privileges of *humans* under its jurisdiction are preserved.

Similar to ethnicity, nationality in multi/race/less/ness is a set of passive raw data that must be actively applied through Creativity if one desires to enact its rights and privileges. To be sure, the definition of nationality can be reduced to "the status of legally belonging to a nation either through birth, naturalization, or some other means." Noble Drew Ali stated,

> The citizens of all free National Governments, according to their national constitutions, are one family, bearing one free National name. Those who fail to recognize the free national name of their Constitutional government are classified as – Undesirables, and are subject to all inferior names and abuses, and mistreatments the citizens care to bestow upon them. And it is a sin for any group of people to violate the National Constitutional Laws of a free National Government; and cling to the names and principles that delude to slavery.[11]

While nationality is a technical mechanism for preservation of rights, privileges, and dignity of *free nationals* and does not serve as anything more on its own, it does establish solid legal basis of the preservation of the *citizen*, not those who identify legally or existentially as one or more "inferior names" (race/trauma). A truly holistic multi/race/less identity in process presupposes nationality.

Nationality in multi/race/less/ness applies to more than geographically demarcated regions known as "nations" and "countries." Of course, the modern definition of "nation" is fairly new, and there are other analogues pre-dating and/or presently existing that are outside of the "common" definition of "nation," such as Hip-Hop Culture. Hip-Hop is seen by many to be a BioDigital Jazz-based global nation consisting of those who practice or adhere to a serious engagement of elements of the culture. This is how one gains citizenship in the nation of Hip-Hop, a "place" outside of yet within any "space." The Hip-Hop Declaration of Peace articulates 18 guidelines/laws Hip-Hop citizens are expected to follow.[12] Nationality in this work is expanded to refer to instances such as these, where members engage in the manifestations of the culture as nationals. Multi/race/less/ness's usage of nationality is one in which the definitional necessity is coupled with a devout interest in the depths of that which said nationality attempts to represent and preserve by "law." In other words, to many, to be a member of the Hip-Hop nation means more than just practicing the art of graffiti. One is expected to perpetually confirm one's nationhood by the continual transformation of one's identity by the Repetition of the craft.

Aesthetic Religion

I argue that nationality and culture are both spaces in which Aesthetic Religion emerges. As I offered in URAR,

Aesthetic Religion focuses on how any particular art form receives and reshapes the world substantially in ways that command the desire for the audience (consisting of both partitioners and observers) to receive the mode of thought and the art form "devoutly" for its giving of perspective, meaning, and novel possibilities to the universe.[13]

Both culture and nationality as described here "receive and reshape the world substantially," and are art forms in this sense. They perpetually establish ULAs and enact Dis/solution on them. Aesthetic Religion is *descriptive* of the ways in which the flux of identity formation deeply impacts the human ever becoming in process. In other words, AR illuminates how the co-creation happening in the "occurrent arts" (Massumi) of culture and nationality displace classical notions of Gods and other deontological systems[14] and are the preliminary means of manufacturing life-guiding centers of significance (Pinn).[15]

Underground Hip-Hop

Underground Hip-Hop in URAR gives a succinct definition of underground Hip-Hop. It is as follows:

> Underground hip-hop be definition is a direct descendant of the social, artistic, and religious kairos society that created what is now known as "hip-hop" culture. Hip-hop culture consists of four aesthetic elements: graffiti (the first element created), b-girling/b-boying (known as "breakdancing" to some, and the second element created), DJing (the third element created), and MCing (or rapping, the final element created). The fifth element, instated by hip-hop pioneer Afrika Baambaataa, is knowledge and understanding, which includes understanding of personal history (also commonly known in hip-hop/underground hip-hop culture as "knowledge of self") and the discovery of ways in which the human can redefine herself/himself in the midst of coercive universal powers that be/come (governments, ideologies, etc.), devaluing revolutionary agency.[16]

Underground Hip-Hop as I define it returns to a synergy between the aforementioned elements long forgotten at the advent of popular rap music, a hijacking of one element of Hip-Hop (and the last element to be created at that) into a marketplace that robs it of the "aura" it knows situated within the InnerSected networks of multiplicity that are the Hip-Hop universe.

Beyond the relational practice of the elements solidified from the late 1960s to the mid-1970s in the Bronx,[17] underground Hip-Hop carries on the understanding articulated by pioneering Hip-Hop DJ and philosopher Afrika Baambaataa in his Zulu Nation that there is something emanating from the relationality of the elements that is more than just the elements themselves. KRS-ONE refers to that obscure yet tangible emergent "collective consciousness" as a new religion.[18] This gets at what Aesthetic Religion describes: art emerges into life emerges into ways of becoming, situating one in the world.

But we can also think of this emergence as a *process* occurrent in every instant of the Culture. Every modicum of the Culture in any given moment after the emergence of the religious element KRS pinpoints could be said to contain the energy of perpetual emergence. This indicates that the cycles of emergence bringing Hip-Hop Culture "on the scene" are always perpetually occurrent. In other words, each particle of the culture can be (un)defined as not fixed in a certain period of emergence but in continual actualization of the *process* of emergence. Each particle loops the past into the present which conjures the future as the loop moves as a tire on paths and picks up novel particles in its journey. This is analogous to the foundational four to six second loop of a Celia Cruz song that might drive a rap song. This loop contains all the potential for a more or less linear rendering of emergence. You can play it once, which is kinda similar to an emanation that doesn't require repetition in the "common" sense." But what happens when you start it again? The Repetition is a remix that reorganizes data previously made available in the four- to six-second clip simply (or complexly) by replaying it repeatedly. Repeated emergence in four to six seconds is infinitely slower than near-instantaneous revolutions I assert occur in the smallest bit of Hip-Hop energy. Think of the sample being played so rapidly that it sounds like garbled garbage to the ears. That's still too slow. But (perhaps) you get the idea. The point is that multi/race/less/ness in underground Hip-Hop is evidenced by emergence as not only a process that happens chronologically but a mode of becoming too rapid to even faintly measure.

Multi/race/less/ness finds its status as a "nontemporal accident" in my philosophy of underground Hip-Hop Culture as a process Aesthetic Religion. I state further,

> Underground hip-hop may be what hip-hop in the commercial world would look like if it did the following things: (1) maintained the unity of the elements and not separated rap from the culture and created an industry out of it on its own (many people falsely assume and perpetuate that hip-hop is rap, when rap is actually an element of hip-hop, as we've just seen); (2) preserved the freedom to access flow's infinite resources of creativity as the individual asserts his agency and in turn lures other individuals to assert their agency, (3) allowed the flourishing of the culture's multi/post/racial utopia (something commercial hip-hop has lost in a drastic way) and (4) kept the mechanism of critique which served as the living example of the antithesis of empire, colonialism, classism, gross and oppressive capitalism, and more, for this mechanism and

how underground hip-hop reshapes what it means to exist as an entity in the world is how it creates God.[19]

Of the four characteristics I identified of underground Hip-Hop, the third (which perhaps could or should be the first) is an organic emergence made possible by the particular histories of the plethora of human events in NYC at the creative moments of the Culture's inception. Many of these humans were from the areas now referred to as the "Caribbean." Many were US descendants of race/trauma schemas of oppression such as chattel slavery. Others had dominant ancestry from Greece and Germany, etc. There is no universal law mandating any sort of automatic or "natural" antagonism or fundamental difference between people who happen to be from different regions of the world. Even though much of the outside world believed that there was, Hip-Hop organically coalesced into the possibility for another way of relational *becoming* as opposed to separatist *being*.

The "line" symbolizes a strict and heavily guarded border between "this" and "that." Canada is not the United States, the United States is not Mexico, and so on. Why is this the case? Because an agreed-upon dividing line "says" so. If one were to remove the lines, especially at the border regions, as Anzaldúa directs our attention to, one side of the line might seem very much like the other with this arbitrary separation between events as the only substantial difference.[20] On the other hand, the "perforation" also comes between one event and another, but offers the possibility of both events going back and forth, enfolding and unfolding so that what was on one side could potentially wind up on the other. The DJs' crossfader at midpoint can cause the two songs reciprocally relating in the fleeting instant to become indistinguishable to the ear. In the moment of the fader at midpoint, they merge into the illusion of one multiplicitous sound because they are *perforated*, not *lined*. This is the sort of "dance" identity underwent in the multiverse of original Hip-Hop that underground Hip-Hop perpetually reveres with what I called "Aesthetic Religious Shrine Organisms" (an honor to the culture by repeating it).[21] Of dance, Erin Manning eloquently says,

> The dancer's body – in the case of relational movement, the two of us moving together – provides a glimpse into the ways in which movement creates the potential for unthinking dichotomies the populate our worlds: abstract, concrete, organic-prosthetic, alive-dead, mind-body, actual-virtual, man-woman. It's not that movement directly undermines these dialectical concepts. It's that movement allows us to approach them from another perspective: a shifting one. When we are no longer still, the world lives differently.[22]

Hip-Hop Culture is the sort of movement Manning is speaking of. It not only caused people to travel out of their neighborhoods to pursue its irresistible energy but also moved them beyond what was familiar to them. In this coming to consciousness, perforations emerged from lines. The characteristics making each event a distinct becoming were still noticeable and practiced in the experiential consciousness of the participant (the "self"). However, a shift in thinking from lines *closing off* outside influence to perforations *opening up* the possibility for influence "allows us to approach . . . from another perspective: a shifting one." In the multi/race/less possibilities orchestrated by the fifth element's Creative concrescence of the first four, persuading a multiverse where identity formation is based on skill and contributions to the way of life and not a hierarchy of race/trauma, "the world lives differently."

In *Underground Rap as Religion*, I offered that,

> I felt it was necessary to create a lens through which the reader could view the following chapters. Without it, the examples, references, and histories I access throughout the text might seem very out of place, since much of the discussion in hip-hop studies has never addressed (or admitted) the historical difficulties with a solely Afronormative/Afrocentric/Afro-original understanding of the culture . . . . The Afronormativity that occurs in much of the literature in the field should not be expected in my work, and multi/race/less/ness is my elongated reason why.[23]

Multi/race/less/ness was literally my answer to what I saw (and still see) is a hiccup in much of the scholarship in Hip-Hop studies: the tendency to constrict the dialogue to the race/trauma category of "Blackness." Due to my assertion that Hip-Hop is built on a post-race metaphysic (multi/race/less/ness), I decided that what was being published needed to be complicated by a philosophical outlook, such as process thought.

Challenge: The Origins of Hip-Hop Debate and Its Relation to Multi/race/less/ness

At the writing of this chapter (Aug 2024), there is a current dialogue around which race/trauma and or race-related category is responsible for founding Hip-Hop. To state the question at hand, it is this: Were "Black" "Americans" responsible for the creation of Hip-Hop with "Caribbean" people (Co-Creation Narrative or CCN) or was it totally a "Black" "American" Culture many "Caribbean" people came into after it was already established (the Sole Narrative or SN)? There are those on the side of the CCN, such as KRS-ONE (MC/philosopher), Busta Rhymes (MC), Crazy Legs (B-Boy), Thirstin' Howell III (MC), Fat Joe (MC), Pete Rock (producer) Grandmaster Caz (one of Hip-Hop's pioneering MCs), Derrick Colón (historian), etc. The most vociferous proponents of the SN side are Lord Jamar (MC), Tariq

Nasheed (documentarian), and others. The CCN has been "generally" accepted by many followers of Hip-Hop and has been either overtly stated or implied in various songs and movies, with Common's "Like They Used to Say"[24] and *Brown Sugar*, both of which have purchase in both "surface level" and underground manifestations of the Culture.[25]

Due to what has been marked as Hip-Hop's fiftieth anniversary on August 11, 2023,[26] and perhaps the induction of the element of B-Girlin'/B-Boyin' (Breakdancing) into the 2024 Olympics,[27] there has been widespread attention on the Culture. Since many people outside of Hip-Hop were unaware of the actual history of the Culture, the assumption was that it was created by so-called "Blacks," a designation in this case primarily signifying those who would be subclassified as "African American," thus excluding those who could be referred to under the main heading with predominant ancestry in Cuba, Puerto Rico, Jamaica, Barbados, and other nations in the "Caribbean."[28] The key point of contention is that many of the pioneers of the Culture were from or had predominant ancestry from said island regions. A prevalent subfield of the debate is whether the cultures present in these so-called "Caribbean" regions had any impact on the birth of Hip-Hop Culture, or were the participants who happened to emerge from said regions from birth or ancestry taking on the cultural practices they learned from "Black" "Americans." Another issue is how the time frame of creation and period of origin is defined. A parallel is the question of the possibility of Hip-Hop to be thought in the key of race/trauma.

The Ancestries of Hip-Hop's Founders and What Can Be Claimed Because of Them

Historian Tariq Nasheed, director of the 2024 documentary *Microphone Check* (By the way, it's quite exciting to be writing about this while it's happening right in front of us. This is a great instance of philosophy engaging the current motions of the world.), has garnered critical amounts of attention for articulating in interviews and curating in the film what I'll refer to as the Radical Sole Narrative (RSN), or the position that not only were those most readily symbolized by the linguistic economy of race/trauma as "Black" "Americans" the only *creators* of Hip-Hop Culture, but also the position that all of its influences came from those classified as "Black" "American." Nasheed says,

> so we're saying we're not gonna let that [the stealing of credit for so-called "Black" "American" artforms from so-called "Black" "American" people] happen with hip-hop . . . we're gonna tell the definitive history. We got the original pioneers, and we're letting them tell the story from their own words . . . a lot of people were saying, including Caribbeans and Latinos, "That's divisive." Okay, tell us what the Caribbeans brought. They're trying to say for years that we got

the sound system concept [the tradition of DJs attempting the loudest PA set, something Kool Herc, a Jamaican immigrant to the Bronx, conceivably would have seen growing up] from the Caribbean. That's not true. There were sound systems here in Brooklyn . . . Then they tried to say, "Well, we got rapping from Jamaican toasting." Not true. Nobody heard Jamaican toasting [the tradition of DJs talking over reggae instrumentals or "riddims," something Herc also was exposed to in Jamaica] records.[29]

Let's park here for a quick second. Nasheed is right that in *Microphone Check*, the pioneers of the culture are telling the story from their own words. But what's happening here is what I've elsewhere referred to in a forthcoming book chapter as "a laking of the sea," or the reduction of the data by the way in which it is constrained and re-presented.[30] I contend that Nasheed, (in)formed by the background assumption that those classified as "Black" "American" are the sole originators of Hip-Hop, moves into creating his documentary based on a type of confirmation bias. This is a contrast to what Simondon is engaging in what he calls "encyclopedism," or the move to systematize information into a nonhierarchical rhizome. Simondon, speaking of Diderot and d'Alembert's *Encyclopedia*, says,

> If the *Encyclopedia* appeared as a powerful and dangerous work, then it was not because of its veiled or direct attacks on a certain abuse of privilege, nor because of the "philosophical" aspect of certain articles; there were more violent libels and pamphlets than the *Encyclopedia*. The *Encyclopedia* was respectfully feared because it was moved by an enormous force, that of a technical encyclopedism, a force that had brought together powerful and enlightened protectors; this force existed by itself, because it responded to the needs of its time, more than political or financial reforms did; it was this force that was positive and creative, and which realized an equally remarkable assembly of researchers, editors, correspondents by granting a faith to this team composed of men who collaborated without being connected through social or religious communities; a great work had to be carried out.[31]

Many in the mid-twentieth century suspected that the developments of digital technologies would "reshape the human condition." Heidegger critiqued this relationship between technology and the human, asserting the dangers of "Enframing," or humanity's potential to transform nature into mere objects devoid of their own organic expressions of "jazz."[32] For Simondon, the nonhierarchical relationality of divergent bits of data within one encyclopedic "event" as members of an "ensemble" is needed to liberate humanity from increasing levels of compartmentalization. What novelty might emerge if Nasheed were to conduct from the vantage point of encyclopedism or the "ensemble," which Simondon succinctly defines as "the totality . . . of dynamical schemas functioning?"[33]

In a defense of statements made by Fat Joe, one of the most vocal proponents of the CCN, Caz says,

> Some of the first Latinos in Hip-Hop were down with ME (emphasis Caz's). Disco Wiz, Charlie Chase, Joe Conzo, the man who took Hip-Hop's baby pictures, Prince Whipper Whip. Okay? All Latinos, all part of my crew. Okay, so there's no way I could talk about there not being a Latino presence in the culture of Hip-Hop. Now I have stuck my foot in my mouth several times on Vlad interviews, and they probably caught an off... comment or something like that. But let me clear that up for all my brothers, my Latino brothers and sisters in Hip-Hop, I've been an advocate since day one. So knock the bullshit off.[34]

Caz is not only standing in solidarity with Fat Joe but also showing how his words in another interview with VladTV were taken in ways he didn't intend, similar to how I hold they were used by Nasheed. In said video, Caz stated, "Latinos weren't involved directly that much in the early days of Hip-Hop. One or two."[35] However, he goes on to state the involvement of his first DJ partner, DJ Disco Wiz, whose family hails from Puerto Rico and Cuba, and would be classified under the metaphysics of US race/trauma and race-related categories as "Latino/x/é." He also credits those with ancestors from Puerto Rico as being among those who developed B-Girling and B-Boying.[36] The words "involvement in the beginning of" arguably indicate that for Caz, these artists were part of the creation of the culture. And if the testimony of a pioneer, the status Nasheed raises as ranking very high in providing credible information on Hip-Hop's origins, is true, even one counterexample shatters the absolute propositions (1) "there were NO 'Caribbean' influences in the culture" and (2) "those pioneers who happened to be from the 'Caribbean' were merely ingressing 'Black' 'American' cultural forms, not 'Caribbean' cultural expression."

Even if these artists are on the periphery of the Culture, or what Simondon refers to as "supplementary structures (and nowhere in my work do I assert this to be true)," they have incorporated themselves into the totality and have become co-creators.[37] Through an honest return to the mulipicity from which the Culture emerges, we have a multi/race/less counterexample providing us something resembling a post-race/trauma way of understanding the origins. This act of Creativity as encyclopedism composes the impenetrable mystery of the universal lure of Hip-Hop, and all involved are co-creators from the view of multi/race/less/ness with no attempts, as Whitehead says, to engage in "the combat of productive force with productive force or destructive force with destructive force, but it lies in the patient operation of the overpowering rationality."[38]

Hip-Hop as a multi/race/less philosophy doesn't posit a centrality of the race/trauma category "Black" or any other race/trauma or race-related category as a starting point of the Culture. With the convergence of a variety of fluid and multidirectional human events into the multiverse of the Culture, it proves difficult to say what was chronologically first. Maybe there was no definite first. Nasheed argues for historical analogues to elements such as B-Girling/B-Boying in "Black" "American" dances of the 1930s and 1940s, and the early B-Girls and B-Boys attest to these influences. But others were influenced by traditions that predate or were contemporaries of these dances, such as the eternal objects of Groucho Marx routines, kung fu moves, Salsa dances, the dances of the nations in the present-day United States when the colonizers arrived, etc.[39]

Unlike Nasheed, KRS-ONE suggests that Hip-Hop's origins are rhizomic, or a nexus dependent on various non-stratified relations. For KRS, Hip-Hop is a "new civilization," a way of saying that Hip-Hop is "human culture" in its emphasis on the organic and most natural becoming of unbridled identity formations. He says, "It is the first thing humans do when they come into existence."[40] All of Hip-Hop's elements have prehistoric manifestations, which means the Hip-Hop Culture refers to a modern return to ancient modes of *human* becoming. If one accepts the plethora of evidence that homo sapiens originate in the regions we now refer to as "Africa," the most ancient ways of human could be said to be "African." This is of course not specific enough to indicate what proponents of the SN and RSN mean when they use the race/trauma term "Black" and "FBA (or Foundational Black American, which refers to humans with ancestries in the chattel slavery period of the US)." But perhaps it points to a way in which the SN and RSN sheds insights into strands of the CCN. Imani Kai Johnson's concept of "dark matter," drawing from its use in physics as referring to the non-luminous substance composing most of the universe, is used in her work on the B-Girl/B-Boy cypher to describe how the gravitational pull of "Blackness" shapes the Culture.[41] However, multi/race/less/ness experimentally asserts that race/trauma and race/trauma-related terms inadvertently function as parallaxes by definition. This causes them to obscure that which proponents of the SN and RSN desire to more fully appear: a truly authentic Hip-Hop history.

How Are We Defining "Creation?"

Depending on how "creation" is interpreted, the door can either be opened or closed on people potentially admitted. Nasheed defines "creation" as the act of bringing something into becoming (or maybe into "being" for him). For Nasheed, this is the role of "Black" "Americans." Of B-Girling/B-Boying, Nasheed says,

> So what happens is we let people come in and just take the culture and turn us into guests in the culture. Because that's what they're trying to do with the whole Latin situation. They want to go from "Latinos were 50/50" to "Latinos actually created breakdancing and Black folks got it from them." That's where

it's going and that's why a lot of people are like "Hey, let's put a time out on this and back it up and tell the truth."[42]

So, Nasheed has created a slippery slope fallacy in his framing of the issue as "Caribbeans" progressively ousting "FBAs" from creator status in Hip-Hop altogether. From the perspective of multi/race/less/ness, nothing could be further from the data. Along with the impossibility of Hip-Hop to be the event it has become and continues to become since the late 1960s without the direct creative input and influence of "FBAs," none of the proponents of the CCN have ever suggested this. They've merely argued that all creators must be acknowledged. The RSN in its gatekeeping of the idea of creation embodies the very rewriting of history that Nasheed accuses the opposing side of.

Under a chronological mapping of Hip-Hop playing by Nasheed's definition of "creation," we could only attribute two out of the five core elements of Hip-Hop Culture to "FBAs," namely the elements of Graffiti, credited to Philadelphia writer Cornbread,[43] and Emceein', arguably credited to Coke La Rock out of the Bronx.[44] Both Coke La Rock and Cornbread would be classified by Nasheed as "FBAs" Deejayin', widely accepted as the creation of Kool Herc, doesn't fall within the boundaries of either the SN or the RSN, as Herc's nationality is Jamaican.[45] The element of Knowledge and Understanding also doesn't qualify either, as Nasheed himself reminds us that Afrika Baambaataa, its founder, comes from Jamaican and Barbadian ancestry."[46] B-Girlin'/B-Boyin' isn't much help either, since the art's beginning isn't credited to a particular person as the other elements are, and even those who Nasheed refers to as "Latinos" with "Caribbean" ancestries are said by him to have significantly shaped it.[47] The reason Nasheed can defend the SN and RSN is because he incorporates eyewitness and first-hand accounts into his historiographical approach to argue that "Caribbeans" were mimicking "FBAs." There is a marginal position Nasheed raises that accurately credits the Disco DJ Hollywood as a precursor to Kool Herc, as he not only played breakbeats[48] but also performed an early version of rapping over said breaks.[49] This is problematic for the whole of Nasheed's argument, as this stance depends on timelines that aren't false but arguably are not as readily known and accepted as foundational to Hip-Hop's history. Further, Nasheed's historiography relies more on impossible to verify assumptions that the totality of what influenced the art of artists readily considered founders was the cultural productions of so-called "FBAs." Nasheed criticizes historian Derrick Colón for citing pioneering B-Boy figures of Puerto Rican ancestry not known to him and dismisses them as pioneers due to their obscurity *to him*.[50,51] It is hard to see how Nasheed's use of DJ Hollywood would be much different than what he charges Colón for. Ironically, he proceeds to do something similar by attributing the beginning spark of all elements squarely to so-called "FBAs" by what is in my estimation poorly founded and convenient altering of creation stories by using more marginal factual accounts. In other words, "creation" doesn't just indicate the *appearance* of an element of Hip-Hop culture, but its *development* into a ULA with fluidly definite characteristics that seem to maintain a form and considerable influence throughout time.

To use B-Girlin'/B-Boyin' as an example, the emergence of this style of dance has roots in the gang cultures of the era and developed in the parties Kool Herc and others gave in the early 1970s.[52] B-Boys such as Spy (who was of Puerto Rican ancestry but under the categorizations of race/trauma may have been considered "FBA" or "Black")[53] and The Nigga Twins (who would be classified under the categorizations of race/trauma as "Black" or "FBA") were among those to inaugurate the emergence of this form of dance into the context that would become Hip-Hop Culture.[54] In the mid-1970s, dancers such as JoJo, Batch, and Crazy Legs (who were of Puerto Rican ancestry and would be defined under the race-related classifications of the time as "Latino") added styles that would become eternal objects along with those so-called "FBAs" (or those "passing" as such, as in the case of Spy) that are the fluid foundation of what the art of Breakdancing is today.[55] KRS says,

> Hip-Hop cannot, would not have existed specifically without Puerto Ricans. Specifically, Cubans were here. Hattians were here. Dominican Republic was here. Everybody was here. ALL of South America BEEN in the Bronx. (Emphasis KRS) But Puerto Ricans in particular sided with the Black folks here. And the Jamaicans were coming in as well. And this group of Puerto Ricans, Jamaicans, and American Blacks made Hip-Hop. Not American Blacks. Not Puerto Ricans. Not Jamaicans. ALL of 'em! (emphasis KRS)[56]

What KRS gives us here is a short chronology of a process of creation by people identified as various categories of race/trauma thought in the dominant metaphysics of the negotiating of humanity to indicate essential impenetrable differences (the line). In Hip-Hop's fluid foundational characteristics, the possibilities of InnerSectional creativity itself are reimagined through the BioDigital Jazz of the then-burgeoning Aesthetic Religion, thus significantly challenging Nasheed's SN and RSN through a balanced view of the history (the perforation).

Can Hip-Hop Culture Be Thought/Thought of within the Metaphysics of Race/Trauma?

Much of what I've covered so far in this less than comprehensive analysis of the challenges brought up against what I'm interpreting as multi/race/less/ness in Hip-Hop has focused on dividing the crediting of the origins of the Culture by racial lines. Fat Joe's statement that "When hip-hop started, it's Latinos and blacks, – half and half"[57] on the CCN side and Lord Jamar's comment "in the beginning stage of Hip-Hop, in the creation stages of Hip-Hop, this was very much a Black American youth thing that had no outside influences from Puerto Rico, Jamaica, or any type of place that you may name"[58] on the SN and RSN part of the spectrum are both appealing to the categorizations of race/trauma and race-related categories as plausible means of discussing Hip-Hop Culture. But based on the CCN's interpretation of the Culture, one is warranted to ask whether or not this type of linguistic organization of Hip-Hop is appropriate.

On this point, KRS-ONE says in a lecture during the 2014 instance of Canadian Music Week,

> Hip-Hop is that vision. Nowhere else on earth do you see the [Dr, King's] "I Have a Dream" speech actualized but in Hip-Hop. Nowhere. Nowhere else on earth. This is the only international <u>culture</u> that really does not operate by way of race. Every other culture and ethnicity on the globe operates internally based on race . . . . Hip-Hop is the most influential [culture] toward the "I Have a Dream" goal. Most. (emphasis mine)[59]

If Hip-Hop Culture does not operate by way of race, it might skew a truly authentic perspective of Hip-Hop to view it through the lens of race/trauma. Of course, one can say that those whom the society readily refers to "Black" "Americans" created a culture where race was displaced as a primary method of identification. But it could also be said that the framing of the origin and creation stories in this way reinforces race/trauma as a category, which is advantageous for proponents of the SN and RSN who are very interested in maintaining arbitrary colonial "lines" in a postcolonial context. Following the presupposition of this work that the category of race/trauma is by definition and usage intrinsically traumatic, hierarchical, and antagonistic, he puts most of his Dis/solutive emphasis on identity formation in Hip-Hop Culture as that of "nationality."

KRS-ONE says in the same lecture,

> King Martin [Dr. Martin Luther King] believed that the true and just nation was a multicultural nation that had nothing to do with race. Nothing to do with class. It had to do with the character inside of you. It had to do with your skill. It had to do with who you associate yourself with, not your color, not your class, not your religion, none of that.[60]

He also says,

> I'm giving you two different things. 1. keep 1979 [in mind], our rise into technology, rise into the mainstream . . . mainstream is rejecting us, saying 'We don't want your kind around here.' But we're coming up saying [to the

mainstream] 'But we don't want YOUR kind around HERE. And so now a parallel universe is created. But this parallel universe has roots. And its roots go into the 60s civil rights movement separatist attitude, to be honest with you... Instead of using "separatism," let me use the word "nationalism." Hip-Hop comes from out of a nationalistic mentality. BUILD YOUR OWN NATION! (emphasis KRS)[61]

What is interesting is that while Lord Jamar and Tariq Nasheed strongly critique and dismiss KRS and Fat Joe's CCN statements around Hip-Hop's beginnings, they speak highly of Hip-Hop-fostered comradery between so-called "Caribbeans" in general and those with ancestry in Borikén (present-day Puerto Rico) and Xaymaca (present-day Jamaica) in particular, shown not only in the development of the culture but also the displacement of race/trauma lines.[62,63] How much more attuned to this comradery might Jamar, Nasheed, and others be if they were to begin to view Hip-Hop Culture not through the perspective of race/trauma but through multi/race/less/ness' posture of rhizomic perpetual creative recreations? The strength of underground Hip-Hop for so many people is its ability to devalue race/trauma as a necessary or even helpful articulation and concept of human identity in formation while still being able to pinpoint its effects, as is evidenced in the work of various underground Hip-Hop adherents and practitioners striving to maintain the post-race advances of the "next universe" to intensify justice in the world. KRS illustrates how Dr. King embodied this cornerstone of what would become Hip-Hop Culture.

Belize as an Instance of Multi/race/less Nationality

In reference to nationality, which has revealed itself in Hip-Hop Culture, I'd like to explore another "on the ground" instance of it in Belize. This chapter is being written after immersing myself in the culture(s), my familial culture(s), for nearly a month, experiencing its ebbs and flows in my paternal ancestral lands. Writing this "fresh off the boat" from my time just beneath southern Mexico's border at Chetumal has activated eternal objects of poetic wisdom, foods, geography, and dormant energies stashed in my flesh.

The area that is now modern-day Belize is a geographic and theoretical region caught within deep histories of wise and prolific Pre-Columbian civilizations, conquests by the colonization projects of Spain and Britian including but not limited to commodification of valuable resources, piracy, natural wonders, and expressions of metaphysics as seen in the Dugu of the Garifuna and cosmological theology of those history has referred to as the "Maya." During the occupation of Spain in the region commonly called "Central America," modern-day Belize was claimed under its jurisdiction but was never fully colonized due to the vehement resistance of the pre-colonial residents. British awareness and interest increased in the 1600s after ship robbers began hiding themselves and treasure there, and the British soon discovered that mahogany and diewood were prevalent.[64] Britain eventually encroached on the territory, oscillating between making and breaking agreements with Spain to export mahogany and other commodities. This "violation" of Spanish domains sparked several wars with the British over the jurisdiction in the late 1700s, finally culminating in 1798 with the famous *Batalla del Cayo de San Jorge* (the Battle of Saint George's Caye), which declared Britain the victor and marked the last attempt at Spanish control.[65] The territory was officially annexed into the British "Caribbean" in 1862, and became the last Central American demarcation to gain independence in 1981. The regime of Porfirio Diaz, the thirty-third president of the then newly-established Mexico, considered Belize to be a part of its own lands until the late nineteenth century when Diaz ceded all claims to Britain in exchange for a cease of their sale of weapons to "rebels" in the Caste Wars.[66] Also, due to discrepancies in the interpretations of the Treaty of Paris, Guatemala has claimed some or all of the region as its own since its signing. Intermittent ideological, legal, and military conflicts with Guatemala have occurred from the inception of British occupation to the present, with the most recent being the push to take the territorial dispute to the International Court of Justice. A vote among Belizean citizens went in favor of taking the matter to the ICJ, but a date has yet to be set.

What is of supreme importance here is the confluence of a geographical region with a particular amalgam of contrasting influences that converge into culture(s) and is legally represented as a nationality. Pimienta-Bey, in an interview with me, appealed to historian Martin Delaney to assert that a person can only garner full human respect when they are presented to the world in a national capacity, akin to what Noble Drew Ali offered as an alternative to the category of race/trauma.[67] In the multi/race/less instance of Belize, I hold that the legal presentation of nationality is extremely intertwined with the culture(s) in ways that map onto Drew Ali's notion of the idea. Multi/race/less/ness is at all turns a "Moorish" undertaking.

The ethnic data and cultural modes of becoming Belizean nationality, when included and presented in a national capacity, gives off a chimera in that it represents without reducing multiplicity.

Let's flesh out what I mean by "representing without reducing multiplicity," starting with the etymology of the word "Belize." The origins of the name are uncertain, but there are three theories usually offered. One is that it is a Spanish pronunciation of "Wallace," the surname of the legendary (and probably fictitious) Scottish buccaneer Peter Wallace, who is said to have started an early settlement of people not native to the region. "Wallace" is thought to have undergone several transitions in the tongues of Spanish conquistadors and friars from "Wallis" to "Baliz"[68] until it eventually became "Belize" in English.[69] Another is the suggestion that it comes from the Spanish "Bella isla," or "beautiful isle," referencing the numerous cayes (cayos) of the region. Also offered as an origin is that "Belize" is a derivative of the Yucatec *belakin*, which has been popularly rendered as "land facing the sea." However, Matthew Restall argues that a translation more faithful to the actual etymology present in the word would be "road to the east." "Belize" coming from *belakin* was popularized by a pair of Guatemalan writers in the 1950s and introduced into the imagination of Belizeans by George Cadle Price, known as "the father of the country."[70]

Restall's own theory about the origin of the term "Belize" deviates from all three of these origin stories and in my opinion not only makes the most sense etymologically but also conceptually and "mythically" resonates with multi/race/less/ness' suspicion of representation sans the reduction of multiplicity. Restall shows that in the Yucatec, Itza, and Mopan languages, *bel* can be translated as "on the way to," and *itza* is said to possibly reference the northern Guatemalan kingdom of Peten Itza, with "Itza" also being the name of the lineage that conquered the "Yucatán." Peten Itza stood until 1697, when it was finally conquered by the Spanish after several attempts. Spanish pronunciation of the names sometimes encountered difficulty with "t" sounds, so it is quite conceivable that the *bel itza* ("on the way to Itza") could have transformed in speech to *bel iza*, with the Spanish *Belice* followed by the now commonly used "Belize."[71]

Allegorically, could it be said that Belize shares with its name a nexus of human identity formation that is always on the way? Restall states that the objective of pre-contact cartography wasn't to establish the singularity of a particular location but to indicate direction.[72] This sounds like Whitehead's description of Creativity: it evades imagery yet can exhibit it in faint bursts of energy.[73] What does it mean to house identities in the *paths* as opposed to the *destinations*? What if Belize's identity formations are thought of less as a *place* and more as a *process* somehow slowed down by yet still exceeding the imaging of nationality?

Upon first encounter with Belize, many people become bewildered by an overwhelming sense of "circular squares." Since it's the only country in the region referred to as "Central America" where English is the official national language, many visitors are surprised to hear a large if not predominant number of conversations on the streets in Spanish. Secondly, dishes common to Jamaica, such as rice and beans, stew(ed) chicken, and plantains, are thought by many to be just about all you'd find in Belize because it can tend to take on by proxy eternal objects associated with other nations in the postcolonial British "Caribbean." This conception may be confounded in the minds of some that a large part of Belizean cuisine consists of dishes such as empanadas, tamales, garnaches (tostadas with refried beans, a habanero and vinegar-based onion sauce, and various vegetable toppings), and salbutes (a staple in the so-called "Yucatán" consisting of vegetables, beans, and some type of meat on top of a disc of fried masa), for in the cultural imagination of many, they are so-called "Mestizo" and/or "Hispanic" and not British-colonized "Caribbean."

Thirdly, those referred to as the "Maya" and "Creole" (with the latter narrowly defined by many as the descendants of the enslaved and British colonizers, even though this definition misses specifics of the "group") are not essentially defined by/as either "group." Therefore, those who would be classified under each "group" by the confines of the definition itself are not exempt from authentic relation with and transitioning into and out of other "groups." Rather, the "groups" as they are metaphysically situated within the landscape of Belizean culture(s) exemplify authentic relation, which is a Repetition of Dis/solution, transgressing and reshaping of the ethnic content of "groups," content which in conceptual and empirical appearance may more or less remain quite similar. In Belize, panades (empanadas Belizean style) aren't thought of as "Maya" cuisine, though the masa and various other elements from which they are made such as achiote (recado) have been developed in the food of the region for thousands of years by the "Maya." Panades are understood as the indefinite reciprocal relations of the enfolding and unfolding of events encased within perforated receptacles. Thus, panades are not "Maya," "Creole," "Mennonite," "East Indian," "Chinese," "British," "Mestizo," or "Garifuna." They are the Creative Repetitions of becoming "Belizean," an emergence of an InnerSection and virtually a sublation of all the aforementioned "groups" in an ever-becoming national capacity definitionally and existentially.

A wonderful freeze frame of the rapid multidirectional movements legally represented to the world by Belizean nationality is,

> Belize Culture is a colorful latticework of different peoples, being themselves and being with each other. To call it a melting pot at this point is almost wrong, because Belize doesn't have one single culture, but instead one people with many cultures. You can spend a lifetime here and perhaps still not experience it all.[74]

BioDigital Jazz in the InnerSections of Belizean events creates a multi/race/less "on the way" of identity formations that never feigns a fixed destination. In other words, the "latticework" of Belize's cultures is characterized "precisely" by their difficulty to be characterized and their lure into the presentational immediacy of experiencing them as primary/primordial as opposed to clearly defining them. Belizeans are "being themselves and being with each other," a reciprocal relation between perforations. The element of nationality implied in the words "one people with many cultures" illustrates how the given definition of "nationality" makes possible a more equitable conception of identity formation.

Multi/race/less/ness in Light the Absence of "Classical" Race/trauma/ in Belize

But is Belize based in race/trauma enough to be multi/race/less/ness? Obviously, Belize has a sordid colonial history. However, the folk historiography founds modern-day Belize on the narrative of a comradery between the enslaved and the British settlers known as the "baymen" against the Spanish.[75] Many, such as the legendary writer and revolutionary Evan X. Hyde, have dismissed the legend of this "partnership" as a ploy by the power structures to stratify the society, particularly creating and reinforcing the superior status of the "Creole" over the Garifuna.[76] I argue that this sanitized national mythology "erases" the dominant/subordinate human stratification while encoding an automatic uncritical reverence of the colonial power, making this advance possible. This sleight-of-hand is the analogue to race/trauma from which Belizean multi/race/less nationality emerges.

Imperfect strides toward a type of equity are found in the tapestry of Belizean colonial history, such as those of Col. Edward Marcus Despard between 1784 and 1790, who attempted to create an alternative (and unpopular) settlement of mahogany cutters returning to present-day Belize from the then British occupied Mosquito Coast and open to all.[77] Also, slavery ended in the region in 1838, and the "lines" drawn creating and hence separating those who were robbed of their nationalities and personhood (status as property under the race/trauma category "Negro") "perforated" so that the formerly enslaved so-called "Creoles" became the archetypes of British rule. This not only caused a hierarchy with the "Creoles" over the Garifuna, but a hierarchy of the "Creoles" over any other category besides "White."[78] The "Creoles," while not always attaining it and in many instances inheriting serious cases of disenfranchisement from various phases of historical oppression, were not systemically restricted from access to economic and property resources in the ways that non-"Whites" were (and are) in the United States. Further, if one is to think in terms of the decrease in number of an ethnic "group" in relation to the rise of another, one might say that the so-called "Creoles" have not only lost their numerical status as the largest "group" due to not only the rise in birth rates of so-called "Mestizos" in Belize but also the migration of other so-called "Mestizos" from neighboring countries. However, I hold that this is not the way to think of Belize at all. It is more than worth quoting at length O Nigel Bollard's words on this, words I find resonant with my own status as a Belizean born in the United States with "nationality" awarded legally in both countries by descent and place of birth respectively. Bollard says,

> it is an oversimplification to think of these "ethnic groups" as static, fixed identities, as the censuses imply, because the historical forces, particularly economic and political forces, which have been the source of a dynamic process of ethnic group formation and redefinition will surely continue in future. Most ethnic groups in Belize today, including the three that are the most numerous – the Mestizo, Creole, and Garifuna, – are themselves the result of considerable mixtures over several centuries and they are continuing to change. There is intermarriage between members of these groups, as there is also between

Mopan and Kekchi Maya, and the East Indians and other Belizeans. Moreover, recent Central American immigrants are not culturally identical to Belizean Mestizos, and many young Belizean Creoles are increasingly influenced by African American and Afro-Caribbean cultures. Not only is Belize a complex and changing multi-ethnic mosaic, but many individual Belizeans, perhaps even a majority, are in many respects multi-cultural.[79]

Due to the perpetual in-betweenness metaphysically structuring the InnerSections of events in the region, there never solidifies definitive categories similar enough to race/trauma, persuasive enough for humans to measure their becoming against or to transform their *becoming* into *being*. I argue that the relational activity of these historical forces from the relatively loose reigns on mahogany slaves[80] to the vague laws poorly regulating the colony in its early years all set the stage for the emergence of ULAs that bespeak a type of infinite slippage. This slippage is the very context from which this "dynamic process of ethnic group formation" is founded and ingresses change as its constant. While I hesitate at Bollar's uncritical use of the phrase "ethnic group" for reasons stated briefly in this chapter and at more length in Chapter 2, it does convey an event in the process of perpetual formation of personhood regarding the contexts situating and limiting said personhood.

The Kriol phrase "We all de one" is a refrain uttered quite frequently by several Belizeans. This indicates a unity amid contrasting events which many external to the context may observe as being anything but complementary. On top of an indefinite sense of "on the way" identities in relational enfolding and unfolding flowing through the collective consciousness of a plethora of Belizeans, there is the value of the national name emerging as a rhizome indicating the irreducible experience of the InnerSections creating and occurring within the country. Considering the "theory of the perforation" as opposed to the "theory of the line," the ethnic "group," thought in some other contexts to be insular and a strict identity, is perceived as a set of data that flows within and without via the in-between perforations loosely bordering the events in question. For example, Belizean Kriol InnerSects English, Spanish, Igbo, Garifuna, French, various strands of Yucatec Maya, and other pronounced languages, and creates a fluctuating linguistic event that gains and loses elements due to its perforations. Kriol never becomes a stagnant entity, and proficiency in this distinct fluid language[81] is a sign of Belizean nationality to a great number of Belizeans; the "many" becoming "one" in a Whiteheadian sense.[82]

Evidence of Belize's multi/race/less imperfect yet progressively forward-moving situation is depicted vividly in the work of the late Zee Edgell, the nation's preeminent fiction writer. Edgell painstakingly uses literature to subtly raise suppressed ripples in the InnerSectional tapestry, such as "Creole" superiority over the Garifuna in her classic *Beka Lamb*. Even though "Carib [slur for Garifuna] and creole are branches of the same African tree," one of the characters in the novel utters, "I am not saying I could marry a Carib man."[83] As opposed to an intersection of so-called "Creole" and so-called "Carib," which might indicate a mode of thought that completely isolates one from the other, while accurately disclosing this real tension to the reader, Edgell reveals a very accurate primordial InnerSection which imperfectly assents to a "Carib"–"Creole" event evading clear definition. Even more shocking to some is her *Time and the River*, a work of historical fiction based on the life of the historical figure Leah Lawson, a formerly enslaved woman who married her owner and inherited 400 slaves whom she freed at her death.[84] If race/trauma is understood as not human essence but legality, we have a "Negro" "woman" moving into the status of "White" "man." Edgell's *The Festival of San Joaquín*, set in the early 1990s, is the first-person view of the day-to-day of Luz Marina, a young woman recently released from prison for killing her husband in self-defense. In this presentation of the settling and resituating of the ingredients prehended for identity formations in Belize, we see the results of a multi/race/less metaphysic, as the ethnic "groups" mentioned in this section are not emphasized when the characters are described but clues to how said characters may be situated within the framework of classifications may or may not appear. What permeates the rich text full of underlying histories and various explorations of gender oppression is the far from utopic beauty of being "Belizean," the representation of the "latticework" of its InnerSection in a national capacity.[85] This is BioDigital Jazz at the teeming heights of its "Creative" improvisational lack of fixed destination. Rather, Belizean BioDigital Jazz is an indefinite adventure . . . of ideas . . . and their manifestation in the modes of humans *becoming*.

Conclusion

In this section, I strove to provide multi/race/less instances of nationality and culture as alternatives to race/trauma as a foundation for identity formations perpetually *becoming*. Hip-Hop served as an example of the cultural dimension in its focus on the practices which emerged in various parts of NYC as a "next universe," basing self and communal perceptions of personhood in one's contributions to the global society of the Culture. Secondly, Belize is lifted over against race/trauma as an example of nationality in the double sense of (1) definitional legitimacy, hence legal protection of human rights and personhood, and (2) the perpetual cultural remixes of ethnic data that nationality represents. I assert that both culture and nationality in their many manifestations (as Hip-Hop and Belize are just two) offer Useful Lived Abstractions for the processes of Dis/solution and Repetition more conducive than race/trauma to the realization of BioDigital Jazz of identity formations in process. This chapter also aimed to provide an awareness of the novel importance of Belize and Hip-Hop Culture to the discourse of philosophy of race and offer substantial starting points for more in-depth work on both. I now move toward some brief words on genealogy as a third multi/race/less alternative to race/trauma and race-related categories in the final chapter.

8 SELF-STUDY: SCATTERED THOUGHTS ON GENEALOGY AS A FACET OF MULTI/RACE/LESS/NESS

> Study, study, study! And when you have studied well and would ask me what to study next, I would reply; study yourselves!
>
> **NOBLE DREW ALI**[1]

I am *becoming* a Moslem. I am *becoming*. A Moslem.

In various transmutations of my own understandings of what sorts of identities the "I" is capable of, the civic and esoteric teachings of Noble Drew Ali take a special place of precedence in my current psychical architecture. For Drew Ali, to practice Islam, or what he refers to as "Islamism," is not only to practice Love, Truth, Peace, Freedom, and Justice,[2] but to study oneself. In these practices, multi/race/less/ness is "self-study." What does it mean to study oneself? In this final facet of multi/race/less covered in the text, the employment of (1) a sketching of family trees, (2) an amplification of non-biological influences responsible for the family tree as it stands, and (3) an active utilization of (1) and (2) for the perpetual reshaping of humanity is referred to as "genealogy."

Genealogy appears in various places in the corpus of so-called "Western" philosophy, and its usage riffs off of and departs from the general usage of the term in the natural sciences, which can be defined as "the event of sexual antecedents responsible for producing the biology of the human." In relation to the philosophical usage of the term "genealogy," Brian Lightbody says it is "a distinct method of practicing philosophy that examines the historical origin of present-day concepts, ideas, practices, and discourses."[3] We've seen genealogy's philosophical appearance in continental thinkers such as Nietzsche's dismantling of the underpinnings of human ethics in *On the Genealogy of Morals*. It is also evident in Roland Faber's reading of Deleuze and Whitehead as inheriting Nietzsche's deconstruction of morality in *Genealogy*. In light of the various social forces from which the human "subject" emerges, "ontology has to be *genealogically deconstructed* as based on its own becoming, which is always prior to being."⁴ In these instances, we are referring to a genealogy, or origin story, of ideas. In multi/race/less/ness' understanding of genealogy, the event of the human Noble Drew Ali admonishes us to study, we are concerned with the ebbs and flows of not only (1) the empirical evidence of the family tree in space-time (we, its human results, or even ancestral records that mark descent) but also (2 and 3) the ideological and social forces constituting the manifold within which the human becoming can be conceived and perceived. In other words, multi/race/less genealogy travels through notions of family tree and associated ULAs and the Dis/solution of forces to the human *as* an idea. It is in this phase where Creativity remixes and transforms into fluidities that which is ossified due to the coercion of race/trauma's definitional hierarchy for optimal Repetition.

A substantial amount of what constitutes the "human" is an idea, thus rooted beyond the realm of physical experience though conditioned by it. But philosophical theory has in many instances overemphasized the "social construction" aspect of identity formation to the point that the "real" (read experiencing) human is lost.⁵ Also, there is another tendency to argue for an essential "substance" of the human beyond the empirical yet imperfectly manifested in it (Neo-Platonism). This is the foundation of race/trauma to which I offer an alternative for in multi/race/less/ness. Further, there is the position of the human as relatively nothing more than an amalgam of inert physical parts somehow giving off the illusion of something beyond, such as a seeming transcendent awareness of experience. Genealogy, in an Alian multi/race/less/ness "self-study," affirms the idea aspect of the race/trauma/race-related "human" not exterior to but emergent from various negotiations of hegemonic power. This perspective of genealogy doesn't restrict the event producing humans in progression to self-determining identities for subsequent experiments in the chain. Rather, multi/race/less/ness focuses on how self-study opens the possibilities of the reinterpretation of antecedents in a long familial event. Unlike many other philosophies of identity contrasted in the text, multi/race/less genealogy gives more credence to the plausibility of *drastic* self-redefinition apart from the rules constituting race/trauma.

So, how does genealogy as defined here provide a multi/race/less facet of identity formation complementary to what has been said about culture and nationality? To briefly recap, "ethnicity" in multi/race/less/ness refers to the data of eternal objects that emerge from human nexuses of considerable sizes, sometimes coalescing within a particular geographical or conceptual region. "Culture" in multi/race/less/ness refers to the ways in which ethnicity is perpetually mixed and "remixed" and fluidly solidifying modes of *becoming* such as cuisine, the passing on of intangible lessons, relationships to the land, etc. Nationality in multi/race/less/ness indicates the legal articulation of that which culture(s) historically do hermeneutically with the eternal objects of their ethnicity. Nationality and culture's main advantage over race/trauma is that both theoretically set a stage conducive to the adventure of unbridled, non-hegemonic, and nonhierarchical human identity formations due to (1) nationality's presupposition of the humanity of all its possessors and (2) culture's leanings toward the infinite lack of strict definition of the experiencing entity perceived and perceiving the universe abstractly as a "self." Considering these definitions of culture and nationality in multi/race/less/ness, the potential for genealogy as a third facet rests in its ability to not only store dormant pasts of our human events for self-study but also to interpret them in ways that could alter and abolish the ULAs and useless lived abstractions we sometimes deem synonymous to the "self" that is never "really" "there." Faber says of Whitehead, "The starting point for these adventures in thinking *cosmology*, however, may surprise: It is the rigorous claim that 'All is Event!'"[6] Genealogy is both multi/race/less analytical and conscious experiential relationality to the chain of biological and conceptual instances in a familial event.

As we know, Noble Drew Ali's command to us to study ourselves responds to our (I'm using "our" to refer to who Drew Ali deems to be in the set of the more direct descendants of the original peoples of the earth, or ALL people who in relation to the metaphysics of current racial nomenclature are said to be "of color," of which I and several readers from Mexico to Tanzania will be included) potential lack of expansive knowledge about the actual entities of familial events, the Whiteheadian "only reasons" responsible for our existence on and in the scene, to draw from the ontological principle stated in *Process and Reality*.[7] In the racial categories this text has taken head on, there stands the illusion of the collapsing of the multiplicity of the familial event, something that could never actually be reduced. The Prophet (Drew Ali) reminds us of that which is excluded in the *performance* of race/trauma, a fixed label not capable of disclosing "authentic" (read faithful to the perception of lived experience) identity. Rather, Annika Thiem reminds us that it is a power dynamic Judith Butler would compare to a type of "drag" in relation to her deconstructions of gender.[8] Multi/race/less/ness as genealogy causes us to confront the most uncomfortable impulse that looms around our struggles to make race/trauma fit: our desire to subscribe to a metaphysic (Or perhaps quasi-metaphysic) that does not organically correspond with the genealogical data. A lack of attention to genealogy provides the option to peacefully continue in the illusion of race/trauma, reifying the accepted categories when they are challenged by "cancelling" those who transgress them and/or deny their necessary existence.

To "scat" along the lines of the family tree, the present era has opened many avenues for anyone who wants to research. The hope of uncovering even most of the various events contrasting in relation to composing a familial event which fell victim to colonial attack might be far-fetched. However, the considerably wider reach in the present era of DNA-tracing sites such as ancestry.com and africanancestry.com along with the advent of 23 and Me and similar services provides a large quantity of birth, marriage, slave-owning, and property records, among other things. There are ways to "study yourselves" more thoroughly than in past eras. For example, actor Don Cheadle, identified and identifying as the race/

trauma category "Black" and race-related category "African American," discovered that his ancestors were enslaved. You may say, "Why phrase it like that? Most of 'us'[9] were." I phrase it like this to erode the persuasive eternal object of widespread assumption that anyone in the United States with long ancestry and various relations to/with the oppression of systemic racism has ancestors who were at one time enslaved.[10] It's quite possible Cheadle's ancestors have and were aware of their ties to the Moorish bloodlines Pimienta-Bey and Miles discuss in their work and were never enslaved or freed due to this knowledge. I digress. Kinda. Kinda not. Anyway, Cheadle, in self-study through a look at his family tree, discovered that some of his ancestors were enslaved by members of the Chickasaw Nation. Of this, he said,

> I don't how I feel about that . . . it's crazy because really you feel like . . . the two biggest blights on the way this country started . . . slavery and the genocide of the Native Americans and the Trail of Tears and all these horrible stories of what has [sic] happened to the Native people here. And then our family was owned by people who had suffered . . . it's just (pause) . . . that's mind blowing.[11]

There are a variety of forces coalescing in the moment of this quote. One of the most importance to a multi/race/less self-study is the shift of perspective that hits Cheadle when he discovers the assumption he seems to have held uncritically about the experience of his ancestors due to the category of race/trauma ("White" people enslaved his 2x great grandparents) is shattered when his history is engaged as *event* and expanded in the way one might stretch an accordion or a slinky and discover hidden colors and debris amid the coils. Race/trauma has the tendency of flattening multiplicity in its use of bio-shorthand. Conversely, multi/race/less/ genealogy in the key of family tree exposes the obscured and excluded, and as Monica A. Coleman would say of polydoxy (a poststructuralist theological approach and response to the challenges made within some strands of logocentric and phallocentric Christianity that moves toward a religious pluralism advocating for various methods of right belief), "is transparent enough to reveal the many in what appears to be one."[12] What Cheadle learns about the familial event shifts his sense of "self," coming to an awareness which until the point of self-study was coerced into the useless lived abstraction of "Blackness."[13]

Cheadle seems to express an underlying comradery between himself and the who he refers to as "Native Americans" that undergoes a fracture when he discovers his ancestors were enslaved by members of the Chikashsha Iyaakni (original name) Nation. What is communicated to me in the clip is less of an anger that this occurred and more disappointment that those who experienced oppression by the same government that maligned his ancestors would participate in this atrocity against them. As the video continues, we learn that the Chikashsha did not grant citizenship to those it once enslaved.[14] Riffing on William James, Massumi says,

The trigger-object is rarely arrived at as a terminus. The world (experience) normally contents itself with brinking on "really next effects." A terminus is like a basin of attraction that draws you toward it, as by a gravitational pull, but no sooner spins you off, as by centrifugal force. The world doesn't stop at your anger. An angry word or deed snowballs into an unfolding drama sweeping you and all around you along. You are always really living in a centrifugal hurdle next to an effect.[15]

This sense of disappointment that befalls Cheadle is not perceived as an end in multi/race/less/ness. It is actually a door. On the other side of this door lie possibilities for the rescrambling of Cheadle's familial event. He is creatively transformed by prehending it to actively transform himself. Much like Larry L.W. Miles' assertion that the hegemony-sanctioned narratives of those systematized to be "Black" "Americans" excludes much of the story,[16] and Faber's point in commentary on Whitehead, Deleuze, and Butler's varying notions of flux that such exclusions and repressions are in fact creations of an entity illusorily transcending the conditions from which it emerges (such as the "self" of race/trauma),[17] Cheadle learns this information about his familial event on the backdrop of other unfounded or perhaps problematically founded presuppositions. These problematically founded propositions condition what is conceivable for him to do with the information discovered. The obvious presupposition that seems to be in play here is that categories such as "Black" and "Native American" are not in need of serious deconstruction. After this eye-opening discovery is revealed in self-study, the conversation between Cheadle and Henry Louis Gates (the host of the program *Finding Your Roots*, which featured Cheadle's study of his familial event) continues in the key of race/trauma. Something else of interest on the part of Cheadle is the lack of questioning of the depth of his ancestors' relation to the Chikashsha Nation. We've discovered they were enslaved by the nation. But the "exclusion" of records and accounts that "blur" or perhaps "negate" the "line" between the so-called "Indian" and the so-called "Negro" as discussed at length by Pimienta-Bey[18] and Miles[19] and what this information could imply don't seem to occur to either Cheadle or Gates. This conversation symbolizes the reification of difference, not in the key of Deleuze as that which "does not oppose but on the contrary, allows the greatest space possible for the apprehension of resemblances."[20] In the discussion between Gates and Cheadle, what is not said is louder than that which is uttered. "Black" and "Native American" are, through the divisive carvings of the metaphysics of race/trauma, literally thought (not necessarily stated) as fundamentally (read "universally") different in their obscurant *creation* of a mutual exclusion. In other words, it is impossible for accounts that subvert the ULAs supporting the narrative of a fundamental (essential or quasi-essential) and historical difference between so-called "Blacks" and so-called "Native Americans to even be thought clearly," such as Sallop Wellington's *The Negro: A Sketch of the Birth and Education of an African Indian* and historian David MacRitchie's work on the Moorish connections to so-called "Indians" during the time of the "American" Revolution.[21]

A multi/race/less approach to the family tree facet of genealogy might draw from these more "fringe" bits of data excluded by default for their counterintuitive status in the milieu of thought. Cheadle's discovery could potentially unfold possible connections between his familial event and the so-called "Native Americans." First, it might be interesting to discover whether or not his ancestry connects him to the families now systematized as "Native American" by blood, and/or if their descent into slavery was related to a later legal classification as "Negroes" due to a loss of nationhood. Second, if the assumption that Cheadle's family was enslaved by someone who the society would readily refer to as "White" was found to be inaccurate, a revisable platform of Dis/solution for questioning other accepted background assumptions about identity formation and negotiation could be set as precedent. Karen Baker-Fletcher says,

> We fail to acknowledge that much of the ancestral heritage we name as African is also Native American. We allow ourselves to remain largely ignorant of our Native American heritage and the ways in which it continues to influence us. The problem is that we have become lost and disconnected from the people of our Native American heritage who can directly remind us of traditions in any concrete, specific way. What we remember is vague and not tied to any specific Indian communities. It has become a part of the mix of our culture as a new people with a new culture that is distinctively African American. But with all the attention to the ancestors that has been a part of much of our practice historically and emphasized in recent years through practices like Kwanzaa, we need to ask which ancestors to remember. Shouldn't we remember all of those ancestors who have contributed to our survival, wisdom, and positive moral heritage? Is it not disrespectful to disremember our Native American ancestors? For me, this means I need to name Jane Finch not only as an individual but also learn something about the tribe and *nation* she came from in order to understand what an entire community of people have contributed to my family heritage.[22] (italics mine)

What Baker-Fletcher articulates was worth quoting at length as it perfectly demonstrates a multi/race/less genealogical approach in the facet of the family tree. Here, Baker-Fletcher moves similar to Whitehead's thoughts on the consequent nature of his theistically progressive God as exemplification of universal process in the last pages of *Process and Reality*. We are encountering "the judgment of a tenderness which losing nothing that can be saved."[23] Baker-Fletcher ushers us into the often forgotten margins of our familial events, shrouded by the categories of race/trauma, which coerce us without reflection into a "closing off" of those parts of the bio "origami" not suited for simplicity. Rather, she lures us to come to terms with the plasticity of the familial event containing many other complex events. In the words of Simondon on his vision of an authentic relationality between the machine and the human he symbolizes with the concept of the "ensemble," "[hu]man[ity] is the permanent organizer of a society of technical objects that need [them] in the same way musicians in an orchestra need a conductor."[24] Baker-Fletcher not only encourages us to be conductors among (not above, as in a logocentric, phallocentric, and linear sanitizing of the queerings of indefinite energies more close to how we become) our genealogies in the key of the family tree[25] but also shows us how to do this by showing her fresh prehension of her own ancestors.

So, in effect, genealogy in the key of family tree is an awareness of the thick human event which gives off a flat appearance. It is the return of dormant ULAs (suppressed stories, traditions, ancestors, ways of becoming, etc.) to active consciousness.

So, how about genealogy in the key of deconstruction or Dis/solution, or the critical analysis of the historico-biological data composing the familial events of which we are a part? John D. Caputo says of Derrida's infamous watershed "event" in the history of the "West's" philosophies, "Deconstruction is the relentless pursuit of *the* impossible, which means, of things whose possibility is sustained by their impossibility, of things, which instead of being wiped out by their impossibility, are actually nourished and fed by it."[26] From genealogy in the key of the family tree, we are presented with "invisible" and hence imperceivable information that constitutes the "latticework" of our familial event. Sometimes, such data baptizes us in itself, causing us to wonder from whence emerge the light raindrops arousing goosebumps on our breasts. And even when we discover the root of the mysterious liquid, there is still cause to be unsettled. For example, say a present descendant comes to cognizance that large swathes of property in a family whose majority would have been constructed by the power systems as "Colored" or "Negro" during enslavement periods in the "Caribbean" were passed down by a so-called "White" slave owner ancestor somewhere down the familial event. Several questions are potentially left unanswered. Was the entrance of this particular ancestor into this familial event by force or by volition? How did the children of the so-called "Biracial" union in today's terms understand themselves in relation to the metaphysics of race/trauma and race-related categories active in the context? How was gender negotiated within and alongside race/trauma and race-related modes of being? The possible questions that emanate from the family tree like the multiplicitous options open to the master of the language when using the language at hand . . . are the "pursuit of the *impossible!*" We can never know the complete answers to these questions, if we can know them at all. This is, of course, presuming that there is something to *know*.

The concept of "knowing" implies not only the existence of the "known" but also possibly a type of overarching structure determining said known. The computer is "known" as an instrument for the use of the internet, digital graphics, music production, and writing (among other things) because an overarching structure of determination (the creator of the computer in this case) intends this function and discloses itself to our ingressed and co-created expectations of the device. Both user and creator of the computer are entangled in a *process*, an "event" of reciprocal relation, akin to Simondon's hope for the equitable and mutually generative InnerSectional potentialities of cybernetics.[27] In Hegel's Christian-sympathetic dialectic, contra the Kantian strand of idealism, the universe itself is synthesized by a *knowable* overarching structure that brings all into its totality. Unlike Kant's "noumena," Hegel's notion of "absolute spirit," an overlaying of seemingly opposing elements which can't be thought together without contradiction in a Kantian "sanitized" philosophical system, not only encounters but concludes the quest for the knowing of the previously unknowable. Hegel, in the "genealogy" of various transcendental steps from the likes of Fichte and Schelling, has "figured it all out."[28] Hegel preempted and stitched the gaping hole opened by deconstruction in the key of Derrida, little over 150 years before he tore it.

So, why is the hole still there? And why was it torn?

Hegel's notion of absolute spirit as the synthesizer of opposites, or "the identity of identity and non-identity," enacts the power of a drastic restriction very much akin to the reduction of race/trauma and race-related categories.[29] The value of Hegel's dialectic is that it offers an account of difference that does not call for any system that "denies the validity of either the transcendental or the natural point of view."[30] But what it raises in its place is a removal of the need to grapple with the tensions present in this sublation of "opposites," and within an awareness of the tension is where the dynamics of race/trauma are not only lived but also "felt." I call on my former and sadly late professor Vitor Westhelle's invocation of the eschatological bent of Hegel to help here. Westhelle reminds us of Hegel's understanding of the fruition of absolute spirit as not merely a benign orchestration of various phases of divergent energies eventually coming to a close when *any given* mature collective consciousness in *any given* epoch realizes an overarching harmony in "opposites" as eschatological culmination. This can be referred to as the "end of time," which rests on not only Hegel's but also on Fichte and Schelling's notion of an absolute *identity*. As mentioned in Chapter 1, for Hegel, the eschaton of absolute spirit culminates *particularly* in "European" consciousness.[31] This is the same "European" consciousness responsible for developing itself and various strands of oppression projects from the late fifteenth century on, of which race/trauma is one of its greatest "creations." Westhelle says,

> The end of history, its eschatological fulfillment, is indeed the final triumph of Hegel's philosophy. It is final in the sense that it was left without any possibility

of further interpretation, for in realizing it – or declaring it realized – Hegel's system was complete and therefore closed.[32]

Leading us back into the deconstruction vein of genealogy, Westhelle's comments on Hegel relate to the kinds of "closed systems" sustaining uncritical acceptance of potentially incurable "cancers" such as race/trauma. The category exists and is completed. It was created by that which is beyond us, and we have no choice but to ingress whatever of its shadows are appropriate for us. Contrary to Caputo's definition of deconstruction as "the relentless pursuit of the impossible," Hegel's absolute spirit is the passive acceptance of the definite end attained whether or not one wants it and not necessarily comfortable for all. This also hearkens back to Ania Loomba's reflections of caste as race: both indicate an *eschatology* many times simultaneously rejected (due to its role in and as the perpetual reinscription of oppression) and accepted (due to the belief that there is no other choice for identity to "appear" in contexts constructed by race/trauma and race-related categories). Race/trauma as eschatology expands when the secrets tucked in the obscure corners of the familial event are exposed in an enactment of genealogy in the key of family tree. The amalgam of a multitude of "opposing" forces, arguably most blatantly amplified in the infamous "master-slave dialectic" in *Phenomenology of Spirit*, is within the background of the consciousness situating our particular events of becoming. Until it is laid bare in a deconstructive move of multi/race/less genealogy, that is. The moment of exposure sets the groundwork for the impossibility of Dis/solution. Multi/race/less/ness asserts that the most alive instances of rich lived experiences are in the inductive indeterminacy of the *process*, not the deductive satisfaction of the *destination*.

Now, the question of genealogy in the key of deconstruction might ask, "With this recent information I've received about my family tree, can I continue *being* who I thought I *was* or must "I" accept "my" *becoming* other? In the key of the family tree, this was hinted at. We were concerned with the ability to conceive questions which may not have previously occurred to us to even ask. The key of deconstruction intends to act on the "oppositions" we are now becoming able to think, relentlessly following their lead. At the dissipation of Hegelian transcendental essentialism, everything, including the human, becomes not the by-product and component of a closed system but an event wide open to adventures in identity formations of flux. If "the end" (insert Jim Morrison's smoky vocals here at the final groove of the vinyl of the self-titled album) of structured fixed identities gives way to the unstructured "in-between" of emergent human in/defiance of Dis/solution, we find ourselves enmeshed in the fortunate loss of the flattened "I." Here, the pursuit is not for a human resolidifying in place of the race/trauma evaporated by a critical coming to terms with the various particles in the familial event Faber would refer to as *non-difference*, or various events in a "harmonious" relation of irreducibility of any particular one to any particular other.[33] Rather, multi/race/less/ness in the key of deconstruction invites a current experient of the familial event into a closer attunement to the dissonance masked by the perpetual deference of identity Derrida gets at in his concept of Differánce, otherwise more commonly known as the "self." Unlike absolute spirit, differánce "does not resist appropriation, it does not impose an exterior limit upon it."[34]

One can think of the library of the familial event as a long series of appropriations. These appropriations repeatedly defer to one another, ebbing and flowing in the sometimes simultaneous revealing and concealing of defining characteristics associating satisfied and currently experiencing entities with the perpetually evolving event. The grandchild by nature defers to and appropriates the grandparents, definitely in DNA and sometimes in traces of the appearance. Nietzsche's notion of eternal return has an interesting place in thinking through traits that "skip a generation" or five. That penchant for traveling to Spain and Portugal dormant in the last four generations, perhaps due to a person in the familial event with ancestry in these regions, "emerges" seemingly out of nowhere in a person in the fifth. All those in the familial event are *identified* in the deference of relation to its other members. There is potentially nothing new happening here. But things can be remixed, conjuring interesting bursts of novelty, such as a current subjective experient in the family line born and raised on the south side of Chicago, placing and reimagining his experience over against that of his Moorish *antepasados*.

Gayatri Spivak, in the translator's preface to the fortieth anniversary edition of Derrida's *Of Grammatology*, says, "The economic character of differánce in no way implies that deferred presence can also be found again."[35] What might this reveal in reference to the genealogy in the key of multi/race/less/deconstruction? Derrida lets us off precisely on the train platform we need to be at with his notion of "economy," which is "identity constituted by difference."[36] Looking at the familial line through Derridean economic microscopes of Dis/solution as opposed to Hegelian binoculars of resolution, we might think of the identity of a living person in the family deferring to the difference of their parents, who defer to the difference of their parents, and so on. Deference is infinite, and causes us to reconsider the "person" who may have ingressed a quasi-essential race/trauma or race/related category as synonymous with "who they are" as difference itself. If all that can be found of the human is "identity constituted by difference," how much less can the subcategory of race/trauma in its hyperbolic enforcement (hence creation) of hierarchical colonial and postcolonial difference claim to produce the sorts of selves it wants to assert are essential or at least quasi-essential? Genealogy in the key of deconstruction renders difficult an acceptance of the racial "self" as universal and a mandatory mode of thought and *being*, even in allegorical usage.

In thinking through the profound work of Catherine Keller in the beginning stages of multi/race/less/ness in *Underground Rap as Religion*, I say,

The adventure of becoming is traded for the predictable nature of being. The fallacy of misplaced concreteness has been committed with gender and ethnicity. Keller asks the question, "Are we feminists or womanists or mujeristas; negroes or Blacks or African Americans, homosexuals or lesbian/gays or queers?" Keller, in this instance using the social constructions of race and ethnicity, muddles the still waters in such a way that we begin to question how seriously we take the metaphors we use to name ourselves, starting the process toward utilizing such abstractions to further probe the complex multiplicity these categories succeed in failing to exemplify.[37]

In light of what has been discovered in the self-study of genealogy in the key of deconstruction, maybe the eschatological metaphysical act of impossibly concluding in tenuous synthesis the not only irreducible but also irreconcilable categories in the plentiful void known as the categories "Black," "African American," "Latinx," etc. is something that can no longer hold sway. The contradictions of race/trauma are indeed lived within and sublated aside from cognizance. However, there are intermittent periods of what Sartre would refer to as "nausea" due to being subsumed and accepting (without choice) such subordination of fluid identities under diametrically opposing forces constituting racial and race/related categories. DuBois' read of what at that time was somewhat of a precursor to the subsequent "African American" in his term the "American Negro" is a wonderful example.[38] Deconstruction causes us to come to terms with the disappearance of the "text" of the human subject. However, there is some experiencing "thing" at "play" here, and the subjective phase of the experience is paramount. This race/traumatic "thing" must be traded in for the multi/race/less familial "event" irreducible to a singularity of which its components are merely participants as "the sum of the parts." The event of familial identity in genealogy's key of deconstruction reveals an ever emergent unfolding which ingresses fleeting traits that briefly freeze process into *lived abstractions*, either useful or useless according to the doctrine of multi/race/less/ness. Considering the realization that my disclosure to myself and the world emerges from an indefinite and undetermined outflowing as opposed to an eschatological conclusion I ingress through Repetition, I must decide whether not I will agree to *be* these race or race-related categories despite what I learned or take a dangerous adventure in "Repetitive" co-creative and perhaps unpopular and "impossible" conscious[39] *becoming*. This moment of evaluation is a function of Dis/solution.

Speaking of deconstruction in the major key of Dubois, what he refers to as "two warring ideals in one body, whose dogged strength keeps it from being torn asunder," matches the precise tone of this facet of genealogy. The inner struggle resulting from tumultuous contrasts between various elements in the familial line, such as the appearance of Leah Lawson's slave-owning husband in a long procession of people who may have appearances drastically different from his and possibly trigger different experiences, leaves the present human instances with a plethora of difficult questions to ask. If some of my ancestors were slave owners and voluntarily and involuntary identified under race/trauma and race-related categories I would have trouble identifying as, and my subjectivity is made in part by the reference to of theirs, is it possible to still see myself as solely the category ingressed by my slave-holding ancestor or the one I'm most deemed as by societies? Does one category cancel the other out? What about the other categories ingressed by other ancestors in the familial event? Do I now attempt to understand the chain and therefore myself as "Mixed Race" or "multiracial," or do I abandon the symbolism of race trauma altogether and take more initiative in co-creating with my context the "nothing" of my "I" into an embrace of multi/race/less fluidity taking formless form abstractly perceivable in every instant? R&B singer Smokey Robinson, in rare form on BET's Def Poetry Jam, offers a genealogy of the race/trauma term "Black" in light of deconstructionist conversations going on in the public conscious at the time around how identities in formation referred to as "Black" should be negotiated (who is "Black," who is "African American," etc.). While finally reaffirming "Blackness" for *himself*, Robinson, in several strokes of poetic genius, deconstructs the "text" of the linguistic event, highlighting and wrestling with various inconsistencies in the idea of race/trauma and race/related categories usually thought to be static and eschatologically completed in the poem. In this, we see hints of the separation of the language of "Blackness" from those it has been employed to symbolize, as well as a novel co-creation in flux that takes into account the slippage of the categories themselves.[40]

The final energy I'll discuss is that of the utilization of genealogy in the keys of family tree and deconstruction to co-create becomings apart from the eschatological closed circles of race/trauma and race-related categories. After becoming aware of key new information in the familial event (family tree) and examining whether or not this new information can co-exist with our present understanding of ourselves, we are now presented with the "aesthetic aretaic" question of what should we *create* the most significant characteristics of our subjective experience of identity formation to *become*? In an essay entitled "Science and General Education," Whitehead says,

> The interest of a sweeping generalization is the interest of a broad high road to men who know what travel is; and the pleasure of the high road has its roots in the labor of the journey. Again, facts are exciting to the imagination in so far as they illuminate some scheme of thought, perhaps only dimly discerned or realized, some day-dreams begotten by old racial experience, or some clear-cut theory exactly comprehended. The complex of both factors of interest satisfies the cravings inherent in the mysterious reaching out of experience from sensation to knowledge, and from blind instinct to thoughtful purpose.[41]

Here, Whitehead lures the reader toward that which lacks a clear general definition as opposed to that which is easily symbolized. The polemic against "general education" in the sciences voiced in this passage is akin to the "sweeping generalization" of race/trauma and race-related categories. They present a crash course on what it means to exist as a human, and we learn these generalizations and live much of our lives through them because we're systematized into them. What would happen to our becoming if we truly pursued a movement beyond "Blackness," "Whiteness," "Asianness," "Indigenousness," etc., and levitated toward "the labor of the journey of self-study?" We may endlessly *become* Moorish American. We may endlessly *become* Belizean. We may endlessly *become* Hip-Hop. We may endlessly *become* beyond any ULA. We may endlessly *become*...

Clarrissa Pinkola Estés reminds us that

> Naming a force, a creature, person, or thing has several connotations. In cultures where names are chosen carefully for their magical or auspicious meanings, to know a person's true name means to know the life path and the soul attributes of that person. And the reason the true name is often kept secret is to protect the owner of that name so that he or she might grow into the power of that name, to shelter it so that no one will either denigrate it or distract from it, and so that one's spiritual authority can develop to its full potential.[42]

In the context of a beyond-the-confines-of-category exposition of the notion of "Woman" outside of the prescriptions of gender, Estés invites us into InnerSectional energies, releasing what she refers to as the "Wild Woman," an unbridled and free nature encased by the confining expectations of gender. The combination of the words "Wild" and "Woman" "create *llamar a tocar a la Puerta*, the fairy tale knock at the door of the deep female psyche."[43] Placing the word "Wild" in front of the *name* "Woman" sparks an undoing, or what Catherine Keller might refer to as an "unsaying," of the eschatological closure of patriarchy. This creates a passageway to something new. Estés says that any woman in the world will understand the *llama a tocar a la Puerta* conjured in the Creative relationality of the words "Wild" and "Woman," a novel name "chosen carefully." What are the types of names we choose for ourselves and what kinds of names can we choose? This is what I wanted to communicate with the lyric "Sit across the room from yourself after you separate yourself from yourself and ask yourself if you were one to name your essence, would you call it "Black?"[44] It is the assertion of multi/race/less/ness that due to the histories, definitional limitations, and intent behind racial language expounded on all throughout the text, they are "careless choices." And at a general level, this merely means a choice not critically examined, hence "lacking care." As opposed to being an authentic symbol of "the life path and the soul attributes," race/trauma and race-related language inscribes and reinscribes the very impossibility of the appearance of these virtues. They are not special but intentionally general, distilling those who simultaneously align and are aligned with them to shells of what they could *become*. But there are other options.

I place the words "post" and "race" together in a way similar to Estés "Wild Woman." I'ma say a few more things about creation and peace the hell up outta here. My head is hurting and I'm not even sure I agree with the ethos of this restaurant/"sanctuary" I've been writing this in. *A todos modos*, there is a creatively transformational spark that comes from the relationality of responsible "post-racial" philosophical thought. It is not the eschatological move of asserting that we now magically live in a world where race is somehow gone and we need to come to an awareness of that. Hell no. This energy affirms that race is indeed real, and it is indeed traumatic. And despite said trauma, there's another mode, a mode of *becoming* and not *being*, available to us to enact. This *becoming* does not emerge merely by a deductive argument that race is a social construction that falls off once we become aware of it. This *becoming* also does not arise from a transcendent pronouncement of the end of race/trauma and race-related language not sensitive to how race is traumatically lived in the world. However, it can ascend from what Simondon might refer to in his work on the philosophy of technology the "technical" pole demonstrating the logical impossibilities inherent in many if not all demonstrations of race/trauma and race-related language and the "theoretical" pole bringing about progressively equitable ways of synthesizing the multiplicity of familial events without an appeal to race/trauma and race-related categories. This sort of InnerSection, where race/trauma is displaced for nonhierarchical identity formations in process, occurs in Aesthetic Religions such as Hip-Hop Culture, where collective consciousnesses are forged not on race/trauma but on skills, commitment to Hip-Hop and global communities, shared interests in the elements and the philosophical notions that underpin them, etc. Hip-Hop Culture is political in its formation of identities aware of their inevitable flux, and for Simondon, this is quasi-religious as both politics and religion fulfill the same function of creating "a unique world that is both natural and human."[45]

Much of the facets of genealogy offered have given significant attention to coming to terms with one's biological rhizome (think of placing a top-down family tree horizontally on a table and how this might shatter the implication of the older ancestors holding a sort of dominance over all other particles in the familial event) of succession. But a problem could be raised: what is the relationship of the keys of genealogy to a person, say an orphan or an adopted child, who has little or no access to the natural event from which they emerged? This person doesn't have the benefit of searching family databases, visiting ancestral sites, or piecing together more "direct" reasons why they have the color eyes or texture of hair they do. Therefore, someone with access to the biological familial event of which they are part could be said to have "more to work with" in their multi/race/less creation of their becoming. But the orphan or adoptee with little to no biological information about their past has access to other formative sources on their becoming. On the physical pole, a DNA test would reveal possible generalizations of geographical locations and people "groups" from which the recent descendants come. This could serve as a ground for learning about said regions and people "groups" and founding substantial parts of an identity always becoming regarding nationalities and cultures related to their familial events. On the conceptual pole, there may be foster and adoptive parents, mentors, cultures, friends, foods, and more contributing eternal objects constituting their present subjective experience. These are imperfect yet possible grounds for a genealogy of becoming. How can these significant formative sources be prehended as the human pursues substantial, intense, and persuasive (holding considerable sway over the experient so that abstractions of identity ingressed are what we've defined as "useful" in that they provide a functional yet non-totalizing unity of diversity) identities in perpetual formation that do not fall prey to the hierarchical traps of race trauma?

A striking example of non-biological engagement of genealogy in the key of the choosing of one's becoming is that of a young man in Livingstone, Guatemala, known under the race-related classifications of the region as "Indigéna." This young man was taken in by the Garifuna in Livingstone. Philip Flores, one of the residents in the area, says of the young man,

> That's an Indian [meaning those referred to as "Maya" by the accepted systems of classification]. He speaks my language better than me. After the hurricane, we adopted him after his parents died. Now if you tell him he's Indian he deny it. He's Garif[una] . . . He's Mayan. Don't he look like it? . . . He no longer thinks he's Mayan. He's Garifuna.[46]

This simple example discloses the fluidity of one's personal psyche. It doesn't matter how the systems of race/trauma taxonomy stratify the young man; he understands himself and is understood by his community to be Garifuna. This is not an erasure. Without the familial event of the "Maya" of which he is apart, the young man might not have even been in Guatemala to *become* Garifuna. All is preserved and represented. The categories do not ultimately determine what one can *be*. They are open jails one can walk out of, at the very least in terms of a subjective experience/enlightenment lured by *becoming* other than. This returns us to the self-study inspired by Noble Drew Ali at the beginning of this chapter and threaded throughout the text. Multi/race/less/ness is first a personal rejection of the trauma of racial categories. The resonance of said rejection and the co-creation of new modes of subjective experience, exceeding the categories of race/trauma, have the potential to lure others into progressive phases of understanding the novel subjective experience as it is lived authentically by the experient. Multi/race/less/ness hopes to broaden what we can think possible of human identity until a post-race human is no longer automatically deemed nonsensical, utopic, or irresponsible.

If you've seen *Emily in Paris*, you'll get this one. Emily, the main character, is a Chicagoan who takes a job in Paris at a branch of the marketing firm she works for. In her time there, she gets swept away by Gabriel, a man living above her who has a girlfriend named Camille. Both Gabriel and Emily have a magnetic attraction to each other. This is similar to the way in which one may be dissatisfied with race/trauma and feel "wild" lures of identities in formation which can't be reduced to the prescriptions of race/trauma but are authentically felt in the experience. These may happen to overtake them as they move through them, like Emily and Gabriel are overtaken by each other. In the last episode of the first season, Emily chooses to deny the fullness of her feelings, her genealogical potential for becoming other than with the information she's provided by her strong connection to Gabriel. They could throw caution to the side and see where the "adventure" of following intuition takes them. The only ones who stop this exploration into novel possibilities are them.[47]

So, this end is a passageway to another beginning. Will we dare to move from behind the shadows of race/trauma and see what interesting and ir/responsible post-race instabilities we can build? Will we find better and more equitable flings of relational identities in fluid InnerSectional formation? Will we cheat on race/trauma?

BREVE EPÍLOGO

The ideas shared in this text are musings I've thought through, lived, explored, and revised throughout the corpus of my very short time on the planet. Race as a category always deeply disturbed me, as I've always thought it an unnecessary and harmful scourge upon the surface of identities in formation, allowing and prohibiting what expressions of human experiential flux can take shape or exist beyond the confines of shape itself. Again, the preceding pages are a thought experiment asking us to take seemingly mandatory racial and race-related glasses off for the duration of the text and see what the world looks like without them. What I have offered is not necessarily intended to assert that multi/race/less/ness solves the problems associated with the personal and societal ingressions of race/trauma infinitely reinscribed into our ways of thinking and thinking as *being*. I do hold that multi/race/less/ness is a possible step that should be considered as we work to shape more equitable worlds in *becoming*. I have attempted to offer a responsible philosophy of race in conversation with philosophy of religion, process thought, and metaphysics (among other streams of thought) that differs from current and in my estimation quite valuable writings advancing racial eliminativism in that it not only articulates and *prescribes* a meticulously articulated system of multi/race/less/ness in the cyclical *process* of Creativity, Useful Lived Abstraction, Dis/solution, and Repetition, but also adds an audacious and provocative thesis to the discourse: race *is* trauma. Therefore, race *as* trauma is a category of thinking and *needing* abolishing as the options of identity formation become more adventurous indications of a *responsible* post-race future where the existential "traumas" of a belief in racial categories are accounted for. In other words, this project is novel because it asserts a new starting point for philosophy of race in the equivalence of race with trauma and offers a substantial and "clear" proposal for a responsible post-race future.

The project also stands on its own in the milieu of philosophy of race in its position that racial eliminativism is already and has been happening successfully for quite some time. Hence, theory does not have to invent it. Our theories can be informed by post-race examples readily accessible to virtually anyone. Concerning her classes, Naomi Zack stated,

Yes, my classes explore what should and can change. The foundation is the false construction of race itself—not just racist stereotypes, but the absence of a foundation in biology. It's all made up. So we need to approach race as real social construction with roots in discarded science and histories and traditions of white supremacy and nonwhite oppression. That race is made up shows the power of social construction and it also suggests that what has been made can be unmade.[1]

Hip-Hop Culture, Belizean nationality, and the potential of a more philosophically robust view of genealogy are three instances I personally offer of multi/race/less/ness "on the ground." The unmaking has already occurred in some places. There are more than just these (to be clear, genealogy is not specifically applied to any one thing in the text, unlike nationality and ethnicity). You, the reader, may be aware of them. Please amplify them in the world. The "made up" nature of race (and quite bluntly the nonsense of it) Zack discusses is something I was always particularly attuned to since childhood. Perhaps due to the subjective experience of various aspects of my familial event, some of which emerge from the present-day United States, Spain, Portugal, Belize, Nigeria, etc. Perhaps due to my interest in philosophy as a child. Perhaps due to my penchant to never leave well enough alone. My intuition led me to eventually renounce and deconvert from the categories of race/trauma and race-related language. This "unmaking" Zack discusses here is a blatant renouncing of the definitionally hierarchical categories in the face of societies that force them on us. In multi/race/less/ness, a way in which unmaking and remaking can (and does) happen is imperfectly spelled out. It is provided as a path. Maybe it is better described as a route toward a destination, which will perpetually move further in distance once we assume we've arrived. It is up to myself and others interested to perpetually fine-tune this way of becoming from artists to electricians to politicians to restaurant owners to philosophers of race to beach bums (of which I've kinda been during the summer where much of the second half of the text was written, and where I sit now, observing the flux of the ocean in Playas de Tijuana as I muse about the fluidity of the human) to make something of this, of themselves. The future might not be so great if we perpetuate race/trauma for another generation. Perhaps not even for another second. Multi/race/less/ness is literally a retraining and reprogramming of thought so that one does not continue to instinctively (hence uncritically) think and act racially/traumatically.

For the sake of keeping lines of dialogue open between myself and people who readily identify racially, I don't dismiss them when they refer to me by the race/trauma and race/related categories "Black," "African American," "Caribbean," "Latinx," and "Native American." But if someone asks me how I identify myself, I draw from the teachings of Prophet Noble Drew Ali and his emphasis on nationality and respond, "I am a subjective instance of a long familial event and refer to myself as a Belizean-Honduran Chicagoan of Afro-diasporic and other descent." Upon further "self-study," I may expand this through a shortening of words to "Belizean-Honduran Chicagoan of Moorish and other descent," as the teachings of not only Drew Ali but exterior historical information gives evidence that the specific *nationality* of "Moorish" was the national capacity of personhood (not of property) through which a large number of people hailing from the various geographical regions of long lines of my ancestors were perceived and valued as ends in themselves by the nations of the world. The particular formulation of irreducible multiplicity we refer to as the "experiencing" subject will of course vary from person to person. But the objective of this all-too-long text was to get us to think differently, if only for a duration as fleeting as the eternal now. Hopefully, this "revolution of the mind," to reference James Brown one last time, will permanently expand the possibilities of the conceivable.

Finally, inspired by process philosophy from my early days in grad school until now (and perhaps before I had the language of the subfield and even read Whitehead), Multi/race/less/ness is a work that attempts to further an expansion of the edges of what is considered a part of this philosophical tradition by remembering what Whitehead (by his own admission) merely echoed in some key points, such as the philosophies of China and India. Also, the universal flux and reverence of impermanence evident in the philosophical thought and praxis of Nigeria, Benin, and Egypt were also important inspirations. The project pays a huge debt to not only Noble Drew Ali's reminding us of these sacred ways of Asiatic becoming but also to Daykeeper Hunbatz Men, whose expansive and border-collapsing work inspired me to deeply engage the types of reimagining hosted in this text. This "Mayan" way of becoming exemplifies the height of process thought: permanence in flux and flux in permanence, as evidenced in the fully embodied experience of sexual energy, felt fully but beyond the confines of symbol.[2] The be/coming exceeding symbolization in sexual energy is very much akin to the orgiastic indeterminateness of identities in formation I hold are able to conquer the up to this point impenetrable deep-seated systemic, folk, and legal hierarchies of race/trauma.

That's it. Read this and in some ways take it with a grain of salt. But please take it. It certainly won't eliminate your existence if you are to "try it on for size." For the upliftment of all of us who have fallen . . .

NOTES

Prolegomenon to any Future Philosophy of Race

1. Tunnel Rats, "Change RMX," *Tunnel Vision* (Uprok Records, 2001), CD.
2. "Kenny Leon, dir. *American Son* (Ventura: Simpson Street, 2019), https://www.netflix.com/watch/81024100?trackId=255824129&tctx=0%2C0%2Ccb8baf2a-609f-411c-b8ef-c4c2183e06a6-187499151%2Ccb8baf2a-609f-411c-b8ef-c4c2183e06a6-187499151%7C2%2Cunknown%2C%2C%2CtitlesResults%2C%2CVideo%3A81024100%2CminiDpPlayButton
3. Michelle Balaev, "Trauma Studies," in *A Companion to Literary Theory*, ed. David H. Richter (Oxford: John Wiley & Sons Ltd., 2018), 361.
4. Ibid. 362.
5. This by no means indicates that there were not systems of divisive identification before the advent of what theorists understand by the category of race. However, it does indicate the absence of a certain system of classification uniquely accompanying the social constructions that eventually become what we refer to as "race."
6. "Race-related" refers to terms of human classification not thought of squarely as referencing phenotype and ancestry but cultures and/or geographical regions, such as "Asian," "Latinx," "Indigenous," "African American," "Native American," and so on. These terms are considered "suspect" along with racial categories because (1) they are the racial residue of and are determined by colonial systems of naming and (2) they in many instances erroneously presuppose certain appearances and ancestries.
7. Alex Klein, "What to Know about Racial Trauma," medicalnewstoday.com, July 23, 2020, https://www.medicalnewstoday.com/articles/racial-trauma (Accessed August 25, 2024).
8. Henry Lefebvre, *Metaphilosophy*, trans. David Fernbach, ed. Stuart Elden (London: Verso, 2016), 21.
9. Rats, "Chainge RMX."

Introduction

1. David Rogers and Moira Bowman, "A History: The Construction and the Deconstruction of Race," 7, https://www.giarts.org/sites/default/files/conference_websites/2017/documents/construction-of-race-and-racism.pdf (Accessed October 25, 2024).
2. James Baldwin, *James Baldwin: The Last Interview and Other Conversations* (Hoboken: Melville House, 2014), 53.
3. "Octavia Butler interview—Transcending Barriers," *YouTube.com*, video, June 22, 2018, https://www.youtube.com/watch?v=KG68v0RGHsY (Accessed August 5, 2025).
4. Ytasha Womack, *Afrofuturism: The World of Black Sci Fi and Fantasy Culture* (Chicago: Lawrence Hill Books, 2013), 27–8.
5. Sri Aurobindo, *The Life Divine* (Detroit: Lotus Press, 1990), 113.
6. Both "historical" and "identities" are in quotation marks because we can severely question whether even pre-colonial identities are really anything more than the creation of those who said histories and identities correspond to. Granted, these inventions may come about for different reasons than the creation of histories and identities by the "same" people in question during and after colonization.
7. Killah Priest, "From Then 'til Now," *Heavy Mental* (Geffen: 1998), CD.
8. Christopher M. Driscoll and Monica R. Miller, *Method as Identity: Manufacturing Distance in the Academic Study of Religion* (Lanham: Lexington Books, 2018), 126–7.
9. I do not use "primordial" in reference to some "essence," but as a marker of a human/society-made idea that existed before the system of race only because it was created by empirical agents and factors, not from a Platonic/Hegelian model upon which the tangible world is shaped or dialectically reflected.

Chapter 1

1. Friedrich Nietzsche, *Nietzsche and the Death of God: Selected Writings*, trans. Peter Fritzsche (Boston: Bedford/St. Martin's, 2007), 71–2.
2. Anthony B. Pinn and Monica R. Miller, "Introduction: Intersections of Culture and Religion in African-American Communities," *Culture and Religion* 10, no. 1 (2009): 4.
3. Christopher M. Driscoll and Monica R. Miller, *Method as Identity: Manufacturing Distance in the Academic Study of Religion* (Lanham: Lexington Books, 2019), 54.
4. Theodore Walker, *Mothership Connections: A Black Atlantic Synthesis of Neoclassical Metaphysics and Black Theology* (Albany: State University of New York Press, 2004), 10.
5. The Doors, "An American Prayer," *An American Prayer* (Electra/Asylum, 1978), CD.
6. Benjamin Isaac, *The Invention of Racism in Classical Antiquity* (Princeton: Princeton University Press, 2004), 34, 37.
7. Ibid.

8   Ibid.
9   George Frederickson, *Racism: A Short History* (Princeton: Princeton University Press, 2002), 31–5.
10 Ibid., 145.
11 Robert Bernasconi and Tony Lee Lott, eds., *The Idea of Race* (Indianapolis: Hackett, 2000), 2–3.
12 Ibid., viii.
13 Ibid., 27–33.
14 Ivan Hannaford, *Race: The History of an Idea in the West* (Baltimore: The Johns Hopkins University Press, 1996), 206.
15 Bernasconi and Lott, *The Idea of Race*, 80.
16 Ibid., 82.
17 Hannaford, *Race*, 351.
18 Ibid., 354.
19 Ibid., 354–5.
20 James Perkinson, *White Theology: Outing Supremacy in Modernity* (New York: Palgrave Macmillan, 2004), 152.
21 Hannaford, *Race*, 358.
22 Michael James and Adam Burgos, "Race," *The Stanford Encyclopedia of Philosophy*, ed. Edward N. Zalta (Summer 2020 Edition), https://plato.stanford.edu/archives/sum2020/entries/race/.
23 Stephen Cornell and Douglass Hartman, *Ethnicity and Race: Making Identities in a Changing World* (Thousand Oaks: Pine Forge Press), 44–6.
24 Bernasconi and Lott, *The Idea of Race*, 100–7.
25 Charles L. Brace, *Race is a Four-Letter Word: The Genesis of the Concept* (New York: Oxford University Press, 2005), 239.
26 Walter Benjamin, "The Work of Art in the Age of Mechanical Reproduction," in *Illuminations*, ed. Hannah Arendt (New York: Schocken Books, 1968), 223, 229.
27 Ibid., 223.
28 Ibid.
29 Maybe "mechanical mutations" are instances when the racial categories are used by those grouped under them as resistance.
30 Benjamin, "The Work of Art in the Age of Mechanical Reproduction," 233.
31 Ibid., 241.
32 Bernasconi and Lott, *The Idea of Race*, viii.
33 David Hume, "Of National Character," in *Hume: Political Essays*, ed. Knud Haakonssen (Cambridge: Cambridge University Press, 1994), 86.
34 Naomi Zack, *Philosophy of Science and Race* (New York: Routledge, 2002), 13–18.
35 Immanuel Kant, "On the Different Races of Man," in *Race and the Enlightenment: A Reader*, ed. Emmanuel Chukwudi Eze (Malden: Blackwell Publishers, 1997), 38–40.
36 Ibid., 41.

37 Pauline Kleingeld, "On Dealing With Kant's Sexism and Racism," *SGIR Review* 2, no. 2, 2019, 3–22, 26.

38 Ibid., 8–9.

39 James and Burgos, "Race."

40 Brace, *Race is a Four-Letter Word*, 93–103.

41 Arthur de Gobineau, "Essay on the Inequality of the Human Races," trans. A. Collins, in *The Idea of Race*, ed. Robert Bernasconi and Tony Lee Lott (Indianapolis: Hackett, 2000), 45–51.

42 Charles Darwin, "On the Races of Man," in *The Idea of Race*, ed. Robert Bernasconi and Tony Lee Lott (Indianapolis: Hackett 2000), 77–8.

43 Hannaford, *Race*, 273.

44 Daniel P. Jamros, "Hegel on the Incarnation: Unique or Universal?" *Theological Studies* 56 (1995): 277, 281–3.

45 C. J. Friedrich, "Introduction to Dover Edition," in Georg Wilhelm Friedrich Hegel, *The Philosophy of History* (New York: Dover Publications, 1956).

46 Ibid., 357.

47 Ibid., 41.

48 Ibid., 40.

49 Richard Crouter, "Introduction," in Friedrich Schleiermacher, *On Religion: Speeches to its Cultured Despisers*, ed. Richard Crouter (Cambridge: Cambridge University Press, 1988), xiv.

50 Schleiermacher, *On Religion*, 97–8.

51 Ibid., 113.

52 For Hegel, this universal intuition that reveals the totality of the universe through religious feeling in Schleiermacher presents itself as a pure universal logic that is most evidenced in the synthesis of human and divine in the person of Jesus. Schleiermacher focuses on religion as a distinct type of emotional disposition to the vastness of the universe, while Hegel's notion of Absolute Spirit is an ultimate awareness of the essence of things through reason.

53 Fortunately, with the work of scholars such as Spencer Drew's *The Aliites: Race and Law in the Religion of Noble Drew Ali* (Chicago: University of Chicago Press, 2019) and Larry L. W. Miles, *Afro and Indigenous Intersectionality in America as Nomen* (Lanham: Lexington Books, 2023), Noble Drew Ali is again garnering attention in the "ivory tower."

54 Felicia Miyakawa, *Five Percenter Rap: God's Hop Music, Message, and Black Muslim Mission* (Bloomington: Indiana University Press, 2006), 9.

55 Ibid., 9–10.

56 Aminah Beverly McCloud, *African American Islam* (New York: Routledge, 1995), 10–11.

57 José Pimienta-Bey, *Othello's Children in the New World* (Bloomington: AuthorHouse, 2002), 71.

58 McCloud, *African American Islam*, 12.

59 Larry L. W. Miles, *Afro and Indigenous Intersectionality in America as Nomen* (Lanham: Lexington Books, 2023), 11.
60 Pimienta-Bey, *Othello's Children in the New World*, 43.
61 Ibid., 40.
62 Ibid., 41.
63 Miyakawa, *Five Percenter Rap*, 11.
64 *The Holy Koran of the Moorish Science Temple of America*, 3.
65 Pimienta-Bey, *Othello's Children in the New World*, 30–1.
66 Drew, *The Aliites*, 32–3.
67 Ibid., 53.
68 McCloud, *African American Islam*, 11.
69 *The Holy Koran of the Moorish Science Temple of America*, 64–5.
70 Drew, *The Aliites*, 46–65.
71 Pimienta-Bey, *Othello's Children in the New World*, 102–3.
72 "Asiatic" is used by the MSTA to refer mostly to the descendants of slavery labeled "Negro," "Black," and "Colored," but also refers to those labeled "Native American," and those of the continent of "Asia" and "Africa." Its use is derived from the assertion of the MSTA and other groups (such as the Nation of Gods and Earths and the Nation of Islam) that the region now called "Africa" was considered "Asia" in ancient maps.
73 *The Holy Koran of the Moorish Science Temple of America*, 67.
74 It is very important to note that in this speech, Minister Farrakhan does not assert that Noble Drew Ali was the possessor of any definitive or original revelation. The comment could possibly be read to merely give Drew Ali "props" for setting the stage for the more "significant" teachings of W.D. Fard Muhammad and The Honorable Elijah Muhammad, similar to how the MSTA understands Garvey to be a forerunner for the work of Drew Ali.
75 Minister Louis Farrakhan, "Minister Farrakhan Honors Noble Drew Ali," Youtube.com, May 27, 2020, https://youtu.be/td9aXByeTh4.
76 McCloud, *African American Islam*, 18.
77 William Eric Perkins, *Droppin' Science: Critical Essays on Rap Music and Hip Hop Culture* (Philadelphia: Temple University Press, 1996), 186.
78 Pimienta-Bey, *Othello's Children in the New World*, 117–19.
79 Allen Davis (May 11, 2020). "An Historical Timeline of Reparations Payments Made From 1783 through 2020 by the United States Government, States, Cities, Religious Institutions, Colleges and Universities, and Corporations." University of Massachusetts Amherst. https://guides.library.umass.edu/reparations.
80 Connor Friedersorf, "What Do 2020 Candidates Mean When They Say 'Reparations'?" *The Atlantic*, June 5, 2019.
81 Pimienta-Bey, *Othello's Children in the New World*, 117.
82 Jennifer Vest, "Names," *The Canadian Journal of Native Studies*, XXX 1, 2010, https://cjns.brandonu.ca/wp-content/uploads/30-1-08vest.pdf (Accessed August 5, 2025).
83 Pimienta-Bey, *Othello's Children in the New World*, 119.

84 Miles, *Afro and Indigenous Intersectionality in America as Nomen*, 28.

85 Malcom X, *The Autobiography of Malcom X*.

86 José Pimienta-Bey, "Race in America: You are NOT Black (Here's More Reasons Why)", *YouTube.com*, May 4, 2020, https://www.youtube.com/watch?v=f7nypydE0V8 (Accessed August 5, 2025).

87 *The Holy Koran of the Moorish Science Temple of America*, 67.

88 Victor Anderson, *Beyond Ontological Blackness: An Essay on African American Religious and Cultural Criticism* (New York: Bloomsbury Press Anderson), 15.

89 Francisco Bethancourt, *Racisms: From the Crusades to the Twentieth Century* (Princeton: Princeton University Press, 2013), 1.

90 Pimienta-Bey, *Othello's Children in the New World*, 20–2.

Chapter 2

1 Ann Cudd, *Analyzing Oppression* (Oxford: Oxford University Press, 2006), 34.

2 Ibid.

3 Ibid.

4 Ibid., 35–6.

5 Ibid., 36.

6 Ibid.

7 Ibid.

8 Ibid., 37.

9 Ibid., 38.

10 Ibid., 39.

11 Ibid., 41.

12 Ibid., 41–2.

13 Jim Perkinson, *White Theology: Outing Supremacy in Modernity* (New York: Palgrave Macmillan, 2004), 163.

14 Cudd, *Analyzing Oppression*, 41.

15 Kwame Anthony Appiah, "Race, Culture, and Identity: Misunderstood Connections," in Kwame Anthony Appiah and Amy Gutman, *Color Consciousness: The Political Morality of Race* (Princeton: Princeton University Press, 1998).

16 Ibid., 64–6.

17 Alfred North Whitehead, *Modes of Thought* (New York: The Free Press, 1966), 33–4.

18 Of course, as we know, this worked in favor of the colonization period from the late fifteenth to nineteenth centuries, as non-"Whites" in many instances by legal analytic definition had less personhood than "Whites" or no personhood at all.

19 Appiah, "Race, Culture, and Identity," 110.

20 Ibid., 109.

21 Ibid., 128.

22 Ibid., 129.

23 Ibid.

24 Jorge J. E. Gracia and Susan L. Smith, "Analytic Metaphysics: Race and Identity," in *The Routledge Companion to Philosophy of Race*, ed. Paul C. Taylor, Linda Martín Alcoff, and Luvell Anderson (New York: Routledge, 2018), 211.

25 Jorge J. E. Gracia, *Surviving Race, Ethnicity, and Nationality: A Challenge for the Twenty-First Century* (Lanham: Rowman and Littlefield, 2005), xii.

26 Gracia and Smith, "Analytic Metaphysics," 212.

27 Ibid., 211.

28 Gracia, *Surviving Race, Ethnicity, and Nationality*, 85.

29 Ibid., 48.

30 Ibid., 65.

31 For now, it suffices to say that I find this ostensible condition of Miller's "nation" definition too passive, and not quite taking into account the possible problem with conflating national identity with the happenstance occurrence of being born in a particular country, which may work fine in the case of individuals who assent to being categorized as an "American," for example, but may not fit so well with a person who is a descendant of a family that "America" has oppressed and has more affinity with another nation or no nation at all. The former may possibly ascribe to all of Miller's definition of nationhood and be a patriot, while the latter may see themself as merely being born in said nation without any other deeper or metaphysical meaning to the term "nationality." The latter troubles the "active in character" qualification for nationality, and one must critically ask if this person can be accurately said to have the nationality of an "American" if they reject what they perceive to be the ethos and history of the nation and merely live in the geographical confines of "America." When one says that one is of a certain nation, in many instances it is implied that having a certain nationality is more than just lip service. In my reading, Miller's definition does not account for the nuances in the usages of "nationality," where the agency or the lack thereof of the national must be seriously considered.

32 Gracia, *Surviving Race, Ethnicity, and Nationality*, 110.

33 Ibid., 112–13.

34 Ibid., 118.

35 Ibid., 123.

36 Naomi Zach, *Philosophy of Science of Race* (New York: Routledge, 2002), 6, 8.

37 Ibid., 7.

38 Gracia and Smith, "Analytic Metaphysics," 208.

39 "UCF Expressions with J.L. Vest: Poet Philosopher," youtube.com, May 19, 2008, https://youtu.be/jD2778K-tr4.

40 Jennifer Lisa Vest, *Names* (El Cerrito: Indigenous Speak, 1997), 154–5.

41 Hunbatz Men, *Secrets of Mayan Science/Religion* (Rochester: Bear & Company, 1990), 81.

42 Jennifer Lisa Vest, "The Promise of Caribbean Philosophy: Toward a 'New Dialogic' in Philosophy," *Caribbean Studies* 33, no. 2 (July/December): 6.

43 Ibid., 8, 9.
44 Ibid., 9.
45 Ibid., 11.
46 Jennifer Lisa Vest, "Being and Not Being, Knowing and Not Knowing," in *Philosophy and the Mixed Race Experience*, ed. Tina Fernandes Bottes (New York: Lexington Books, 2016), 95.
47 Ibid.
48 Ibid., 97.
49 Ibid., 97–8.
50 Ibid., 98.
51 Ibid., 94.
52 Ibid.
53 Ibid., 96.
54 Ibid., 106.
55 Ibid., 107.

Chapter 3

1 Tomorrow Kings, "Black Power in Hell," *Nigger Rigged Time Machine* (ReSERVED Records, 2013), CD.

3 Pimienta-Bey elaborates on Prophet Noble Drew Ali's statement found in chapter XLVII of the Holy Koran of the Moorish Science Temple of America asserting that the Asiatics of the present-day United States lost their national name in 1774 due to "forsaking the principles of their mother and father." The Articles of Association, written in 1774, marked to Noble Drew Ali a voluntary loss of nationality of those of Moorish ancestries under new legal system, which would render them "Negro" and "Colored," precursors of the racial category "Black." For more information, consult Pimienta-Bey's *Othello's Children in the "New World:" Moorish History & Identity in the African American Experience* (Bloomington: AuthorHouse, 2002), 116–48.

4 This is in reference to Noble Drew Ali's assertion that all those referred under any legal term other than "White" have connections to the ancient Moorish empire and are hence members of an extensive global family.

5 I do not hold that Pimienta-Bey provides a "smoking gun" for this case, but the information he and other scholars provide is well-researched and plausible based on the provided evidence.

6 The area encompassing much of what is now referred to as the "Middle East," including much of the regions that are modern-day Egypt, Iran, the Arabian Peninsula, etc. and what is now referred to as "northern Africa," is the region the MSTA holds the original humans emerged from. The teachings of Noble Drew Ali refer to Pangea as "Asia," and those original humans who spread throughout the continent before the landmass separated are known as "Asiatics."

7   The leadership of the MSTA has been the site of major and sometimes deadly contestations of power. After the death of Noble Drew Ali in 1929, leadership was passed on to the Supreme Grand Sheik Edward Mealy El. E. Mealy El was the highest official in the organization at the time, respectively appointed to the offices of Assistant Chairman, Grand Sheik, and Supreme Grand Sheik by Drew Ali himself. Mealy El's leadership was unanimously approved by the organization's Supreme Grand Council and legal paperwork was changed to reflect this in 1929. C. Kirkman-Bey, Grand Advisor to Noble Drew Ali, went to the courts to contest Mealy El's leadership of the MSTA and lost repeatedly, with a final court ruling in favor of Mealy El on May 7, 1931. This split the organization and prompted Kirkman-Bey to found his own faction of the movement called the Moorish Science Temple of America, Inc. Moorish Americans practicing the Science in temples under the lineage of Mealy El refer to said temples as "authorized" and temples and incorporations emerging from the line of Kirkman-Bey or any other ancestry as "unauthorized." This has a striking resemblance to the Sunni/Shia split within the Islam of the "Middle East" and Northern "Africa." For more on factions in/of the MSTA, consult Sheik Way-El, *Noble Drew Ali and the Moorish Science Temple of America: The Movement that Started it All* (City unknown: Moorish Science Temple of America, 2013).

8   The title of an album I recorded with DPEL in 2009 and released by Chicago independent label The Secret Life of Sound in 2012.

9   In many MSTA temples, the US flag is displayed at the left front of the room and the Moorish flag is to the left right, denoting the current government first and what Moorish Americans believe to be the former government second (following reading from left to right in languages such as English and Spanish). Bro. Pettis-El speaks of a time when the Moorish governance will return and the status of the United States will take a secondary role. It is to be noted that while many offshoots of the teachings of Noble Drew Ali reject the legitimacy of the US government, the MSTA accepts it as the lawful current administration of these lands.

10 For a critical analysis of the Yacub story resonating with what Brother Pettis-El has stated but more extensive due to its sole focus on this topic from the perspective of the critical study of religion, refer to the chapters "I Am That I Am" and "Troglodytes" in Christopher M. Driscoll's *White Devils, Black Gods: Race, Masculinity, and Religious Codependency* (London: Bloomsbury Academic, 2023), 67–84.

11 Aesop Rock is a popular underground MC who under the racial designations of the United States would be referred to as "White."

12 This argument is made in reference to the Moorish presence in Sicily during the time of their occupation of present-day Spain in ninth to eleventh centuries.

13 The book Pettis-El is referring to is Aminah Beverly McCloud's *African American Islam* (New York: Routledge, 1995).

14 Refer to Chapter 1 for a more detailed history of the stages of the MSTA oversaw by Noble Drew Ali from the Holy Moorish Temple of Science to the Moorish Science Temple of America.

15 Unity Hall, during the time of Noble Drew Ali, was social club on Chicago's South Side that has existed since 1887. During the early twentieth century, Unity Hall served as a meeting place for community organizing and forward thinking

motions among so-called "Blacks" for social upliftment. One of the most famous pictures of Noble Drew Ali with his followers in Chicago was taken in front of Unity Hall during the 1928 Annual Convention. Lomax-Bey is in this photo.

16 The Nation of Islam begins on July 4, 1930, approximately 17 years after Noble Drew Ali founded the Canaanite Temple in Newark, New Jersey in 1913.
17 "Fruit of Islam" is a term signifying the men in the Nation of Islam.
18 I take this to be in reference to the stage area of the auditorium of the headquarters of the Nation of Islam in Chicago, IL.
19 "G7" is short for my rap alias, "Gilead7."
20 This is in reference to Frank Cherry, widely credited with the founding of the Hebrew Israelite movement along with William Saunders Crowdy.
21 One of the Moorish surnames used by members of the MSTA. "El," as in "Dominic Pettis-El," is the other surname used by the organization.
22 The person giving Pettis-El this information about the previous affiliation of one of the founders of the Hebrew Israelite movement may have been referring to a possible later influence, as Hebrew Israelitism can be traced back to 1886, close to 25 years prior to Drew Ali's first temple, which was formed in 1913.

Chapter 4

1 Since race is largely a matter of the state, this is appropriate.
2 Jonah E. Bromwich, "Everyone Is Cancelled," *The New York Times*, June 28, 2018, https://www.nytimes.com/2018/06/28/style/is-it-canceled.html (accessed April 9, 2024).
3 "Cancel Culture Top 3 Pros and Cons," ProCon.org, August 16, 2023, https://www.procon.org/headlines/is-cancel-culture-or-callout-culture-good-for-society/.
4 Sarah McCammon, "Remembering Bishop Carlton Pearson, Who Believed in 'Universal Salvation,'" npr.org, November 26, 2023, https://www.npr.org/2023/11/26/1215227713/remembering-bishop-carlton-pearson-who-believed-in-universal-salvation (accessed October 26, 2024).
5 Bromwich, "Everyone Is Cancelled."
6 Jean Paul Sartre, *Nausea*, trans. R. Baldick (Hammondsworth: Penguin Books, 1965), 183.
7 Jean Paul Sartre, *Being and Nothingness*, trans. H. E. Barnes (New York: Routledge, 1958), xxxi.
8 Catherine L. Albanese, *America, Religions and Religion* (Boston: Wadsworth Publishing Company, 1981), 10.
9 Christopher M. Driscoll and Monica R. Miller, *Method as Identity: Manufacturing Distance in the Study of Religion* (Lanham: Lexington Books, 2018), 62.
10 InnerSection is my way of identifying varying regions are by nature a part of coalescing multiplicity. I use this term as opposed to "intersection," which could be said to presuppose a fundamental distinction between two entities that come into contact due to the confluences of various forces. In InnerSection, there is not

necessarily one substance as in Spinoza. However, InnerSection, similar in some ways to the various strands of monism in the Āshtika Indian philosophies, does identify all-encompassing process as the inclusion of that which we sometimes call "things," thus stripping said "things" of the fundamental distinctions that create militarized partitions between races and revealing a primordial relationality. InnerSection is influenced by the philosophies of Hunbatz Men, Alfred North Whitehead, Jennifer Lisa Vest, and others.

11 David West, *An Introduction to Continental Philosophy* (Cambridge: Polity Press, 1996), 141.

12 Slavoj Žižek, *The Parallax View* (Cambridge, MA: MIT Press, 2009), 78.

13 Miguel de Unamuno, *Tragic Sense of Life* (New York: Dover Publications, 1954), 1–18.

14 Tunnel Rats, "Just Words," *Experience* (Brainstorm Recordings, 1996), CD.

15 Žižek, *The Parallax View*, 78–9.

16 James Ward, *Zero Victim: Overcoming Injustice with a New Attitude* (Warrenton: Freiling Publishing, 2021), 5.

17 Ethan Alter, "Kanye West Said, "George Bush Doesn't Care about Black People" on This Day in 2005," Yahoo!, September 2, 2023, www.yahoo.com/entertainment/kanye-west-said-george-bush-doesnt-care-about-black-people-on-this-day-in-2005-130006321.html?guccounter=1&guce_referrer=aHR0cHM6Ly93d3cuZ29vZ2xlLmNvbS8&guce_referrer_sig=AQAAAJFwzG5sjfHhC26sSpiBOZPriVlH9SaPprd5uCl8PaRcKv_PZ0PL8oh7zOq-SL_TR9gP--OAjQbL5-Ir3-C3qTbpZtsBiV32B4SZotmzdCcyp7IzVLjpeaOGqYFiQt_E73eb3CN46VGbtIOuNq0ZC9GWYj09Oi3whKxCvMn5LPYX (accessed April 9, 2024).

18 Xavi Sancho, "The Rise and Fall of Kanye West," *EL PAÍS English*, October 31, 2022, english.elpais.com/culture/2022-10-31/the-rise-and-fall-of-kanye-west.html (accessed April 9, 2024).

19 Javier P. Martín, "How Kanye West Uses Instagram to Settle Scores," *EL PAÍS English*, March 14, 2022, english.elpais.com/culture/2022-03-14/how-kanye-west-uses-instagram-to-settle-scores.html (accessed April 9, 2024).

20 Harmeet Kaur, "Kanye West Just Said 400 Years of Slavery Was a Choice," CNN, May 4, 2018, www.cnn.com/2018/05/01/entertainment/kanye-west-slavery-choice-trnd/index.html (accessed April 9, 2024).

21 "Kanye West TMZ Full Interview," TMZ, YouTube, May 2, 2018, 0:38–1:42, www.youtube.com/watch?v=1LIGh91mloA (accessed April 9, 2024).

22 Frantz Fanon, *The Wretched of the Earth*, trans. Richard Philcox (New York: Grove Press, 2004), 56.

23 "Kanye West TMZ Full Interview," 3:26–3:58.

24 Ibid., 4:09–4:51.

25 Alfred North Whitehead, *Symbolism: Its Meaning and Effect* (New York: Fordham University Press, 1927), 19.

26 Talib Kweli and Jasmin Leigh, dirs. *Van Lathan And Talib Kweli Discuss His TMZ Kanye West Incident*, YouTube, September 28, 2019, 10:07–10:08, https://www.youtube.com/watch?v=mrryp3vF0Pg (accessed January sixteen, 2024).

27 Whitehead, *Symbolism*, 19.

28 Ibid.

29 "Preexistent" in this instance does not indicate a primordial and unconditioned fact but something that possesses an antithesis at the moment of its existence. For example, in the moment of the mental and conceptual labeling of commodified humans as "Negro" existed the possibility for the mental rejection of said status by those given it, even though the existential situation would have made its awareness extremely difficult. I of course understand that this would have done very little in the instant of realization, but I would argue that this realization of "I am not a Negro" stimulated the Haitian Revolution, the Nat Turner revolt, the exploits of Harriet Tubman, etc.

30 "Kanye West TMZ Full Interview," 17:12–18:14.

31 Jean Paul Sartre, *Being and Nothingness: An Essay on Phenomenological Ontology* (New York: Washington Square Press, 1969), 53–4.

32 "Kanye West TMZ Full Interview," 23:13–24:03.

33 Whitehead, *Symbolism*, 8.

34 Ibid., 21.

35 Ibid., 33, 37.

36 Dana Ford and Greg Botelho, "Who Is Rachel Dolezal?" CNN, Cable News Network, June 17, 2015, www.cnn.com/2015/06/16/us/rachel-dolezal/.

37 Ibid.

38 Ibid.

39 Ibid.

40 Chris McGreal, "Rachel Dolezal: 'I Wasn't Identifying as Black to Upset People. I Was Being Me,'" *The Guardian*, Guardian News and Media, December 13, 2015, www.theguardian.com/us-news/2015/dec/13/rachel-dolezal-i-wasnt-identifying-as-black-to-upset-people-i-was-being-me (accessed April 10, 2024).

41 Ibid.

42 Hilton Als, "Hilton Als on Writing and Race: Vice Podcast 025," interviewed by Reihan Salam, YouTube, December 18, 2013, www.youtube.com/watch?v=EzqmaaDYOQg&t=336s (accessed April 10, 2024).

43 Ibid.

44 Rich Benjamin, "Shades of Influence," *The New York Times*, November 8, 2013, www.nytimes.com/2013/11/10/books/review/white-girls-by-hilton-als.html?pagewanted=1 (accessed April 10, 2024).

45 Hilton Als, *White Girls* (San Francisco: McSweeney's, 2014), 28–9.

46 Sartre, *Being and Nothingness*, 1969 103.

47 "Race vs. State of Mind: Rachel Dolezal's Thoughts on Whiteness," YouTube, November 2, 2015, 0:36–0:39, www.youtube.com/watch?v=54QrcxCKo1o (accessed April 10, 2024).

48 Monica R. Miller, "Left of Black with Monica R. Miller," interviewed by Mark Anthony Neal, YouTube, October 5, 2015, 23:21–23:25, https://www.youtube.com/watch?v=zi8rZhN8Xek (accessed April 10, 2024).

49. "Race vs. State of Mind: Rachel Dolezal's Thoughts on Whiteness," 4:24–5:11 (accessed April 10, 2024).

50. Als, *White Girls*.

51. James Cone, *Black Theology and Black Power* (Maryknoll: Orbis Books, 1969), 151–2.

52. Dick Gregory, Brainy Quotes, https://www.brainyquote.com/quotes/dick_gregory_472450 (accessed April 10, 2024).

53. Miller, "Left of Black with Monica R. Miller," 25:17–28:22.

54. In many usages of the word "Jew," a nonracial term/idea can and does take on racial expectations that ground who are and are not members of the set.

55. "Nick Cannon and Professor Griff, 'Hebrew Israelite,' 'Anti-Semitism' & 'Identity,'" YouTube, June 30, 2020, 1:11–1:46, www.youtube.com/watch?v=CGXGuWCRSh4 (accessed April 10, 2024).

56. Ibid., 4:39–4:46.

57. "Anti-Semitism Definition & Meaning," Merriam-Webster, Merriam-Webster, www.merriam-webster.com/dictionary/anti-Semitism (accessed February 19, 2024).

58. "Nick Cannon and Professor Griff, 'Hebrew Israelite,' 'Anti-Semitism' & 'Identity,'" 4:39–5:50 (accessed April 10, 2024).

59. Ibid., 6:47–7:22.

60. Ibid., 7:26–7:58.

61. Ibid., 8:04–9:02.

62. "Dr Yosef Ben Jochannan and Rabbi Arthur Seltzer," YouTube, September 11, 2021, 22:55–23:51, www.youtube.com/watch?v=oCdEAzX85VA (accessed April 10, 2024).

63. Adam Reinherz, "Ethiopian-Born Israeli Researcher and Activist to Speak at Pitt," *Pittsburgh Jewish Chronicle*, April 10, 2023, jewishchronicle.timesofisrael.com/ethiopian-born-israeli-researcher-and-activist-to-speak-at-pitt/ (accessed February 29, 2024).

64. Lewis Gordon, *Black Existentialism and Decolonized Knowledge*, ed. Rozena Maart, Sayan Dey, and Louis Gordon (London: Bloomsbury Academic, 2023), 181.

65. Levin Marc, dir., *Brooklyn Babylon* (Santa Monica: Bac Films/Artisan Entertainment, 2001), DVD.

66. Gordon, *Black Existentialism and Decolonized Knowledge*, 177.

67. "Nick Cannon Humbled by Rabbi Cooper | Cannon's Class with Rabbi Cooper | "Anti-Semitism" Response," YouTube, August one, 2020, 1:10:04–1:12:15, www.youtube.com/watch?v=_6UIv868SB8&t=3085s (accessed April 10, 2024).

68. "***exclusive*** Rabbi Noam Marans Interviews Nick Cannon | Nick Cannon Says He's a Sacrificial Lamb!" YouTube, August 12, 2020, 40:01–41:41, www.youtube.com/watch?v=eilqQK33jZ0 (accessed April 10, 2024).

69. Gary Hatfield, "Introduction," in Immanuel Kant, *Prolegomena to any Future Metaphysic*, trans. and ed. Gary Hatfield (Cambridge: Cambridge University Press, 1997), xxxiii.

Chapter 5

1. Martin Heidegger, *Basic Writings: From Being and Time (1927) to The Task of Thinking (1964)* (New York: HarperPerrenial, 2008), 165, 170, 175–81.

2. Miles uses this term in contradistinction to racial and race-related terms that largely if not mostly chart the history of a people starting with when they were dominated and renamed (e.g., African American, Latinx, Native American, etc.). Drawing from the assertion that there was a strong pre-Columbian "American" presence of people who would under the racial distinctions of modernity and postmodernity be referred to as "Black" as well as numerous amounts of evidence suggesting that these people are one the central roots of those now referred to as "Native Americans" among other nomenclatures, Miles seeks to provide a fuller narrative separate from the dominant histories which tell the information through the lens of a narrative beginning with the colonial names and identities of race/trauma that happened to these people.

3. Larry L. W. Miles, *Afro and Indigenous Intersectionality as Nomen* (Lanham: Lexington Books, 2023), 103.

4. "Black or African American? Neither (Here's Why)," YouTube.com, September 9, 2019, https://www.youtube.com/watch?v=7N330vc6A3U&t=249s (accessed July 9, 2024).

5. Thandeka, *The Embodied Self: Friedrich Schleiermacher's Solution to Kant's Problem of the Empirical Self* (Albany: State University of New York Press, 1995), 1, 68–9.

6. Ibram Kendi, *How to Be an Antiracist* (New York: ONEWORLD, 2023), 41.

7. Ibid., 9.

8. By "quasi-essential" I refer to ideas that the thinker doesn't necessarily believe exist mandatorily but remain a part of a library of ideas because said idea is a pervasive force in the world. Race is a good example of this.

9. "The Difference Between Being 'Not Racist' and Antiracist | Ibram X. Kendi," YouTube.com, June 17, 2020, 0:00–3:37, https://www.youtube.com/watch?v=KCxbl5QgFZw (accessed July 10, 2024).

10. Kendi, *How to Be an Antiracist*, 256.

11. Amrita Mindal, "How to Be an Antiracist: NIH Big Read Discussion with Ibram Kendi," The NIH Catalyst, 30:6, November–December 2022, https://irp.nih.gov/catalyst/30/6/how-to-be-an-antiracist (accessed July 9, 2024).

12. "Black or African American? Neither (Here's why)."

13. "Mind Bugs | Mahzarin R. Banaji | TEDxBari," YouTube.com, January 10, 2018, 0:00–3:14, https://www.youtube.com/watch?v=AFEaCFFsM2U (accessed July 14, 2024).

14. Ibid., 3:45–4:22.

15. Ibid., 8:02–16:21.

16. Ibid., 16:14–16:17.

17. Mahzarin R. Banaji and Anthony G. Greenwald, *Blindspot: Hidden Biases of Good People* (New York: Bantam Books, 2016), xii.

18. Ibid.

19 Nowhere in this work do I suggest that creating a more equitable world happens instantly and can come into existence by the mere abolishing of racial language. However, the work is based on examining how one of many crucial steps in realizing this more progressive world would very well be the dismantling and eventual obsolescence of the category of race in discourse, thought, and practice.

20 Cornel West, *Race Matters, 25th Anniversary* (Boston: Beacon Press, 2017), 26–8.

21 Ibid., 23.

22 Ibid., 28.

23 West is an heir of Cone's philosophy of race mentioned in chapter 4 in relation to Rachel Dolezal. For Cone, to be "Black" meant you fought and put yourself at mortal risk for the freedom of the oppressed. Unfortunately, neither Cone or West fully investigate the postracial and poststructural implications of this position.

24 It goes without saying that both Thomas and Hill's membership in the group "Blackness" under West's definition has been and is the subject of much debate since many of their critics see their politics and stances of live as being different than the goals of "Black" liberation. This is especially true for Thomas. I raise them in this chapter for concerns that only peripherally relate to this issue and will not proceed to investigate something West already brilliantly did in *Race Matters*.

25 Ibid., 43.

26 Cornel West, *Prophesy Deliverance: An Afro-American Revolutionary Christianity* (Louisville: Westminster John Knox Press, 2022), 17.

27 Judith Butler, *Gender Trouble: Feminism and the Subversion of Identity* (New York: Routledge, 2007), 1.

28 Ibid., 2.

29 Ibid., 2–3.

30 Ibid.

31 Ania Loomba, "Racism in India," in *The Routledge Companion to the Philosophy of Race*, ed. Paul C. Taylor, Linda Martín Alcroft, and Luvell Anderson (New York: Routledge, 2018), 181.

32 Ibid., 185–7.

33 Ibid., 185–7, 192.

34 Ibid., 185.

35 Ibid., 188.

36 Ibid., 181, 189.

37 Peter Griffin, dir., *The Lord of the Rings: The Fellowship of the Ring* (Burbank: New Line Cinema, 2001), Amazon, 5:06–5:23.

38 Ibid., 1:36–1:41.

39 Gilbert Simondon, *On the Mode of Existence of Technical Objects*, trans. Cecile Malaspina and John Rogove (Minneapolis: University of Minnesota Press, 2017), 28.

40 Elaina Dockerman, "There's a Deeper Meaning Behind Wizards in The Rings of Power," time.com, October 14, 2022, https://time.com/6222110/wizard-istar-the-rings-of-power/ (accessed July 16, 2024).

41 Griffin, *The Fellowship of the Ring*, 1:20:54–1:21:09.

42 Ibid., 1:27:56–59.
43 "Nazgûl," fandom.com, https://lotr.fandom.com/wiki/Valar (accessed July 16, 2024).
44 "KRS-One Gives Detailed Breakdown of Hip-Hop's Prehistoric Roots," YouTube.com, January 22, 2015, 11:14–11:27, https://www.youtube.com/watch?v=0PCsYktWGiI (accessed July 17, 2024).
45 Mark C. Taylor, *Deconstruction in Context: Literature and Philosophy* (Chicago: University of Chicago Press, 1986), 33–4.
46 Griffin, *The Fellowship of the Ring*, 31:11–23.

Chapter 6

1 James Brown, "King Heroin," *There It Is* (Polydor Records, 1972), LP.
2 Jon Ivan Gill, *Underground Rap as Religion: A Theopoetic Examination of a Process Aesthetic Religion* (New York: Routledge, 2019), 27–8.
3 Jacques Derrida, *Of Grammatology*, trans. G. C. Spivak (Baltimore: Johns Hopkins University Press, 1976), 26.
4 Gill, *Underground Rap as Religion*, 30.
5 This term has come under attack due to its use as a description of how the world is currently. For me, this is irresponsible. Post-race, like Kendi's "antiracist," is a conscious movement toward such a future, and I am critical of any post-racial philosophies that do not responsibly address how race/trauma is still very much a lived reality. Its use here is quite the opposite.
6 Brian Massumi, *Semblance and Event: Activist Philosophy and the Occurrent Arts* (Cambridge, MA: MIT Press, 2011), 82.
7 Alfred North Whitehead, *Process and Reality*, corrected edition, ed. David Ray Griffin and Donald Sherburne (New York: The Free Press, 1978), 20.
8 Ibid., 31.
9 Frantz Fanon, *The Wretched of the Earth* (New York: Grove Press, 2004), 2.
10 Ibid.
11 I am aware of the differences in Fanon's context of colonialism and the United States where much of this work has up until now been focused. Despite the important differences, Fanon's assertion that the metaphysical epistemologies of colonization need to be struggled against so that they do not repeat themselves in the bodies of the colonized post-colonization is the kernel I am connecting to the Creativity phase of multi/race/less/ness.
12 Fanon, *The Wretched of the Earth*, 2.
13 Richard Polt, *Heidegger: An Introduction* (New York: Routledge, 1999), 78, 177.
14 Gloria Anzaldúa, *Borderlands/La Frontera: The New Mestiza* (San Francisco: Aunt Lute Books, 2007), 108.
15 Whitehead, *Process and Reality*, 21.
16 Gilbert Simondon, *On the Mode of Existence of Technical Objects*, trans. Cecile Malaspina and John Rogove (Minneapolis: University of Minnesota Press, 2017), 71.

17 Ibid., 259.

18 Jay McDaniel, "John Cobb on Eternal Objects," openhorizons.org, https://www.openhorizons.org/eternal-objects.html (accessed July 23, 2024).

19 Massumi, *Semblance and Event*, 15.

20 Ibid.

21 Crop Circles720, "The Listener," *Existentialism* (Echoes of Oratory Music, 2012), CD.

22 Whitehead, *Process and Reality*, 159.

23 Ibid.

24 Rafael Reyes, "All Are Abstractions: Reading Alfred North Whitehead's Critique of the Sciences," medium.com, December 6, 2014, https://medium.com/process-imagining/all-are-abstraction-reading-alfred-north-whiteheads-critique-on-the-sciences-17b50b6e75e8 (accessed July 26, 2024).

25 Lao Tzu, *Tao Te Ching*, Chapter 28, trans. Steffan Stenudd, taoistic.com, https://www.taoistic.com/taoteching-laotzu/taoteching-28.htm (accessed July 27, 2024).

26 Victor Montejo, *Mayalogue: An Interactionist Theory of Indigenous Cultures* (Albany: SUNY Press, 2021), 99.

27 Ibid., 97.

28 Whitehead, *Process and Reality*, 7.

29 Ibid., 164.

30 To limit a largely metaphysical and separate from the world understanding of God in favor of a neoclassical concept that moves within and beyond but is simultaneously the world (panentheism), Whitehead must assert that the eternal objects lie within some actual entity to be consistent. Whitehead's ontological principle simply asserts that actual entities, not transcendent ideas or Gods, are the only reasons.

31 It must be noted that Whitehead's aim could be interpreted as intending to focus on the "how" as opposed to the "why" of creativity, as the latter is a quest beyond where the asserted philosophy could go.

32 John B. Cobb, Jr., "A Whiteheadian Doctrine of God," in *Process Philosophy and Christian Thought*, ed. Delwin Brown, Ralph James, and Gene Reeves, religion-online.org, https://www.religion-online.org/book-chapter/chapter-12-a-whiteheadian-doctrine-of-god-by-john-b-cobb-jr/ (accessed July 24, 2024).

33 Thomas Hidya Tjaya, "Creativity and God in Whitehead's Process Philosophy," *Diskursus—JurnalFilsafatdanTeologi STF Driyarkara* 11, no. 2 (2012): 141–59, https://doi.org/10.36383/diskursus.v11i2.133 (accessed July 27, 2023).

34 Ibid., 140–3.

35 Montejo, *Mayalogue*, 131–6.

36 "Philip Clayton – How Can Emergence Explain Reality?" YouTube.com, August 23, 2014, 3:35–3:45, https://www.youtube.com/watch?v=nzWclhC7WmE (accessed July 24, 2024).

37 Javier Leach, "Emergence and Transcendence in Philip Clayton: His Moderate Ideas Place Him in an Ideal Position for Dialogue," *Pensamiento* 64, no. 242 (2008): 1109, https://revistas.comillas.edu/index.php/pensamiento/article/download/17970/15826 (accessed July 26, 2024).

38 "KRS-ONE Gives Detailed Breakdown of Hip-Hop's Prehistoric Roots," YouTube.com, January 22, 2015, 1:52–1:57, https://www.youtube.com/watch?v=0PCsYktWGiI&t=688s (accessed July 25, 2024).

39 Philip Clayton, *Mind and Emergence: From Quantum to Consciousness* (Oxford: Oxford University Press, 2004), 167.

40 Whitehead, *Process and Reality*, 340.

41 Lamon Manuel, "Sh*t. Everything We Have Together Is Falling Apart," *Music to Feel Like Shit to* (ReSERVED Records, 2016), CD.

42 Christopher John Fuller, *The Camphor Flame: Popular Hinduism and Society in India* (Princeton: Princeton University Press, 2004), 58.

43 I realize it could be said that race/trauma has survived its various deconstructive opponents because it is still quite influential and hence qualifies as a ULA. However, I have already argued at length why race/trauma exerts a type of influence that permeates but is not useful (read able to be used in service of a nonhierarchical process of identity formation post-race). Therefore, at this point, the reader is to take this as not something that needs to be argued again here.

44 Hunbatz Men, *Secrets of Mayan Science/Religion* (Santa Fe: Bear and Company Publishing, 1990), 25.

45 There is some pushback to the notion that what has come to be known as "Mayan philosophy" is totally physicalist, as some scholars would argue that a close analysis of the philosophical metaphysics in question would imply a very different conclusion. For more on this, please refer to Alexus McLeod, *Philosophy of the Ancient Maya: Lords of Time* (Lanham: Lexington Books, 2018), 152–8.

46 Jennifer Lisa Vest, "Being and Not Being, Knowing and Not Knowing," in *Philosophy and the Mixed Race Experience*, ed. Tina Fernandes Botts (Lanham: Lexington Books, 2016), 107–10.

47 Ibid., 105.

48 Noel Ignatiev, *Treason to Whiteness is Loyalty to Humanity*, in *Oppression, Privilege, and Resistance: Theoretical Perspectives on, Racism, Sexism, and Heterosexism*, ed. Lisa Heldke and Peg O'Conner (New York: McGraw Hill, 2004), 610.

49 "The C.O.W.S. w/Noel Ignatiev," YouTube.com, May 20, 2012, 18:35–21:10, https://www.youtube.com/watch?v=y04fGuSo1tU&t=868s (accessed July 26, 2024).

50 Alfred North Whitehead, *Symbolism: Its Meaning and Effect* (New York: Fordham University Press, 1955), 11.

51 Quetzil E. Casteñada, ""We Are Not Indigenous!:" An Introduction to the Maya Identity of the Yucatán," *The Journal of Latin American Anthropology* 9, no. 1 (2004): 36–63.

52 Kwame Anthony Appiah, *The Ethics of Identity* (Princeton: Princeton University Press, 2023), xxiv.

53 Ibid.

54 Ibid.

55 Jacques Derrida, "Différance," in *Deconstruction in Context: Literature and Philosophy*, ed. Mark C. Taylor (Chicago: University of Chicago Press, 1986), 400–2.

56 John D. Caputo, *The Prayers and Tears of Jacques Derrida: Religion Without Religion* (Bloomington: Indiana University Press, 1997), 118.

57 "Envisioning the Future of Theology and Ethics: A Womanist Perspective," YouTube.com, April 20, 2017, 1:05:13–1:06:30, https://www.youtube.com/watch?v=J7rBYfTjznY&t=4619s (accessed July 26, 2024).

58 In *Difference and Repetition*, Deleuze lays out three types of repetition, habit, the easily accessible images of things emerging from habitual experience with what gives rise to them, and the more elusive (yet not all illusory, as Deleuze asserts the first two are) possibility of what he refers to as "difference in itself." Multi/race/less ness is directly related to the latter. For a thorough exploration of the concepts of difference and repetition in Deleuze, refer to the source in the following footnote.

59 James Williams, *Gilles Deleuze's Difference and Repetition: A Critical Introduction and Guide* (Edinburgh: Edinburgh University Press, 2013), 4–12.

60 Gilles Deleuze, *Difference and Repetition*, trans. Paul Patton (London: Continuum, 2001), 1.

61 I use this to mean the same as "quasi-essential," an awareness that the experience or idea in question isn't at all fixed but carrying on as if it is.

62 José Francisco Morales Torres, *Wonder as a New Starting Point for Theological Anthropology* (Lanham: Lexington Books, 2023), 26.

Chapter 7

1 "Tron Legacy (2010) – BioDigital Jazz," YouTube.com, May 20, 2023, 0:00–1:51, https://www.youtube.com/watch?v=mA0gm1EFZtk (accessed July 29, 2024).

2 Joseph Kosinski, dir., *Tron: Legacy* (2010; Burbank, Walt Disney Studios), 5:01–5:04, https://www.amazon.com/gp/video/detail/B004R63MWQ/ref=atv_plr_detail_play.

3 Ibid., 5:06–5:14.

4 Alfred North Whitehead, *Process and Reality*, corrected edition, ed. David Ray Griffin and Donald Sherburne (New York: The Free Press, 1978), 5.

5 Walter Benjamin, *Illuminations: Essays and Reflections*, trans. Harry Zohn, ed. Hannah Arendt (Boston: Mariner Books, 2019), 176.

6 "Harmony" and "harmonious" here does not necessarily refer to a utopic "getting along" with everyone but references the openness of events to influences which sets the stage for Whitehead's notion of "reciprocal relation."

7 By "forceful," I take Montejo to mean what Whitehead refers to in the philosophy of organism as the "lure," or the pervading persuasiveness of a set of possibilities, which is more compatible with a process approach cautious of implicit determinism. This less traditional reading of the idea of "force" seems to go along with the relational and emergent picture given in this quote.

8 Victor Montejo, *Mayalogue: An Interactionist Theory of Indigenous Cultures* (Albany: SUNY Press, 2021), 45, 46.

9. Ennis Barrington Edmonds, *Rastafari: From Outcasts to Culture Bearers* (Oxford: Oxford University Press, 2003), 64.
10. "Ethnic Minorities: Defining Ethnicity and Race," scotpho.org.uk, June 25, 2023, https://www.scotpho.org.uk/population-groups/ethnic-minorities/defining-ethnicity-and-race/#:~:text=Ethnicity%20has%20been%20defined%20as,1 (accessed July 30, 2024).
11. M.S.T.A. Pamphlet, "A Warning from the Prophet," 1928.
12. "The Hip-Hop Declaration of Peace, Hip-Hop Principles," chosenhiphop.com, https://chosenhiphop.com/principles (accessed August 17, 2024).
13. Jon Ivan Gill, *Underground Rap as Religion: A Theopoetic Examination of a Process Aesthetic Religion* (New York: Routledge, 2019), 154.
14. Brian Massumi, *Semblance and Event: Activist Philosophy and the Occurrent Arts* (Cambridge, MA: MIT Press, 2011), 110.
15. Anthony B. Pinn, *The End of God-Talk: An African-American Humanist Theology* (Oxford: Oxford University Press, 2012), 43.
16. Ibid., 46.
17. At least this is the accepted narrative. Many of the origin stories of Hip-Hop are being critiqued, and the traditional position of Hip-Hop having a solely Bronx foundation is one of the stories on which counterexamples are currently being offered.
18. KRS-ONE, *The Gospel of Hip-Hop: The First Instrument* (New York: powerHouse Books, 2009), 12.
19. Ibid., 46.
20. Gloria Anzaldúa, *Borderlands/La Frontera: The New Mestiza* (San Francisco: Ann Lute Books, 2007), 102, 104–5, 107.
21. Gill, *Underground Rap as Religion*, 47.
22. Erin Manning, *Relationscapes: Movement, Art. Philosophy* (Cambridge, MA: MIT Press, 2012), 15.
23. Ibid., 35.
24. Common, "Like They Used to Say" (Rawkus Records, 1999), CD.
25. Rick Famuyiwa, *Brown Sugar* (2002; Los Angeles: Fox Searchlight Pictures, 2002), DVD.
26. "Tariq Nasheed Dismantles Revisionist Hip-Hop History," YouTube.com, June 6, 2024, 2:16–5:25, https://www.youtube.com/watch?v=qxDzdT5bADs (accessed August 1, 2024).
27. "@MRTariqNasheed Reveals the Hidden Lies Behind Hip-Hop's Origins!" YouTube.com, June 30, 2024, 1:10–1:28, https://www.youtube.com/watch?v=DXUTY9JNWcg (accessed August 1, 2024).
28. The assumption that Hip-Hop was created by solely those the system of racial classification would refer to as "Black" (usually referring to those the system of race/classification would subclassify as "African American") is due to a misconception that rap is synonymous with Hip-Hop and a sort of analytic a-priori concluding that because of the way most commercial rappers identity and are identified under the system of race/trauma, this must be accurate.
29. Ibid., 2:01–2:08.

30. Jon Ivan Gill, "The Multiplicitious Theopoetic Humanism of Becoming: An Anzaldúan Reflection on Process 'Caribbean' Identity," in *God and the World in Crisis*, ed. Roland Faber and Jeffrey Lang (forthcoming), 6.

31. Gilbert Simondon, *On the Mode of Existence of Technical Objects*, trans. Cecile Malspina and John Rogove (Minneapolis: University of Minnesota Press, 2017), 109–10.

32. Martin Heidegger, "The Question Concerning Technology," in *The Question Concerning Technology and Other Essays*, trans. William Lovitt (New York: Harper & Row, 1977), 28–30.

33. Simondon, *On the Mode of Existence of Technical Objects*, 35.

34. "Grandmaster Caz RESPONDS To Fat Joe Claims That Blacks & Latinos Created Hip-Hop (MUST WATCH)," YouTube.com, August 30, 2022, 1:09–2:20, https://www.youtube.com/watch?v=0uBdzKgKtMI (accessed August 1, 2024).

35. "The World's First Rapper Grandmaster Caz on Latino's Role in Hip-Hop (Flashback)," YouTube.com, August 20, 2022, 1:54–2:00, https://www.youtube.com/watch?v=ipy1TnIlTf0 (accessed August 1, 2024).

36. Ibid., 2:02–2:27.

37. Simondon, *On the Mode of Existence of Technical Objects*, 35.

38. Whitehead, *Process and Reality*, 346.

39. "The Freshest Kids: The History of the B Boy (2002)," YouTube.com, January 11, 2015, 11:06–13:28, https://www.youtube.com/watch?v=RxoWyGFSGuk&t=1066s (accessed August 1, 2024).

40. "KRS-ONE Gives Detailed Breakdown of Hip-Hop's Prehistoric Roots," YouTube.com, January 22, 2015, 0:00–16:33, https://www.youtube.com/watch?v=0PCsYktWGiI&t=688s (accessed, July 25, 2024).

41. Imani Kai Johnson, *Dark Matter in Breaking Cyphers: The Life of Africanist Aesthetics in Global Hip-Hop* (Oxford: Oxford University Press, 2023), 19.

42. "Tariq Nasheed: Fat Joe is Disrespectful Saying Blacks and Latinos Created Hip-Hop 50/50 (Part 5)," YouTube.com, July 28, 2024, 1:51–2:14, https://www.youtube.com/watch?v=16vXIEZmoWk (accessed August 1, 2024).

43. Gill, *Underground Rap as Religion*, 22.

44. Emmett Price, *Hip-Hop Culture* (Santa Barbara: ABC-CILO, 2006), 108.

45. Gill, *Underground Rap as Religion*, 23–4.

46. Richard Iton, *In Search of the Black Fantastic: Politics and Popular Culture in the Post-Civil Rights Era* (Oxford: Oxford University Press, 2006), 250.

47. Gill, *Underground Rap as Religion*, 22–3.

48. This term refers to the four- to eight-bar drum-heavy portions in records the B-Girls and B-Boys would "break" to, which Kool Herc eventually extended indefinitely by playing the same break on two turntables and going back and forth between them with a mixer. Herc's co-creation of playing the same break repeatedly is where the electronic and sample-based music of today emerges from.

49. "Tariq Nasheed Dismantles Revisionist Hip-Hop History," 21:50–23:48.

50. "Tariq Nasheed Debates Dr. Derrick Colón About Latinos in Early Hip-Hop," YouTube.com, January 2, 2024, 0:00–33:27, https://www.youtube.com/watch?v=xvIowgZGRio (accessed August 1, 2024).

51. Ironically, in the world of Breakin.' the B-Boys Colón tells Nasheed about such as Trac 2 and Batch are not only known but supremely respected. For more information on them, see Israel, dir., *The Freshest Kids: A History of the B-Boy* (2002; Image Entertainment), DVD.

52. Gill, *Underground Rap as Religion*, 23.

53. Daniel Girma, "The Beat Goes On: Interviews with Kurtis Blow and Crazy Legs," laidoffnyc.com, July 5, 2020, https://www.laidoffnyc.com/kurtis-blow-and-crazy-legs-break-down-40-years-of-hip-hop-history/ (accessed August 3, 2024).

54. "The Freshest Kids," 11:07–12:00.

55. Luicana Mazza, "Back to Roots of Hip-Hop," streetopia.me, March 26, 2021, https://www.streetopia.me/m/news/605e2aa8694366087554329b/back-to-roots-of-hip-hop (accessed August 3, 2024).

56. "KRS One: 'People Who Downplay Latino's Roles in HipHop Are So Stupid,'" YouTube.com, June 18, 2024, 0:11–0:49, https://www.youtube.com/watch?v=ZCPwPiQ0U_A (accessed August 3, 2024).

57. Wshakes, "Fat Joe's Botched Attempt at Cultural Appropriation Reveals the Delusional Psychology of Racists," medium.com, October 20, 2023, https://medium.com/@wshakes28/fat-joes-botched-attempt-at-cultural-appropriation-reveals-the-delusional-psychology-of-racists-7f8e4dd3def6 (accessed August 3, 2024).

58. "Lord Jamar Calls Out Fat Joe and KRS-One for Lying About Puerto Ricans Creating Hip-Hop," YouTube.com, July 11, 2024, 0:31–0:50, https://www.youtube.com/watch?v=UfyTUwzlQO8 (accessed August 3, 2024).

59. "2008 KRS-One Keynote Address," YouTube.com, December 4, 2014, 12:49–13:35, https://www.youtube.com/watch?v=T9GrwKqRCgE&t=1262s (accessed August 3, 2024).

60. Ibid., 9:54–10:33.

61. Ibid., 10:40–11:29.

62. "LORD JAMAR Responds to KRS-ONE 'Beef' and Debate about Who Started Hip-Hop," YouTube.com, June 19, 2024, 9:53–10:44, https://www.youtube.com/watch?v=WmsFYt-R-5Q (accessed August 3, 2024).

63. "Tariq Nasheed Dismantles Revisionist Hip-Hop Histoty," 20:49–20:55.

64. Matthew Restall, "Creating Belize: The Mapping and Naming History of a Liminal Locale," *Terrae Incognito* 00, no. 00 (2019): 3, https://doi.org/10.1080/00822884.2019.1573962 (accessed August 8, 2024).

65. Víctor Manuel Durán, ed., *An Anthology of Belizean Literature: English, Spanish, Creole, Garifuna* (Lanham: University Press of America, 2007), ii–iii.

66. "Understanding the 1893 Mariscal-Spencer Treaty between Mexico and England," belizehub.com, https://www.belizehub.com/the-1893-mariscal-spencer-treaty/ (accessed August 8, 2024).

67 José Pimienta-Bey, interviewed by Jon Ivan Gill, *All Things Cosmic*, podcast audio, August 15, 2022, 55:16–55:50, https://podcasts.apple.com/us/podcast/all-things-cosmic-w-jon-ivan-gill-s2-e5-jos%C3%A9-pimienta-bey/id1568692649?i=1000576107349.

68 Restall, "Creating Belize," 14.

69 Hubert Howe Bancroft, *History of the Pacific States of North America*, vol. 2 (San Francisco: A.L. Bancroft & Co., 1883), 624.

70 Restall, "Creating Belize," 25–6.

71 Ibid., 26–8.

72 Ibid., 30.

73 Whitehead, *Process and Reality*, 7.

74 "Belize Culture: Ethnic Groups Explained (2023 Update)," belize-travel-blog.chaacreek.com, August 15, 2023, https://belize-travel-blog.chaacreek.com/2016/08/belize-culture/ (accessed August 12, 2023).

75 O Nigel Bolland, *Colonialism and Resistance in Belize* (Benque Viejo del Carmen, Belize: Cubola Productions, 2004), 17–18.

76 Durán, *An Anthology of Belizean Literature*, ii.

77 Bolland, *Colonialism and Resistance in Belize*, 34.

78 Ibid., 205.

79 Ibid., 209.

80 Ibid., 55–6.

81 Kriol happens in different formations in different regions in the "Caribbean" based on the various strands of data in said region. So, the English-derived language holds common features such as words and accents but can have several particular elements from dialects spoken in the region in question. For example, the Kriol of Belize will have elements of Spanish due to Belize's history under Spanish jurisdiction, Spanish speakers moving to the area and impressing Spanish upon Kriol, etc. This is not linear and "emerges" in ways that make locating a definitive starting point difficult if not impossible.

82 Whitehead, *Process and Reality*, 7.

83 Zee Edgell, *Beka Lamb* (Long Grove: Waveland Press, 2015), 67.

84 Masood Raja-Urdu, "*Time and the River* by Zee Edgell: A Belizean Novel| Postcolonial Fiction," YouTube.com, April 13, 2021, 0:00–11:29, https://www.youtube.com/watch?v=diWR5RIDxdg (accessed August 17, 2024).

85 Zee Edgell, *The Festival of San Joaquín* (London: Macmillan, 2007), 14, 22.

Chapter 8

1 Noble Drew Ali, "24 Quotes from Noble Drew Ali and Marcus Garvey," ed. Isheka N. Harrison, moguldom.com, October 1, 2020, https://moguldom.com/307573/24-quotes-from-noble-drew-ali-and-marcus-garvey/ (accessed August 19, 2024).

2 Ibid.

3   Brian Lightbody, "Reconstructing Philosophical Genealogy from the Ground Up: What Truly is Philosophical Genealogy and What Purpose Does it Serve?" *Genealogy* 7, no 98 (December 10, 2023): 2.

4   Roland Faber, "Introduction: Negotiating Becoming," in *Secrets of Becoming: Negotiating Whitehead, Deleuze, and Butler*, ed. Roland Faber and Andrea M. Stephenson (New York: Fordham University Press, 2011), 7.

5   Michael Halewood, "Butler and Whitehead on the (Social) Body," in *Secrets of Becoming: Negotiating Whitehead, Deleuze, and Butler*, ed. Roland Faber and Andrea M. Stephenson (New York: Fordham University Press, 2011), 109.

6   Faber, "Introduction," 10.

7   Alfred North Whitehead, *Process and Reality*, corrected edition, ed. David Ray Griffin and Donald Sherburne (New York: The Free Press, 1978), 24.

8   Annika Thiem, *Unbecoming Subjects: Judith Butler, Moral Philosophy, and Critical Responsibility* (New York: Fordham University Press, 2008), 177.

9   Another reference to the challenging of the assumed "sticking power" of social groups addressed in Chapter 2 and referred to throughout the text.

10 Larry L. W. Miles, *Afro and Indigenous Intersectionality in America as Nomen* (Lanham: Lexington Books, 2023), 94.

11 "Don Cheadle Finds out Native Americans Owned His Ancestors," YouTube.com, August 16, 2017, 1:32–1:57, https://www.youtube.com/watch?v=b5YEKPiNwu0 (accessed August 20, 2024).

12 Monica A. Coleman, "Invoking Oya: Practicing a Polydox Soteriology Through a Postmodern Womanist Reading of Tananarive Due's The Living Blood," in *Polydoxy: Theology of Multiplicity and Relation*, eds. Catherine Keller and Laurel Schneider (New York: Routledge, 2011), 186.

13 Faber, "Introduction," 24.

14 "Don Cheadle Finds out Native Americans Owned His Ancestors," 2:50–2:59.

15 Brian Massumi, *Semblance and Event: Activist Philosophy and the Occurrent Arts* (Cambridge, MA: MIT Press, 2011), 32.

16 Miles, *Afro and Indigenous Intersectionality in America as Nomen*, 18.

17 Faber, "Introduction."

18 José Pimienta-Bey, *Othello's Children in the 'New World:' Moorish History & Identity in the African American Experience* (Bloomington: AuthorHouse Books, 2002), 70.

19 Miles, *Afro and Indigenous Intersectionality in America as Nomen*, 121–30.

20 Gilles Deleuze, *Difference and Repetition*, trans. Paul Patton (New York: Columbia University Press, 1994), 12.

21 Pimienta-Bey, *Othello's Children in the 'New World'"*, 70–1.

22 Karen Baker-Fletcher, *Sisters of Dust, Sisters of Spirit: Womanist Wordings on God and Creation* (Minneapolis: Fortress Press, 1998), 43.

23 Whitehead, *Process and Reality*, 346.

24 Gilbert Simondon, *On the Mode of Existence of Technical Objects*, trans. Cecile Malaspina and John Rogrove (Minneapolis: University of Minnesota Press, 2017), 17.

25 Ibid., 18.

26 John D. Caputo, "A Commentary: Deconstruction in a Nutshell," in *Deconstruction in a Nutshell: A Conversation with Jacques Derrida*, ed. John D. Caputo (New York: Fordham University Press, 2021), 33.

27 Simondon, *On the Mode of Existence of Technical Objects*, 121.

28 Vitor Westhelle, *Eschatology and Space: The Lost Dimension in Theology's Past and Present* (New York: Palgrave Macmillan, 2012), 37–8.

29 Georg Wilhelm Friedrich Hegel, *The Difference Between the Fichtean and the Schellingean Systems of Philosophy* (Albany: State University of New York Press, 1988), 46.

30 Ibid.

31 Westhelle, *Eschatology and Space*, 38.

32 Ibid., 39.

33 Roland Faber, *God as Poet of the World: An Exploration of Process Theologies* (Louisville: Westminster John Knox Press, 2008), 327.

34 Jacques Derrida, *On Grammatology*, trans. Gayatri Chakrovorty Spivak (Baltimore: Johns Hopkins University Press, 2016), 155.

35 Gayatri Chakravorty Spivak, "Translator's Preface," in *On Grammatology*, trans. Gayatri Chakrovorty Spivak (Baltimore: Johns Hopkins University Press, 2016), LVX.

36 Ibid., LXIII.

37 Jon Ivan Gill, *Underground Rap as Religion: A Theopoetic Examination of a Process Aesthetic Religion* (New York: Routledge, 2019), 17.

38 W. E. B. Dubois, *The Souls of Black Folks*, ed. Brent Hayes Edwards (Oxford: Oxford University Press, 2007), 8.

39 The word "conscious" is important. Since process philosophies hold that all is event, even those operating under the static category of race/trauma are identities in flux. Multi/race/less/ness holds that there is something particularly transformative about an active awareness and decision-making in the direction of becoming.

40 "A Black American by Smokey Robinson Def Poetry Jam," YouTube.com, August 23, 2016, https://www.youtube.com/watch?v=hy-dOm5ZgrQ (accessed August 21, 2024).

41 Alfred North Whitehead, "Science in General Education," in *Essays in Science and Philosophy* (New York: Philosophical Library, 1948), 142.

42 Clarrissa Pinkola Estés, *Women Who Run With the Wolves* (New York: Ballantine Books, 1995), 128.

43 Ibid., 5.

44 Gilead7 & Subtrax, "Piece Offering," *Peaces of War* (Echoes of Oratory Muzik, 2016), LP.

45 Simondon, *On the Mode of Existence of Technical Objects*, 226.

46 "The Guatemala The Don't Want You to See," YouTube.com, June 19, 2021, 16:39–17:03, https://www.youtube.com/watch?v=9VcE5iV1Wm4 (accessed August 22, 2024).

47 *Emily in Paris*, Season 1, Episode 10, "Cancel Couture," directed by Peter Lauer, written by Grant Sloss, aired October 2, 2020, 0:00-35:09, https://www.netflix.com/watch/81289290?trackId=200257859.

Breve Epílogo

1. Colleen Lutolf, "The Philosophy of Race: 10 Questions with Professor Naomi Zack," lehman.edu, January 10, 2020, https://lehman.edu/news/The-Philosophy-of-Race-10-Questions-with-Professor-Naomi-Zack.php (accessed August 23, 2024).
2. Hunbatz Men, *Secrets of Mayan Science/Religion* (Rochester: Bear & Company, 1990), 145.

BIBLIOGRAPHY

"***exclusive*** Rabbi Noam Marans Interviews Nick Cannon | Nick Cannon Says He's a Sacrificial Lamb!" YouTube, August 12, 2020. www.youtube.com/watch?v=eilqQK33jZ0 (accessed April 10, 2024).

"@MRTariqNasheed Reveals the Hidden Lies Behind Hip-Hop's Origins!" YouTube.com, June 30, 2024. https://www.youtube.com/watch?v=DXUTY9JNWcg (accessed August 1, 2024).

"2008: KRS-One Keynote Address." YouTube, December 4, 2014. https://www.youtube.com/watch?v=T9GrwKqRCgE&t=539s (accessed April 9, 2024).

"2008 KRS-One Keynote Address." YouTube.com, December 4, 2014. https://www.youtube.com/watch?v=T9GrwKqRCgE&t=1262s (accessed August 3, 2024).

Albanese, Catherine L. *America, Religions and Religion*. Boston: Wadsworth Publishing Company, 1981. Dick Gregory, Brainy Quotes, https://www.brainyquote.com/quotes/dick_gregory_472450 (accessed April 10, 2024).

Ali, Noble Drew. "24 Quotes from Noble Drew Ali and Marcus Garvey." Edited by Isheka N. Harrison. moguldom.com, October 1, 2020. https://moguldom.com/307573/24-quotes-from-noble-drew-ali-and-marcus-garvey/ (accessed August 19, 2024).

Als, Hilton. "Hilton Als on Writing and Race: Vice Podcast 025." Interviewed by Reihan Salam. YouTube, December 18, 2013. www.youtube.com/watch?v=EzqmaaDYOQg&t=336s (accessed April 10, 2024).

Als, Hilton. *White Girls*. San Francisco: McSweeney's, 2014.

Alter, Ethan. "Kanye West Said, 'George Bush Doesn't Care about Black People' on This Day in 2005." Yahoo!, September 2, 2023. www.yahoo.com/entertainment/kanye-west-said-george-bush-doesnt-care-about-black-people-on-this-day-in-2005-130006321.html?guccounter=1&guce_referrer=aHR0cHM6Ly93d3cuZ29vZ2xlLmNvbS8&guce_referrer_sig=AQAAAJFwzG5sjfHhC26sSpiBOZPriVlH9SaPprd5uCl8PaRcKv_PZ0PL8oh7zOq-SL_TR9gP--OAjQbL5-Ir3-C3qTbpZtsBiV32B4SZotmzdCcyp7IzVLjpeaOGqYFiQt_E73eb3CN46VGbtIOuNq0ZC9GWYj09Oi3whKxCvMn5LPYX (accessed April 9, 2024).

Anderson, Victor. *Beyond Ontological Blackness: An Essay on African American Religious and Cultural Criticism*. New York: Bloomsbury Press, 2016.

"Anti-Semitism Definition & Meaning." Merriam-Webster. www.merriam-webster.com/dictionary/anti-Semitism (accessed February 19, 2024).

Anzaldúa, Gloria. *Borderlands/La Frontera: The New Mestiza*. San Francisco: Ann Lute Books, 2007.

Appiah, Kwame Anthony. *The Ethics of Identity*. Princeton: Princeton University Press, 2023.

Appiah, Kwame Anthony. "Race, Culture, and Identity: Misunderstood Connections." In Kwame Anthony Appiah and Amy Gutman, *Color Consciousness: The Political Morality of Race*. Princeton: Princeton University Press, 1998.

Aurobindo, Sri. *The Life Divine*. Twin Lakes: Lotus Press, 2006.

Author unknown. "Rachel Dolezal: 'I Wasn't Identifying as Black to Upset People. I Was Being Me.'" *The Guardian*, December 13 2015, www.theguardian.com/us-news/2015/dec/13/rachel-dolezal-i-wasnt-identifying-as-black-to-upset-people-i-was-being-me (accessed April 10, 2024).

Baker-Fletcher, Karen. *Sisters of Dust, Sisters of Spirit: Womanist Wordings on God and Creation*. Minneapolis: Fortress Press, 1998.

Balaev, Michelle. "Trauma Studies," in *A Companion to Literary Theory*. Ed. David H. Richter. Oxford: John Wiley & Sons Ltd., 2018.

Baldwin, James. *James Baldwin: The Last Interview and Other Conversations*. Brooklyn: Mellville House, 2014.

Banaji, Mahzarin R., and Anthony G. Greenwald. *Blindspot: Hidden Biases of Good People*. New York: Bantam Books, 2016.

Bancroft, Hubert Howe. *History of the Pacific States of North America*. Vol. 2. San Francisco: A.L. Bancroft & Co., 1883.

"Belize Culture: Ethnic Groups Explained (2023 Update)." belize-travel-blog.chaacreek.com, August 15, 2023. https://belize-travel-blog.chaacreek.com/2016/08/belize-culture/ (accessed August 12, 2023).

Benjamin, Rich. "Shades of Influence." *The New York Times*, November 8, 2013. www.nytimes.com/2013/11/10/books/review/white-girls-by-hilton-als.html?pagewanted=1 (accessed April 10, 2024).

Benjamin, Walter. *Illuminations: Essays and Reflections*. Translated by Harry Zohn. Edited by Hannah Arendt. Boston: Mariner Books, 2019.

Benjamin, Walter. "The Work of Art in the Age of Mechanical Reproduction." In *Illuminations*, edited by Hannah Arendt. New York: Schocken Books, 1968.

Bernasconi, Robert, and Tony Lee Lott, eds. *The Idea of Race*. Indianapolis: Hackett, 2000.

Bethancourt, Francisco. *Racisms: From the Crusades to the Twentieth Century*. Princeton: Princeton University Press, 2013.

"Black or African American? Neither (Here's why)." YouTube.com, September 9, 2019. https://www.youtube.com/watch?v=7N330vc6A3U&t=249s (accessed July 9, 2024).

"A Black American by Smokey Robinson Def Poetry Jam." YouTube.com, August 23, 2016. https://www.youtube.com/watch?v=hy-dOm5ZgrQ (accessed August 21, 2024).

Bolland, O Nigel. *Colonialism and Resistance in Belize*. Benque Viejo del Carmen, Belize: Cubola Productions, 2004.

Brace, Charles L. *Race is a Four-Letter Word*. New York: Oxford University Press, 2005.

Brooker Charlie, and Konnie Huq, writers. *Black Mirror*. Season 1, episode 2, "Fifteen Million Merits." Directed by Euros Lyn. Aired December 11, 2011. https://www.netflix.com/watch/70264858.

Brown, James. "King Heroin." *There It Is*. Polydor Records, 1972.

Butler, Judith. *Gender Trouble: Feminism and the Subversion of Identity*. New York: Routledge, 2007.

Caputo, John D. "A Commentary: Deconstruction in a Nutshell." In *Deconstruction in a Nutshell: A Conversation with Jacques Derrida*, edited by John D. Caputo. New York: Fordham University Press, 2021.

Caputo, John D. *The Prayers and Tears of Jacques Derrida: Religion Without Religion*. Bloomington: Indiana University Press, 1997.

Casteñada, Quetzil E. "'We Are Not Indigenous!:' An Introduction to the Maya Identity of the Yucatán." *The Journal of Latin American Anthropology* 9, no. 1 (2004).

Clayton, Philip. *Mind and Emergence: From Quantum to Consciousness*. Oxford: Oxford University Press, 2004.

Cobb Jr., John B. "A Whiteheadian Doctrine of God." In *Process Philosophy and Christian Thought*, edited by Delwin Brown, Ralph James, and Gene Reeves. religion-online.org. https://www.religion-online.org/book-chapter/chapter-12-a-whiteheadian-doctrine-of-god-by-john-b-cobb-jr/ (accessed July 24, 2024).

Coleman, Monica A. "Invoking Oya: Practicing a Polydox Soteriology Through a Postmodern Womanist Reading of Tananarive Due's The Living Blood." In *Polydoxy: Theology of Multiplicity and Relation*. New York: Routledge, 2011.

Common. "Like They Used to Say." Rawkus Records, 1999. CD.

Cone, James. *Black Theology and Black Power*. Maryknoll: Orbis Books, 1969.

"The C.O.W.S. w/Noel Ignatiev." YouTube.com, May 20, 2012. https://www.youtube.com/watch?v=y04fGuSo1tU&t=868s (accessed July 26, 2024).

Crop Circles720. "The Listener." *Existentialism*. Echoes of Oratory Music, 2012.

Crouter, Richard. "Introduction." In Friedrich Schleiermacher. *On Religion: Speeches to its Cultured Despisers*, edited by Richard Crouter. Cambridge: Cambridge University Press, 1988.

Cudd, Ann. *Analyzing Oppression*. Oxford: Oxford University Press, 2006.

Darwin, Charles. "On the Races of Man." In *The Idea of Race*, edited by Robert Bernasconi and Tony Lee Lott. Indianapolis: Hackett 2000.

Davis, Allen. "An Historical Timeline of Reparations Payments Made From 1783 through 2020 by the United States Government, States, Cities, Religious Institutions, Colleges and Universities, and Corporations." University of Massachusetts Amherst, May 11, 2020. https://guides.library.umass.edu/reparations.

Deleuze, Gilles. *Difference and Repetition*. Translated by Paul Patton. New York: Columbia University Press, 1994.

Deleuze, Gilles. *Difference and Repetition*. Translated by Paul Patton. London: Continuum, 2001.

Derrida, Jacques. "Différance." In *Deconstruction in Context: Literature and Philosophy*, edited by Mark C. Taylor. Chicago: University of Chicago Press, 1986.

Derrida, Jacques. *Of Grammatology*. Translated by Gayatri Chakrovorty Spivak. Baltimore: Johns Hopkins University Press, 1976.

Derrida, Jacques. *On Grammatology*. Translated by Gayatri Chakrovorty Spivak. Baltimore: Johns Hopkins University Press, 2016.

"The Difference Between Being 'Not Racist' and Antiracist | Ibram X. Kendi." YouTube.com, June 17, 2020. https://www.youtube.com/watch?v=KCxbl5QgFZw, 0:00-3:37 (accessed July 10, 2024).

Dockerman, Elaina. "There's a Deeper Meaning Behind Wizards in The Rings of Power." Time.com, October 14, 2022. https://time.com/6222110/wizard-istar-the-rings-of-power/ (accessed July 16, 2024).

"Don Cheadle Finds out Native Americans Owned His Ancestors." YouTube.com, August 16, 2017. https://www.youtube.com/watch?v=b5YEKPiNwu0 (accessed August 20, 2024).

The Doors. "An American Prayer." *An American Prayer*. Electra/Asylum, 1978. CD.

"Dr. Yosef Ben Jochannan and Rabbi Arthur Seltzer." YouTube, September 11 2021. www.youtube.com/watch?v=oCdEAzX85VA (accessed April 10, 2024).

Drew, Spencer. *The Aliites: Race and Law in the Religion of Noble Drew Ali*. Chicago: University of Chicago Press, 2019.

Driscoll, Christopher M. *White Devils, Black Gods: Race, Masculinity, and Religious Codependency*. London: Bloomsbury Academic, 2023.
Driscoll Christopher M., and Monica R. Miller. *Method as Identity: Manufacturing Distance in the Study of Religion*. Lanham: Lexington Books, 2018.
Dubois, W. E. B. *The Souls of Black Folks*. Edited by Brent Hayes Edwards. Oxford: Oxford University Press, 2007.
Durán, Víctor Manuel, ed. *An Anthology of Belizean Literature: English, Spanish, Creole, Garifuna*. Lanham: University Press of America, 2007.
Edgell, Zee. *Beka Lamb*. Long Grove: Waveland Press, 2015.
Edgell, Zee. *The Festival of San Joaquín*. London: Macmillan Caribbean, 2007.
Edmonds, Ennis Barrington. *Rastafari: From Outcasts to Culture Bearers*. Oxford: Oxford University Press, 2003.
"Envisioning the Future of Theology and Ethics: A Womanist Perspective." YouTube.com, April 20, 2017. https://www.youtube.com/watch?v=J7rBYfTjznY&t=4619s (accessed July 26, 2024).
Estés, Clarrissa Pinkola. *Women Who Run With the Wolves*. New York: Ballantine Books, 1995.
"Ethnic Minorities: Defining Ethnicity and Race." scotpho.org.uk, June 25, 2023. https://www.scotpho.org.uk/population-groups/ethnic-minorities/defining-ethnicity-and-race/#:~:text=Ethnicity%20has%20been%20defined%20as,1 (accessed July 30, 2024).
Faber, Roland. *God as Poet of the World: Exploring Process Theologies*. Louisville: Westminster John Knox Press, 2008.
Faber, Roland. "Introduction: Negotiating Becoming." In *Secrets of Becoming: Negotiating Whitehead, Deleuze, and Butler*, edited by Roland Faber and Andrea M. Stephenson. New York: Fordham University Press, 2011.
Famuyiwa, Rick. *Brown Sugar*. 2002; Los Angeles, Fox Searchlight Pictures. DVD.
Fanon, Frantz. *The Wretched of the Earth*. Translated by Richard Philcox. New York: Grove Press, 2004.
Farrakhan, Minister Louis. "Minister Farrakhan Honors Noble Drew Ali." Youtube.com, May 27, 2020. https://youtu.be/td9aXByeTh4.
Ford, Dana, and Greg Botelho. "Who Is Rachel Dolezal?" CNN, Cable News Network, June 17, 2015. www.cnn.com/2015/06/16/us/rachel-dolezal/ (accessed April 10, 2024).
Frederickson, George. *Racism: A Short History*. Princeton: Princeton University Press, 2002.
"The Freshest Kids: The History of the B Boy (2002)." YouTube.com, January 11, 2015. https://www.youtube.com/watch?v=RxoWyGFSGuk&t=1066s (accessed August 1, 2024).
Friedersorf, Connor. "What Do 2020 Candidates Mean When They Say 'Reparations'?" *The Atlantic*, June 5, 2019.
Friedrich, C. J. "Introduction to Dover Edition." In Georg Wilhelm Friedrich Hegel, *The Philosophy of History*. New York: Dover Publications, 1956.
Fuller, Christopher John. *The Camphor Flame: Popular Hinduism and Society in India*. Princeton: Princeton University Press, 2004.
Gilead 7 & Subtrax. "Piece Offering." *Peaces of War*. Echoes of Oratory Muzik, 2016. LP.
Gill, Jon Ivan. "The Multiplicitious Theopoetic Humanism of Becoming: An Anzaldúan Reflection on Process 'Caribbean' Identity." In *God and the World in Crisis*, edited by Roland Faber and Jeffrey Lang. Forthcoming.
Gill, Jon Ivan. *Underground Rap as Religion: A Theopoetic Examination of a Process Aesthetic Religion*. New York: Routledge, 2019.

Girma, Daniel. "The Beat Goes On: Interviews with Kurtis Blow and Crazy Legs." laidoffnyc.com, July 5, 2020. https://www.laidoffnyc.com/kurtis-blow-and-crazy-legs-break-down-40-years-of-hip-hop-history/ (accessed August 3, 2024).

Gobineau, Arthur de. "Essay on the Inequality of the Human Races." Translated by A. Collins. In *The Idea of Race*, edited by Robert Bernasconi and Tony Lee Lott. Indianapolis: Hackett 2000.

Gordon, Lewis. *Black Existentialism and Decolonized Knowledge*. Edited by Rozena Maart, Sayan Dey, and Louis Gordon. London: Bloomsbury Academic, 2023.

Gracia, Jorge J. E. *Surviving Race, Ethnicity, and Nationality: A Challenge for the Twenty-First Century*. Lanham: Rowman and Littlefield, 2005.

Gracia, Jorge J. E., and Susan L. Smith. "Analytic Metaphysics: Race and Identity." In *The Routledge Companion to Philosophy of Race*, edited by Paul C. Taylor, Linda Martín Alcoff, and Luvell Anderson. New York: Routledge, 2018.

"Grandmaster Caz RESPONDS To Fat Joe Claims That Blacks & Latinos Created Hip-Hop (MUST WATCH)." YouTube.com, August 30, 2022. https://www.youtube.com/watch?v=0uBdzKgKtMI (accessed August 1, 2024).

Gregory, Dick. *Brainy Quotes*. https://www.brainyquote.com/quotes/dick_gregory_472450 (accessed April 10, 2024).

Griffin, Peter, dir. *The Lord of the Rings: The Fellowship of the Ring*. 2001; Burbank: New Line Cinema, 2001. Amazon.com.

"The Guatemala The Don't Want You to See." YouTube.com, June 19, 2021. https://www.youtube.com/watch?v=9VcE5iV1Wm4 (accessed August 22, 2024).

Halewood, Michael. "Butler and Whitehead on the (Social) Body." In *Secrets of Becoming: Negotiating Whitehead, Deleuze, and Butler*, edited by Roland Faber and Andrea M. Stephenson. New York: Fordham University Press, 2011.

Hannaford, Ivan. *Race: The History of an Idea in the West*. Baltimore: The Johns Hopkins University Press, 1996.

Hatfield, Gary. "Introduction." In Immanuel Kant, *Prolegomena to any Future Metaphysic*, translated and edited by Gary Hatfield. Cambridge: Cambridge University Press, 1997.

Hegel, Georg Wilhelm Friedrich. *The Difference Between the Fichtean and the Schellingean Systems of Philosophy*. Albany: State University of New York Press, 1988.

Heidegger, Martin. "The Question Concerning Technology." In *The Question Concerning Technology and Other Essays*, translated by William Lovitt. New York: Harper & Row, 1977.

"The Hip-Hop Declaration of Peace, Hip-Hop Principles." chosenhiphop.com. https://chosenhiphop.com/principles (accessed August 17, 2024).

The Holy Koran of the Moorish Science Temple of America.

Hume, David. "Of National Character." In *Hume: Political Essays*, edited by Knud Haakonssen. Cambridge: Cambridge University Press, 1994.

Ignatiev, Noel. *How the Irish Became White*. New York: Routledge, 1995.

Ignatiev, Noel. *Treason to Whiteness is Loyalty to Humanity*. In *Oppression, Privilege, and Resistance: Theoretical Perspectives on, Racism, Sexism, and Heterosexism*. Edited by Lisa Heldke and Peg O'Conner. New York: McGraw Hill, 2004.

Isaac, Benjamin. *The Invention of Racism in Classical Antiquity*. Princeton: Princeton University Press. 2004.

Iton, Richard. *In Search of the Black Fantastic: Politics and Popular Culture in the Post-Civil Rights Era*. Oxford: Oxford University Press, 2006.

James, Michael, and Adam Burgos. "Race." In *The Stanford Encyclopedia of Philosophy* (Summer 2020 Edition), edited by Edward N. Zalta. https://plato.stanford.edu/archives/sum2020/entries/race/.

Jamros, Daniel P. "Hegel on the Incarnation: Unique or Universal?" *Theological Studies* 56 (1995): 277, 281–3.

John Hope Franklin Center at Duke University. "Left of Black with Monica R. Miller," October 5, 2015. https://www.youtube.com/watch?v=zi8rZhN8Xek (accessed April 10, 2024).

Johnson, Imani Kai. *Dark Matter in Breaking Cyphers: The Life of Africanist Aesthetics in Global Hip-Hop*. Oxford: Oxford University Press, 2023.

Kant, Immanuel. "On the Different Races of Man." In *Race and the Enlightenment: A Reader*, edited by Emmanuel Chukwudi Eze. Malden: Blackwell Publishers, 1997.

"Kanye West TMZ Full Interview." *TMZ*. YouTube, May 2, 2018. www.youtube.com/watch?v=1LIGh91mloA (accessed April 9, 2024).

Kaur, Harmeet. "Kanye West Just Said 400 Years of Slavery Was a Choice." CNN, Cable News Network, May 4, 2018. www.cnn.com/2018/05/01/entertainment/kanye-west-slavery-choice-trnd/index.html (accessed April 9, 2024).

Kendi, Ibram. *How to Be an Antiracist*. New York: ONEWORLD, 2023.

Killah Priest. "From Then 'Til Now," *Heavy Mental*. Geffen, 1999. CD.

Klein, Alex. "What to Know about Racial Trauma" medicalnewstoday.com, July 23, 2020. https://www.medicalnewstoday.com/articles/racial trauma. Accessed August 25, 2024.

Kleingeld, Pauline. "On Dealing With Kant's Sexism and Racism." *SGIR Review* 2, no. 2, 3–22, 26.

Kosinski, Joseph, dir. *Tron: Legacy*. 2010; Burbank: Walt Disney Studios. https://www.amazon.com/gp/video/detail/B004R63MWQ/ref=atv_plr_detail_play (accessed August 2, 2024).

KRS-ONE. "2008: KRS-ONE Keynote Address at Canadian Music Week." Youtube.com, March 8, 2008. https://youtu.be/T9GrwKqRCgE.

KRS-ONE. *The Gospel of Hip-Hop: The First Instrument*. New York: powerHouse Books, 2009.

"KRS One: 'People who Downplay Latino's Roles in HipHop are So Stupid.'" YouTube.com, June 18, 2024. https://www.youtube.com/watch?v=ZCPwPiQ0U_A (accessed August 3, 2024).

"KRS-One Gives Detailed Breakdown of Hip-Hop's Prehistoric Roots." YouTube.com, January 22, 2015. https://www.youtube.com/watch?v=0PCsYktWGiI (accessed July 17, 2024).

"KRS-ONE Gives Detailed Breakdown of Hip-Hop's Prehistoric Roots." YouTube.com, January 22, 2015, https://www.youtube.com/watch?v=0PCsYktWGiI&t=688s (accessed July 25, 2024).

Kweli, Talib, and Jasmin Leigh, dirs. "Van Lathan and Talib Kweli Discuss His TMZ Kanye West Incident." YouTube, September 28, 2019. https://www.youtube.com/watch?v=mrryp3vF0Pg (accessed January 16, 2024).

Lamon Manuel. "Sh*t. Everything We Have Together Is Falling Apart." *Music to Feel Like Shit to*. ReSERVED Records, 2016.

Lao Tzu. *Tao Te Ching*. Chapter 28. Translated by Steffan Stenudd. taoistic.com. https://www.taoistic.com/taoteching-laotzu/taoteching-28.htm (accessed July 27, 2024).

Leach, Javier. "Emergence and Transcendence in Philip Clayton: His Moderate Ideas Place Him in an Ideal Position for Dialogue." *Pensamiento* 64. no. 242 (2008): 1109–13.

Lefebre, Henry. *Metaphilosophy*. Trans. David Fernbach. Ed. Stuart Elden. London: Verso, 2016.

Leon, Kenny, Dir. *American Son*. Ventura: Simpson Street, 2019. https://www.netflix.com/watch/81024100 trackId=255824129&tctx=0%2C0%2Ccb8baf2a-609f-411c-b8ef-c4c2183e06a6-187499151%2Ccb8baf2a-609f-411c-b8ef-c4c2183e06a6-187499151%7C2

%2Cunknown%2C%2C%2CtitlesResults%2C%2CVideo%3A81024100%2CminiDpPlayButton.

Levin, Marc, dir. *Brooklyn Babylon*. 2001; Santa Monica: Bac Films/Artisan Entertainment, 2001. DVD.

Lightbody, Brian. "Reconstructing Philosophical Genealogy from the Ground Up: What Truly is Philosophical Genealogy and What Purpose Does it Serve?" *Genealogy* 7 (December 10, 2023): 98.

Loomba, Ania. "Racism in India." In *The Routledge Companion to the Philosophy of Race*, edited by Paul C. Taylor, Linda Martín Alcroft, and Luvell Anderson. New York: Routledge, 2018.

"Lord Jamar Calls Out Fat Joe and KRS-One for Lying About Puerto Ricans Creating Hip-Hop." YouTube.com, July 11, 2024. https://www.youtube.com/watch?v=UfyTUwzlQO8 (accessed August 3, 2024).

"LORD JAMAR Responds to KRS-ONE 'Beef' and Debate about Who Started Hip-Hop." YouTube.com, June 19, 2024. https://www.youtube.com/watch?v=WmsFYt-R-5Q (accessed August 3, 2024).

Loring, Brace, C. *Race is a Four-Letter Word: The Genesis of the Concept*. New York: Oxford University Press, 2005.

Lutolf, Colleen. "The Philosophy of Race: 10 Questions with Professor Naomi Zack." lehman.edu, January 10, 2020. https://lehman.edu/news/The-Philosophy-of-Race-10-Questions-with-Professor-Naomi-Zack.php (accessed August 23, 2024).

M.S.T.A. Pamphlet. "A Warning from the Prophet," 1928.

Malcom X, *The Autobiography of Malcom X*.

Manning, Erin. *Relationscapes: Movement, Art. Philosophy*. Cambridge, MA: MIT Press, 2012.

Martín, Javier P. "How Kanye West Uses Instagram to Settle Scores." *EL PAÍS English*, March 14, 2022. english.elpais.com/culture/2022-03-14/how-kanye-west-uses-instagram-to-settle-scores.html (accessed April 9, 2024).

Massumi, Brian. *Semblance and Event: Activist Philosophy and the Occurrent Arts*. Cambridge, MA: MIT Press, 2011.

Mazza, Luicana. "Back to Roots of Hip-Hop." streetopia.me, March 26, 2021. https://www.streetopia.me/m/news/605e2aa8694366087554329b/back-to-roots-of-hip-hop (accessed August 3, 2024).

McCloud, Aminah Beverly. *African American Islam*. New York: Routledge, 1995.

McDaniel, Jay. "John Cobb on Eternal Objects." openhorizons.org. https://www.openhorizons.org/eternal-objects.html (accessed July 23, 2024).

McGreal, Chris. "Rachel Dolezal: 'I Wasn't Identifying as Black to Upset People. I Was Being Me.'" *The Guardian*, December 13, 2015. www.theguardian.com/us-news/2015/dec/13/rachel-dolezal-i-wasnt-identifying-as-black-to-upset-people-i-was-being-me (accessed April 10, 2024).

McLeod, Alexus. *Philosophy of the Ancient Maya: Lords of Time*. Lanham: Lexington Books, 2018.

Men, Hunbatz. *Secrets of Mayan Science/Religion*. Santa Fe: Bear and Company Publishing, 1990.

Miles, Larry L. W. *Afro and Indigenous Intersectionality in America as Nomen*. Lanham: Lexington Books, 2023.

Miller, Monica R. "Left of Black with Monica R. Miller." Interviewed by Mark Anthony Neal. YouTube, October 5, 2015. https://www.youtube.com/watch?v=zi8rZhN8Xek (accessed April 10, 2024).

"Mind Bugs | Mahzarin R. Banaji | TEDxBari." YouTube.com, January 10, 2018. https://www.youtube.com/watch?v=AFEaCFFsM2U (accessed July 14, 2024).

Miyakawa, Felicia. *Five Percenter Rap: God's Hop Music, Message, and Black Muslim Mission*. Bloomington: Indiana University Press, 2006.

Montejo, Victor. *Mayalogue: An Interactionist Theory of Indigenous Cultures*. Albany: SUNY Press, 2021.

Morales Torres, José Francisco. *Wonder as a New Starting Point for Theological Anthropology*. Lanham: Lexington Books, 2023.

"Nazgûl." fandom.com. https://lotr.fandom.com/wiki/Valar (accessed July 16, 2024).

"Nick Cannon Humbled by Rabbi Cooper | Cannon's Class with Rabbi Cooper | 'Anti-Semitism' Response." YouTube, August 1, 2020. www.youtube.com/watch?v=_6UIv868SB8&t=3085s (accessed April 10, 2024).

"Nick Cannon and Professor Griff 'Hebrew Israelite,' 'Anti-Semitism' & 'Identity.'" YouTube, June 30, 2020. www.youtube.com/watch?v=CGXGuWCRSh4 (accessed April 10, 2024).

Nietzsche, Friedrich. *Nietzsche and the Death of God: Selected Writings*. Translated by Peter Fritzsche. Boston: Bedford/St. Martin's, 2007.

Perkins, William Eric. *Droppin' Science: Critical Essays on Rap Music and Hip Hop Culture*. Philadelphia: Temple University Press, 1996.

Perkinson, James. *White Theology: Outing Supremacy in Modernity*. New York: Palgrave Macmillan, 2004.

"Philip Clayton – How Can Emergence Explain Reality?" YouTube.com, August 23, 2014. https://www.youtube.com/watch?v=nzWclhC7WmE (accessed July 24, 2024).

"Philip Clayton – Why is Emergence Significant?" YouTube.com, October 24, 2023. https://www.youtube.com/watch?v=1rwm61R3gNY&t=18s (accessed July 29, 2024).

Pimienta-Bey, José. Interviewed by Jon Ivan Gill. *All Things Cosmic*. Podcast audio, August 15, 2022. https://podcasts.apple.com/us/podcast/all-things-cosmic-w-jon-ivan-gill-s2-e5-jos%C3%A9-pimienta-bey/id1568692649?i=1000576107349.

Pimienta-Bey, José. *Othello's Children in the 'New World:' Moorish History & Identity in the African American Experience*. Bloomington: AuthorHouse Books, 2002.

Pimienta-Bey, Jose. "Race in America: You are NOT Black (Here's More Reasons Why)." Youtube.com, May 4, 2020. https://youtu.be/f7nypydE0V8.

Pinn, Anthony B. *The End of God-Talk: An African American Humanist Theology*. Oxford: Oxford University Press, 2012.

Pinn Anthony B., and Monica R. Miller. "Introduction: Intersections of Culture and Religion in African-American Communities." *Culture and Religion* 10, no. 1 (2009): 1–9.

Polt, Richard. *Heidegger: An Introduction*. London: Routledge, 1999.

Price, Emmett. *Hip-Hop Culture*. Santa Barbara: ABC-CILO, 2006.

"Race vs. State of Mind: Rachel Dolezal's Thoughts on Whiteness." YouTube, November 2, 2020. www.youtube.com/watch?v=54QrcxCKo1o (accessed April 10, 2024).

Raja-Urdu, Masood. "*Time and the River* by Zee Edgell: A Belizean Novel| Postcolonial Fiction." YouTube.com, April 13, 2021. https://www.youtube.com/watch?v=diWR5RIDxdg (accessed August 17, 2024).

Rasheed, Kameelah Janan. "You are Not Negroes, Colored Folks, Black People or Ethiopians." *Mapping The Spirit*, June 8, 2017. https://www.mappingthespirit.com/stories/msta/act-6-divine-constitution.

Reinherz, Adam. *Ethiopian-Born Israeli Researcher and Activist to Speak at Pitt. Pittsburgh Jewish Chronicle*, April 10, 2023. jewishchronicle.timesofisrael.com/ethiopian-born-israeli-researcher-and-activist-to-speak-at-pitt/ (accessed February 29, 2024).

Restall, Matthew. "Creating Belize: The Mapping and Naming History of a Liminal Locale." *Terrae Incognito* 00, no, 00 (2019). https://doi.org/10.1080/00822884.2019.1573962 (accessed August 8, 2024).

Reyes, Rafael. "All Are Abstractions: Reading Alfred North Whitehead's Critique of the Sciences." medium.com, December 6, 2014. https://medium.com/process-imagining/all-are-abstraction-reading-alfred-north-whiteheads-critique-on-the-sciences-17b50b6e75e8 (accessed July 26, 2024).

Rogers, Brian Wayne. "Heidegger on What it Means to Dwell." planksip.com, March 19, 2023. https://www.planksip.org/heidegger-on-human-dwelling/ (accessed July 21, 2024).

Rogers, David and Moira Bowman. "A History: The Construction and the Deconstruction of Race." https://www.giarts.org/sites/default/files/conference_websites/2017/documents/construction-of-race-and-racism.pdf. Accessed October 25, 2024.

Sancho, Xavi. "The Rise and Fall of Kanye West." *EL PAÍS English*, October 31, 2022. english.elpais.com/culture/2022-10-31/the-rise-and-fall-of-kanye-west.html (accessed April 9, 2024).

Sartre, Jean Paul. *Being and Nothingness: An Essay on Phenomenological Ontology*. New York: Washington Square Press, 1969.

Sartre, Jean Paul. *Nausea*. Translated by R. Baldick. Hammondsworth: Penguin Books, 1965.

Simondon, Gilbert. *On the Mode of Existence of Technical Objects*. Translated by Cecile Malaspina and John Rogove. Minneapolis: University of Minnesota Press, 2017.

Sloss, Grant, writer. *Emily in Paris*, Season 1, Episode 10, "Cancel Couture." Directed by Peter Lauer. Aired October 2, 2020. https://www.netflix.com/watch/81289290?trackId=200257859.

Stephen, Cornell, and Douglass Hartman. *Ethnicity and Race: Making Identities in a Changing World*. Thousand Oaks: Pine Forge Press.

"Tariq Nasheed: Fat Joe is Disrespectful Saying Blacks and Latinos Created Hip-Hop 50/50 (Part 5)." YouTube.com, July 28, 2024. https://www.youtube.com/watch?v=16vXIEZmoWk (accessed August 1, 2024).

"Tariq Nasheed Debates Dr. Derrick Colón About Latinos in Early Hip-Hop." YouTube.com, January 2, 2024. https://www.youtube.com/watch?v=xvIowgZGRio (accessed August 1, 2024).

"Tariq Nasheed Dismantles Revisionist Hip-Hop History." YouTube.com, June 6, 2024. https://www.youtube.com/watch?v=qxDzdT5bADs (accessed August 1, 2024).

Taylor, Mark C. *Deconstruction in Context: Literature and Philosophy*. Chicago: University of Chicago Press, 1986.

Thandeka. *The Embodied Self: Friedrich Schleiermacher's Solution to Kant's Problem of the Empirical Self*. Albany: State University of New York Press, 1995.

Thiem, Annika. *Unbecoming Subjects: Judith Butler, Moral Philosophy, and Critical Responsibility*. New York: Fordham University Press, 2008.

Tjaya, Thomas Hidya. "Creativity and God in Whitehead's Process Philosophy." *Diskursus - Jurnal Filsafat dan Teologi STF Driyarkara* 11 no. 2 (2012): 141–59. https://doi.org/10.36383/diskursus.v11i2.133 (accessed July 27, 2023).

Tolkein, J. R. R. *The Fellowship of the Ring*. New York: Ballantine Books, 1982.

"Tron Legacy (2010) – BioDigital Jazz." YouTube.com, May 20, 2023. https://www.youtube.com/watch?v=mA0gm1EFZtk (accessed July 29, 2024).

Tunnel Rats. "Just Words." *Experience*. Brainstorm Recordings, 1996. CD.

Tunnel Rats, "Chainge RMX." *Tunnel Vision*. Uprok Records, 2001.

"UCF Expressions with J.L. Vest: Poet Philosopher." YouTube.com, May 19, 2008. https://youtu.be/jD2778K-tr4 (accessed October 25, 2024).

Unamuno, Miguel de. *Tragic Sense of Life*. New York: Dover Publications, 1954.

"Understanding the 1893 Mariscal-Spencer Treaty between Mexico and England." belizehub.com. https://www.belizehub.com/the-1893-mariscal-spencer-treaty/ (accessed August 8, 2024).

Van Sertima, Ivan. *They Came Before Columbus: The African Presence in Ancient America*. New York: Random House, 2003.

Vest, Jennifer Lisa. "Being and Not Being, Knowing and Not Knowing." In *Philosophy and the Mixed Race Experience*, edited by Tina Fernandes Bottes. New York: Lexington Books, 2016.

Vest, Jennifer Lisa. *Names*. El Cerrito: Indigenous Speak, 1997.

Vest, Jennifer Lisa. "The Promise of Caribbean Philosophy: Toward a 'New Dialogic' in Philosophy." *Caribbean Studies* 33, no. 2 (July/December 2005): 6.

Walker, Theodore. *Mothership Connections: A Black Atlantic Synthesis of Neoclassical Metaphysics and Black Theology*. Albany: State University of New York Press, 2004.

Ward, James. *Zero Victim: Overcoming Injustice with a New Attitude*. Warrenton: Freiling Publishing, 2021.

Way-El, Sheik. *Noble Drew Ali and the Moorish Science Temple of America: The Movement that Started it All*. City unknown: Moorish Science Temple of America, 2013.

West, Cornel. *Prophesy Deliverance: An Afro-American Revolutionary Christianity*. Louisville: Westminster John Knox Press, 2022.

West, Cornel. *Race Matters, 25th Anniversary*. Boston: Beacon Press, 2017.

West, David. *An Introduction to Continental Philosophy*. Cambridge: Polity Press, 1996.

Whitehead, Alfred North. *Modes of Thought*. New York: The Free Press, 1966.

Whitehead, Alfred North. *Process and Reality*. Corrected edition. Edited by David Ray Griffin and Donald Sherburne. New York: The Free Press, 1978.

Whitehead, Alfred North. "Science in General Education." In *Essays in Science and Philosophy*. New York: Philosophical Library, 1948.

Whitehead, Alfred North. *Science and the Modern World*. New York: The Free Press, 1967.

Whitehead, Alfred North. *Symbolism: Its Meaning and Effect*. New York: Fordham University Press, 1955.

Williams, James. *Gilles Deleuze's Difference and Repetition: A Critical Introduction and Guide*. Edinburgh: Edinburgh University Press, 2013.

"The World's First Rapper Grandmaster Caz on Latino's Role in Hip-Hop (Flashback)." YouTube.com, August 20, 2022. https://www.youtube.com/watch?v=ipy1TnIlTf0 (accessed August 1, 2024).

Womack, Ytasha L. *Afrofuturism: The World of Black Sci Fi and Fantasy Culture*. Chicago: Lawrence Hill Books, 2013.

Wshakes. "Fat Joe's Botched Attempt at Cultural Appropriation Reveals the Delusional Psychology of Racists." medium.com, October 20, 2023. https://medium.com/@wshakes28/fat-joes-botched-attempt-at-cultural-appropriation-reveals-the-delusional-psychology-of-racists-7f8e4dd3def6 (accessed August 3, 2024).

Zack, Naomi. *Philosophy of Science and Race*. New York: Routledge, 2002.

Žižek, Slavoj. *The Parallax View*. Cambridge, MA: MIT Press, 2009.

INDEX

Absolute spirit (Hegel)   21, 174, 175–6
aesthetic movement, race as   13
"African American" category   2, 152, 170, 177–8, 184
"African" category   13, 25, 27–9, 47, 112, 155, 25, 143, 167
Afrofuturism   143
  The World of Black Sci-Fi and Fantasy Culture (Womack)   4
Agassis, Louis   21
Al-Andalus   14, 23
Ali, Noble Drew (Timothy Drew)   ix, 1, 2, 5, 6, 12, 24, 26–7, 29–30, 34, 54, 57, 60–3, 67, 69–71, 73, 106, 147, 160, 167–9, 181, 184, 185
American Association of Physical Anthropologists (AAPA)   17
American Son (film)   x–xi
Anderson, Victor   29
Aniyunwiyah (Cherokee)   24
antiracism (Kendi)   8, 101, 104, 105, 111, 125
Appiah, Kwame Anthony   6, 31, 37–40, 43–4, 49, 51–2, 138, 139
Arkansas   1
Arnold, Matthew   39
Aryan race   16
"Asian" category   xiv, 3, 7, 11, 15, 34, 111, 146, 179
"Asian American" organizations   35
Asiatics (Noble Drew Ali's term)   26, 34, 53, 60–2, 64–7
Atlantis   25
Aura (Benjamin)   17–18, 144, 48
Aurobindo, Sri   4

Baker-Fletcher, Karen   172–3
Balaev, Michelle   xiii

Baldwin, James   3
Banaji, Mahzarin R.   8, 101–107, 109
Belgrano, Elisabeth   ix
Belize   ix, 1, 2, 3, 9, 41, 66, 136, 144–5, 159–66, 179, 184–5
Ben Jochannan, Yosef   1, 95
Benjamin, Walter   17, 18
aBernier, François   14–15, 18
Bethencourt, Francisco   29
"Bey" surname   24–5, 53, 121
Bhabha, Homi   50
biological determinism   13
  UNESCO rejection of (1950)   17
"Black"   xi–xvi, 1–9, 11–13, 20–21, 24–31, 33–5, 38–43, 45, 49, 51, 54, 56–63, 72, 75, 76–102, 105, 108, 109, 112, 117, 126, 131–2, 138–9, 151–5, 157–8, 170–2, 177–9
"Black Lives Matter"   5, 29
"Black Power"   40, 53, 90
Blumenbach, Johann Friedrich   15, 21
Boas, Franz   16
Bottes, Tina Fernandes   48
Britton, Christopher   ix
Butler, Judith   xiv, 8, 101, 109–111, 169
Butler, Octavia   4

Canaanite Temple (1913)   24
Canaanites   25
Cancel culture   1, 7, 75, 76–7, 79–80, 84, 86, 89, 92, 97, 100
Cannon, Nick   7, 75, 92, 92–6, 97, 100
Caputo, John   9, 139, 173, 175
Caribbean philosophy   47, 48
Carlsson Redell, Petra   ix
Carter, J. Cameron   24
Caste   4, 8, 75, 112–15, 160, 175
"Caucasian" term (Blumenbach)   15

Chahta (Choctaw)   1
Chamberlain, Houston Stewart   15
Cheadle, Don   169-2
Chicago   1, 24, 35, 45, 54, 62, 69-70, 80, 176, 182, 185
Citizenship   9, 28, 59, 146-7, 170
Clay, Elonda   ix
Clayton, Philip   ix, 134-5
Coleman, Monica A.   xiv, 9, 139, 170
Colonization projects   2, 5, 8, 100, 159
"Colored" category   6, 25, 26, 27, 28, 29, 56, 59, 62-3, 65, 173
Common-Bundle View (Gracia)   40-2
complex subjectivity (Pinn)   12
"Coolie" category   3
cosmopolitan right (Kant)   20
cranium size   15-16
critical race theory   2, 12, 17
crystal Radio   ix
Cudd, Ann   6, 31-7, 51, 52
Cushites   25

Darwin, Charles   15, 21
"Death of God" (Nietzsche)   11, 24
DeGeorge, Richard   33
Deleuze, Gilles   xiv, 140, 167, 171
Derrida, Jacques   118-19, 123, 139, 173-4, 176
Dolezal, Rachel   7, 75, 86-92, 97, 100
Drew, Timothy. *See* Ali, Noble Drew
Driscoll, Christopher M.   ix, 7, 12, 77
DuBois, W. E. B.   39, 177

Echoes of Oratory Muzik   130
Edgell, Zee, 164-5
Emergence theory (Clayton)   9, 134, 149-50, 162-4
"Ethiopian" category (Blumenbach)   15
ethnicity   2, 6, 28, 40, 41-3, 51, 57, 122, 125, 146-7, 158, 163, 177, 184
eugenics   15, 16
    Galton's introduction of term   15
externalist compatibilism   33

Faber, Roland   xiv, 167, 169, 171, 175
Farrakhan, Louis   27, 57, 71, 72, 94
fascism (Benjamin)   18
Ferdinand and Isabella   14
Fokuz, I. B. *See* Pettis-El, Dominic
Fourteenth Amendment   28

Fredrickson, George   14
Freedom vs. Nature (Hegel)   22
Freud, Sigmund   xiii

Galton, Francis   15
Garvey, Marcus   26, 71, 73
Genealogy   9, 18, 132, 141, 144, 166, 169-70, 172-84
Genetic Common-Bundle View (Gracia)   40-1
Ghana   25
Gilbert, Margaret   34-6
Gobineau, Arthur de   21
Goldberg, Theo   49
Gracia, Jorge   6, 31, 37, 40-4
Grant, Madison   16
Greene-Bey, Claude D.   27
Guatemala   136, 160, 161, 181

Hadford, Connesia   xv
Ham (son of Noah)   25
Hamites   25
Harding, Warren   41
Harris, Cheryl   49
Hegel, G. W. F.   xii, 21-3, 118, 174, 175-6
Hinojosa-Cisneros, Carolina   45
Hip-Hop Culture/Kulture   8, 9, 83, 121, 124, 144-5, 147-9, 151-66, 183
"Hispanic" category   7, 8, 31, 34, 40, 54, 161, 75, 99, 121
Historical-Familial View (Gracia)   42-3, 51
Hodge, Daniel White   ix
Holy Moabite Temple of the World   24
Honduras   1, 2, 66, 136
Hume, David   xii, 19-20, 85, 130, 131
Hunbatz Men   9, 46, 136, 185

Ice Cube   1
"Indigenous" category   xiv, 7, 31, 133, 138-9, 146, 179
InnerSection, 54, 77, 89, 100, 102, 111, 115, 132, 144, 157, 162, 164-5, 174, 179, 180, 182
Internalist compatibilism   33
Isaac, Benjamin   13
Islam   ix, 18, 24-7, 43, 67-72, 94, 167
Itzpapolotl   viii

Jamaica   19, 152-3, 156-9, 161
Japanese reparations   6

Jefferson, Thomas 39
Jesus Christ 21, 62, 73
Judaism 14, 16, 94–5

Kant, Immanuel xii, 5, 20, 21, 76, 79, 82, 85, 96, 103, 117, 125, 174
Keller, Catherine 176–77, 179
Kendi, Ibram X 8, 101, 104–5, 107, 114, 123, 125, 138
Kinouani, Guiliane xv
Klein, Alex xv
Knörrer, Matthias ix
in lak'ech (Maya concept) 46

"Latina/o/x" categories xiv, 3, 7, 8, 9, 11, 31, 33–4, 54, 127, 152, 154, 156–7, 184
Lefebvre, Henri xv
Limpieza de sangre (purity of blood) 14
Lincoln, Abraham 41
Living While Black (Kinouani) xv
Long, Charles 7, 12
Loomba, Ania 8, 101, 112–14
Loving vs. Virginia (1967) 16

McCutcheon, Russell 12, 85
"Malay" category (Blumenbach) 15
Malcolm X (Malcolm Little) 28
Mali 25
Manning, Erin xiv, 150
Marrero, Ariel D. xv
Martin, Trayvon 45
Massumi, Brian xiv, 9, 121, 126, 129–30, 148, 170
Mauritania 25
May, Larry 33
Mbiti, John 48
Mechanical reproduction (Benjamin) 17–18
Men, Hunbatz. See Hunbatz Men
Mexico 35, 45, 136, 150, 159–60, 169
  cultural identity formations 143, 156
Middle Passage 1, 13, 61, 62
Miles, Larry L. W. 7, 28, 102, 170–1
Miller, David 43
Miller, Monica R. 7, 9, 12, 43, 77, 86, 87, 90, 91–2
"Mind bugs" (Banaji) 8, 105–7, 109, 113
Miscegenation 16
Mississippi 1, 60

Mixed Race identity 6, 45, 48–50, 52, 99, 137, 178
Moabites 25, 26
"Mongolian" category (Blumenbach) 15
Monogenesis 5, 19–21
Montagu, Ashley 16–17
Montejo, Victor 133, 145
Moorish American identity(relating to the MSTA) 26–7, 29, 34, 53, 54, 59, 60, 62, 64, 72
Moorish Divine and National Movement of North America 24
Moorish Holy Temple of Science 24, 70
Moorish Science Temple of America (MSTA) 2, 5, 6, 7 12, 24–27, 29, 30, 35, 54, 58, 60–3, 66–8, 70, 72, 73
Moors (relating to Northern Africa) 14, 25, 26, 29, 117
Morales Torres, José Francisco 140–1
Morocco 24–6, 61
Morrison, Jim 13, 175
Mozambique 25
MSTA. See Moorish Science Temple of America

Nation of Islam (NOI) 27, 53, 60, 67, 68, 70–2, 94
Nationality 6, 8, 9, 24–9, 40, 42–4, 51, 54, 55, 57, 58, 59, 60, 62–7, 72, 73, 122, 125, 132, 141, 144–8, 156, 158–69, 184, 185
"Native American" category xiv, 6, 7, 11, 20, 31, 33–5, 47, 132, 139, 170–2, 184
Natural selection (Darwin) 15–17, 21
New Dialogic (Vest) 45, 47–8
Nietzsche, Friedrich 11, 24, 27, 32, 89, 167, 176
Niger 25, 60, 143
Noble Drew Ali. See Ali, Noble Drew

"Of National Characters" (Hume) 19
"Of the Different Races of Man" (Kant) 20
"On the Natural Variety of Mankind" (Blumenbach) 15
One drop rule 41
Outlaw, Lucius 44

"Pacific Islander" category 7
"people of color" 3, 138

Perkinson, Jim   16, 35
Pettis-El, Dominic   6, 53–74
Phantom Thrett   1
Pimienta-Bey, José   5, 12, 25, 26, 28, 29, 59, 63, 69, 103, 105–7, 160, 170
Pinn, Anthony B.   12, 118, 148
Polygenesis. *See* Monogenesis *vs.* polygenesis debate
post-race, responsible   3, 141, 183
Price, George   161
process philosophy   8, 9, 12, 14, 122, 127–36, 139–49, 151, 157, 161, 163–6, 172, 174, 175, 177, 180, 183, 185
Public Enemy   7
Puerto Cortés, Honduras   1
Puerto Rico   152, 154, 158, 159
Purity of blood. *See* Limpieza de sangre

racial eliminativism   49, 51, 102, 183
"Red" category   3, 20
the Reformation   16
Reparations   6, 27, 28, 53, 62, 63
Reynosa, Dax   xi, xv
Rice, Tamir   45
Rogers, J. A.   41
Rowe, Sheila Wise   xv

Saint Peter Good Neighbor Council   ix
Sartre, Jean-Paul   32, 76, 77, 84, 89, 177
Schleiermacher, Friedrich   22–3, 103
Semantic deference (Appiah)   37
Seminole Nation   45–6
Senegal   25
Serious Cartoons Records and Tapes   1
Sixpence None the Richer   1
Slavery   xiv, 7, 13, 20, 25, 28, 29, 62, 71, 79, 80–5, 108, 117, 147, 150, 155, 163, 170, 172
Social Darwinism   15
Social groups   6, 9, 31, 32–6, 40, 41, 51, 77, 79, 80, 107
Spain   2, 4, 8, 18, 22, 29, 46, 48, 66, 100, 159, 160, 176, 184
Standing Rock   35
Structuralists *vs.* intentionalists   32–3
Sudan   25

Temple No. 1 (MSTA)   6, 54
Third Space (Bhabha)   50
Tomorrow Kings   6, 39, 54
Torquemada   14
Toward Perpetual Peace (Kant)   20
Transatlantic slave trade   4, 27
Trauma   xi–xvi, 5, 9, 30, 34, 75, 78–80, 83, 86–7, 97, 99–101, 104, 106–133, 137–141, 144, 146–7, 150–2, 154–5, 157–185
Treaty between United States and Morocco (1787)   26
Tunnel Rats   x, xi, 78

Underground Rap as Religion (Gill)   8, 101, 117, 118, 121–3, 141, 147, 148, 151, 176
UNESCO statement on race (1950)   17
Universal Negro Improvement Organization (UNIA)   26

Van Sertima, Ivan   1
Vest, Jennifer Lisa   6, 28, 32, 45–50, 52, 99, 121, 136–8

Walker, Theodore   12–13
Washington, Kerry   xi
Weber, Max   32
Weisenfeld, Judith   7
West, Cornel   8, 101, 107–10, 114, 138
West, Kanye. *See* Ye
Whitehead, Alfred North   xiv, 8, 9, 38, 82, 85, 121–35, 138, 141, 144, 154, 161, 164, 167, 169, 171, 172, 178, 179, 185
"Whiteness"   xiii, 2, 8, 11, 16, 19, 35, 49, 58, 88, 89, 91, 102, 118, 138, 179
Womack, Ytasha   4
Woods, Joe   ix

Ye (Kanye West)   7, 75, 79–85, 97, 100

Zack, Naomi   6, 31, 37, 44, 45, 48–51, 100, 101, 183–4
Zanzibar   25